NEGOTIATION AND RESISTANCE

NEGOTIATION AND RESISTANCE

PEASANT AGENCY IN HIGH MEDIEVAL FRANCE

CONSTANCE BRITTAIN BOUCHARD

CORNELL UNIVERSITY PRESS

Ithaca and London

First published 2022 by Cornell University Press

Library of Congress Cataloging-in-Publication Data

Names: Bouchard, Constance Brittain, author.
Title: Negotiation and resistance : peasant agency in high Medieval France / Constance Brittain Bouchard.
Description: Ithaca [New York] : Cornell University Press, 2022. | Includes bibliographical references and index.
Identifiers: LCCN 2022002803 (print) | LCCN 2022002804 (ebook) | ISBN 9781501766572 (hardcover) | ISBN 9781501766589 (paperback) | ISBN 9781501766602 (epub) | ISBN 9781501767258 (pdf)
Subjects: LCSH: Peasants—France, Northern—Social conditions—To 1500. | Peasants—France, Northern—Economic conditions—To 1500. | Autonomy (Psychology)—France—History—To 1500. | Civilization, Medieval. | France—History—Medieval period, 987-1515.
Classification: LCC HD1536.F8 B765 2022 (print) | LCC HD1536.F8 (ebook) | DDC 305.5/633094427—dc23/eng/20220214
LC record available at https://lccn.loc.gov/2022002803
LC ebook record available at https://lccn.loc.gov/2022002804

Contents

PREFACE

Peasants in the high Middle Ages constituted by far the majority of the population. Yet relatively little attention has been given to their history, compared to that of aristocrats (knights and nobles) and members of the church. Popular works and even some scholarly studies often depict peasants as an undifferentiated mass of impoverished and powerless workers, about whom it is impossible to learn very much, other than that they were maltreated. Just as medieval women were once assumed to be silent and marginal, so peasants are now routinely treated as passive victims. But the records in which they appear tell a different story.

A number of common assumptions about the medieval peasantry need to be reexamined. French peasants of the high Middle Ages, the focus of this book, had far more scope for action, self-determination, and resistance to oppressive treatment—that is, for agency—than they are usually credited with having. Although of course peasants lived in conditions that would now be considered intolerable by Western standards (as for that matter did most aristocrats), I here argue that they were neither silent nor helpless.

The argument is primarily based on documents from northern France in which powerful lay and ecclesiastical people made agreements with each other—agreements in which peasants frequently played a significant but underappreciated role. While the documents I analyze here cannot provide a comprehensive look at medieval peasants, these sources do offer glimpses, and sometimes sustained looks, into the various ways in which peasants sought, surprisingly often successfully, to make their own decisions about their own lives, and the extent to which the powerful treated such peasant agency as normal.

Thus my focus here is on peasants as active agents, principally in negotiation with or in opposition to the more powerful. The Latin charters of agreement that constitute the book's principal sources do not provide intimate details of a peasant's personal life. The reader should therefore not expect a reconstruction of a typical daily round for a peasant, or a description of a peasant's clothing or cottage, or a recipe for rustic bread.[1] Rather, the sources show peasants claiming rights, bargaining for advantage, or offering themselves for service, taking action at what might have been some of the most fraught moments of their lives. In doing so, these sources reveal the responsibilities, activities, and ceremonies that tied peasants to their families, their communities, and broader society.

The eleventh and twelfth centuries in France, the heart of this book, constituted a period of rapid economic expansion, one of the factors that may have given the peasantry the leverage needed to act and to have their acts recorded. Overall economic developments are not my focus, however, and so I will have little to say about agricultural practices, or expansion of the arable, or medieval technology. These are of course important topics in medieval economic history and have been covered widely, both in survey accounts and in more specialized studies. Yet some accounts of the economic developments of the high Middle Ages may suggest a rather disembodied series of land clearances, new technologies, and establishment of trade routes without direct reference to the people carrying these out. By focusing on the peasants themselves, in particular their ability to shape their own lives, I intend to populate these developments with actual individuals. Once one begins to look for evidence of peasant agency in the documents, one will find it everywhere.

The decisions and actions of lower-status people, along with their ability to resist coercion, are of social and political concern in the twenty-first century as well as of historical concern. Still, I here keep my eyes on the Middle Ages, leaving it to the reader to decide whether any of the peasants who bought their way out of serfdom, took their complaints to the highest courts, or negotiated for self-governance have contemporary relevance. The broader issues have been examined by historians and social scientists using material spanning two millennia and half a dozen continents, but for a book intended to fill a historiographic gap I have kept the focus on high medieval peasants. Writing a book during a pandemic with very limited library access is, as I'm sure scores of colleagues can also attest, quite a challenge. I decided to embrace those limitations by making most of the book an in-depth conversation with the charters in which peasants appear, going about their lives.

This book began with an invitation to give the Warren Hollister lecture at the annual meetings of the Haskins Society, held at the University of North

---

1. Although one will still not find a bread recipe, one will find a wealth of information on what medieval people grew and ate in the article by Kathy L. Pearson, "Nutrition and the Early Medieval Diet," *Speculum* 72 (1997), 1–32.

Carolina in November 2017. I was encouraged by the positive reaction to the lecture to decide that this was a topic that needed further development and to expand my ideas into a book. The editors of the society journal have graciously allowed me to use some material from that lecture, printed in the journal.[2] I would like to thank Mahinder Kingra of Cornell University Press for his enthusiasm for this project and the three anonymous readers for the press for their many suggestions that helped clarify my arguments.

Although for most of my scholarly life I have focused on the medieval church and the aristocracy, peasants kept showing up in the documents I consulted. Editing cartularies from the Burgundy-Champagne region, the region on which this book primarily focuses, made me look carefully at documents that I might once have overlooked as irrelevant to what I was then researching. And this, I decided, was the problem—if one goes into the archives with a good sense of what one wants to find, that is all one will find.

Historians are necromancers. We make the dead sit up and speak. When people have been dead for eight hundred years or more, it is only fair to give them their chance to speak, even if we have not anticipated what they will say.

Wooster, Ohio, September 2021

---

2. "Medieval French Peasants: The New Frontier?" *Haskins Society Journal* 30 (2018), 213–30. The journal is published by Boydell & Brewer Ltd.

ABBREVIATIONS

BnF   Bibliothèque nationale de France
GC   Gallia Christiana in provincias ecclesiasticas distributas
MGH   Monumenta Germaniae Historica
       Capit.   Capitularia
       SS   Scriptores
PL   J.-P. Migne, ed., Patrologiae cursus completus, series Latina

NEGOTIATION AND RESISTANCE

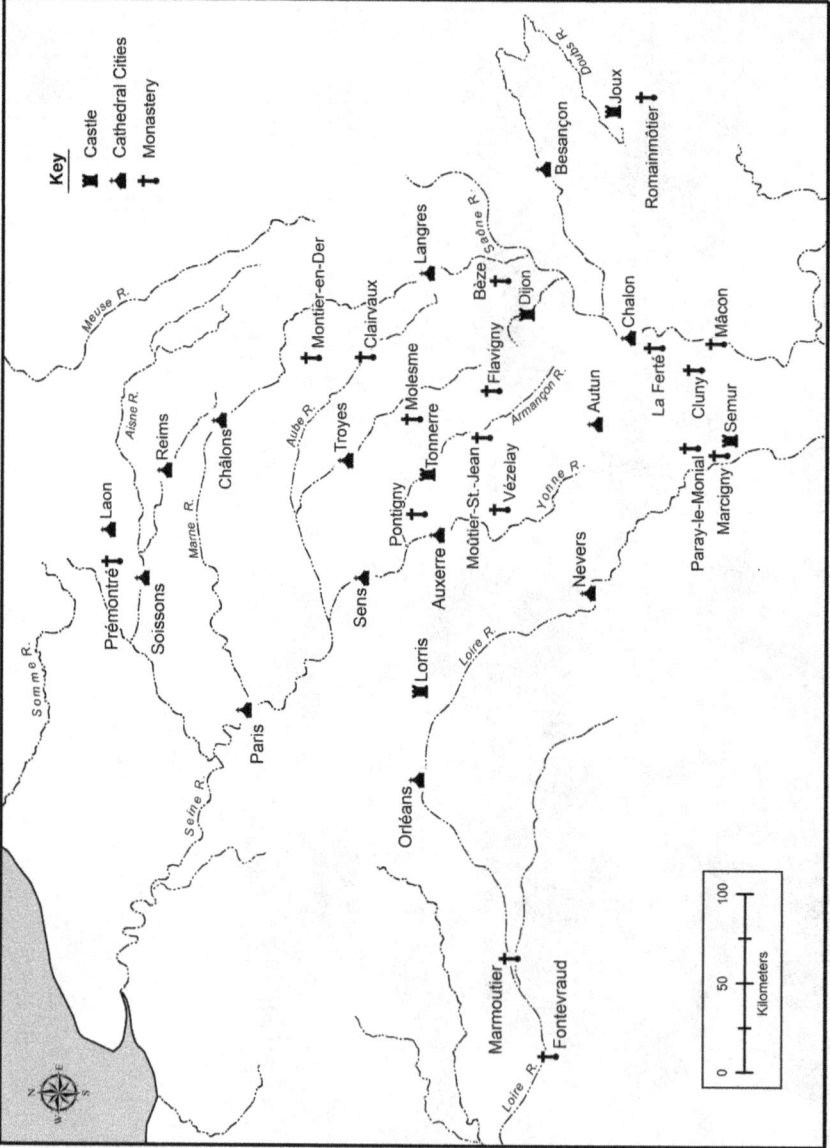

Castles, Cathedrals, and Monasteries in France

Introduction

Around the year 1100 the count of Brienne in Champagne gave the monastery of Molesme a woman (*femina*) as a gift, for his father's soul and for his own.[1] At first glance she appears to fit the stereotype of the downtrodden peasant, someone unfree—a woman at that, making it worse—who is treated as property, something to be given as a gift, by a powerful lord much more interested in prayers for his late father's soul than the welfare of a living woman. And yet this brief charter undercuts the stereotype.

She has the dignity of her own name, Rocelina. She is not labeled a serf (*ancilla*) but rather a woman (*femina*), a term that could also be used for a much more powerful person of the same sex. And, most significantly, before she starts providing her rents and labor to the monks, she comes before the abbot and half a dozen witnesses, several of whom appear to be knights, and places a penny in the abbot's hand "in recognition" (*recognitio*) of her new position. The penny carries symbolic weight on several levels and, it should be noted, was offered by her hand, not, as the stereotype of servitude would suggest, on her head. It does anticipate the dues she will be paying, though also showing that peasants had access to coins. But most importantly

---

1. *Cartulaires de l'abbaye de Molesme*, ed. Jacques Laurent, vol. 2, *Texte* (Paris, 1911), p. 131, no. 1.134.

it demonstrates that she had to be seen as accepting her new status, clearly crucial, because there would not be a need for such a ceremony if she had no say in the matter.

Rocelina was not alone. Many other peasants in the high Middle Ages insisted that they be taken seriously in decisions that affected them, and the powerful treated this as normal. Yet for far too long historians presented medieval peasants as passive, marginalized, and silent, with little ability to shape their own lives and little impact in the records. Scholarship on them has lagged far behind that on other sectors of society.[2] If one presumes peasants' actions were not recorded, then of course one will not look for them in the sources. But just as was once the case for the study of medieval women, one gets a very different picture if one does not begin by taking a lack of power or influence for granted.

Those who had already concluded that women were not to be found in the sources did not, unsurprisingly, suddenly discover that women had a voice. In the same way, those who failed to look for peasant self-determination were unlikely to find it. But as I shall demonstrate, the documents indicate that despite forces of coercion and constraint, medieval peasants exercised a good deal of autonomy in their choices and in ordering their own lives. Focusing on peasants of northern France, especially the Burgundy-Champagne region in the high Middle Ages (late tenth through early thirteenth centuries), I argue that difficult as their experience must have been, peasants had agency: that is, they were always capable of making their own decisions and fighting back against oppression. And while they may not have always prevailed, they did so surprisingly often.

My central argument then is that peasants during the high Middle Ages were active agents in their society and recognized as such by the more powerful. This argument is based principally on charters, most from monastic houses in north-central France. In support, I weave three major themes throughout the chapters that follow. The first of course is that medieval peasants were more than the helpless and downtrodden beings often portrayed in popular accounts and even some scholarly works. Rather, they carried out their own plans, even in the face of oppression and humiliation, through a combination of negotiation, stubborn resistance, and collective action.

Second, I intend to make the French peasants specifically of the high Middle Ages far more visible. The long eleventh and twelfth centuries are

---

2. The Library of Congress classification HD 1330, supposedly designating books giving the history of peasants and landlords, is nearly unused in all but the largest American libraries and is primarily populated by books about twentieth-century Asia.

considered the heart of the Middle Ages, a time of economic and cultural flourishing that witnessed everything from the origin of universities to the growth of towns to the development of epics and romances to the spread of reformed monasticism. Yet, with a few notable exceptions, scholars have largely overlooked peasants for this period. Most serious studies of the medieval peasantry focus either on the ninth century with its polyptyques or else on the fourteenth and fifteenth centuries, when manorial rolls (especially in England) provide plentiful sources, unlike anything earlier.

But there are other, underappreciated sources from the high Middle Ages in which peasants regularly appear. Here, and this is my third major theme, by using the sort of charters produced by and preserved by churches, charters that on their face are often not about peasants at all, I demonstrate that peasants as individuals, indeed highly active individuals, can be commonly found in the documents if one knows to look for them.

Medieval historians have long been finding new groups to study and new questions to ask the sources. The days when the rise of the nation-state was the principal focus of the field are long gone. In the last generation or two, first women and gender and, subsequently, saints have become significant topics of study in their own right. More recently scholars have turned to racial and religious differences in medieval Europe. Yet in all these cases it was once assumed that we could not obtain what was considered useful information on these issues. Women, it was earlier concluded, were marginal and ineffective, having no real impact either in medieval society or in the written sources, and whatever the sources said about saints was imaginary if not hopelessly derivative and thus best ignored.[3] Just as medievalists have come to realize that overlooking the female half of the population could be considered deliberate obtuseness,[4] so they have recognized that the study of medieval saints is improved by not imposing modern visions of proper religion on the past.[5] Analysis of minority groups has challenged the

---

3. Georges Duby's "A History of Women" series titled its second volume *Silences of the Middle Ages*, ed. Christiane Klapisch-Zuber (Cambridge, Mass., 1992). See also Georges Duby, *Love and Marriage in the Middle Ages*, trans. Jane Dunnett (Chicago, 1994); originally published as *Mâle moyen âge*. The seminal work for the serious study of saints' lives was that of Patrick J. Geary, *Furta Sacra: Thefts of Relics in the Central Middle Ages*, 2nd ed. (Princeton, 1990); originally published in 1978. See also Felice Lifshitz, "Beyond Positivism and Genre: 'Hagiographical' Texts as Historical Narrative," *Viator* 25 (1994), 95–113.

4. Indeed, Judith M. Bennett suggests that the important role of medieval women has become so widely acknowledged that feminist scholars have decided to move on to more recent periods, a development she deplores; *History Matters: Patriarchy and the Challenge of Feminism* (Philadelphia, 2006).

5. The study of Merovingian-era saints especially has become something of a scholarly growth industry; for discussion and references, see Constance B. Bouchard, "Restructuring Sanctity and

stereotype of medieval Europe as uniformly white and Christian, arguing for a more complicated reality.[6] Here I would like to propose peasants as the next group that needs to be recognized for their role in shaping events for their families and communities, rather than overlooked as silent victims.

The rapid economic expansion of the high Middle Ages, the period under discussion here, has often been assumed to have presented lords with new opportunities to oppress their peasantry. The "feudal revolution" debate of the 1990s turned on the question of whether the economic and social changes of the early eleventh century were accompanied by an abrupt imposition of new forms of servitude or whether there was only gradual change, with significant continuities in peasant subjugation from the tenth century.[7] I intend, contrary to both positions, to argue that the high Middle Ages were a period of peasant opportunity and (potential) freedom. If the powerful found in an expanding economy an opening for new forms of oppression, I argue, the peasantry found then an opening to fight back even more determinedly and often successfully.

The Medieval Peasantry

The challenges of studying medieval peasants are exacerbated by the lack of an agreed upon meaning for the word "peasant" among scholars. Like

---

Refiguring Saints in Early Medieval Gaul," in *Studies on Medieval Empathies*, ed. Karl F. Morrison and Rudolph M. Bell (Turnhout, 2013), pp. 91–114.

6. Geraldine Heng, *The Invention of Race in the European Middle Ages* (Cambridge, 2018). William Chester Jordan, *The Apple of His Eye: Converts from Islam in the Reign of Louis IX* (Princeton, 2019).

7. The debates on the "mutations" of the early eleventh century had their starting point with the work by Jean-Pierre Poly and Eric Bournazel, *The Feudal Transformation, 900–1200*, trans. Caroline Higgitt (New York, 1991); originally published in French in 1980. Curiously, only one twenty-page chapter in this four-hundred-page book is devoted to peasants. R. I. Moore has sought to label the eleventh and twelfth centuries a "revolution" without invoking the adjective "feudal," by concentrating instead on changes in the source and exercise of power; *The First European Revolution, c. 970–1215* (Oxford, 2000). The debates on feudal mutations have now more or less died out, after exhausting the principals. The (perhaps) final arguments on this topic, including extensive bibliography, may be found in Dominique Barthélemy, *The Serf, the Knight, and the Historian*, trans. Graham Robert Edwards (Ithaca, N.Y., 2009), originally published in French in 1997; and Thomas Bisson, *The Crisis of the Twelfth Century: Power, Lordship, and the Origins of European Government* (Princeton, 2009). Bisson is one of the last to continue to argue for a feudal revolution, even though he now distances himself from the word "feudalism." Curiously, his recent work does not cite two books, published simultaneously, that seriously undercut the argument; Richard E. Barton, *Lordship in the County of Maine, c. 890–1160* (Woodbridge, Suff., 2004); and Jeffrey A. Bowman, *Shifting Landmarks: Property, Proof, and Dispute in Catalonia around the Year 1000* (Ithaca, N.Y., 2004). Charles West has revisited the topic but has sought to change it from a debate about the eleventh century to a discussion of the ninth; *Reframing the Feudal Revolution: Political and Social Transformation between Marne and Moselle, c. 800–c. 1100* (Cambridge, 2013), pp. 1–9.

"feudalism," it has been used with very different implications depending on whether one is discussing the Middle Ages or the eighteenth and nineteenth centuries. In popular usage those engaged full-time in agriculture are called peasants only if they live in backward or undeveloped countries. Terms like "farmer" or "tenant" or "villager" have been proposed as less pejoratively loaded than "peasant," but I use the word "peasant" in this book as meaning at its most basic a country person (a *paysan* is someone of the *pays*, the countryside), someone low on the socioeconomic scale.[8] Most typically peasants grew their own food and paid some sort of rents or dues. But they differed from modern tenant farmers in that their rents and dues, rarely uniform even in the same village, were generally paid in a diverse combination of labor, coin, animal products (such as eggs or wool), and produce (such as grain or wine), rather than simply in money—and some medieval peasants paid no rent at all. I discuss the term "peasant" itself and the status of peasants more fully in chapter 1.

Peasants were far from an undifferentiated group, with significant variations in property holdings and legal status. Although the majority were directly involved in agriculture or animal husbandry, many peasants undertook work in trades such as carpentry, baking and brewing, or milling instead of (or in addition to) their farm labor. Some peasants were well-to-do or held positions of real authority, such as bailiff or village mayor.

Peasants constituted by far the majority of the medieval population and were fundamental to the economy. In the modern West, where only a tiny fraction (under 4 percent in the United States) of the population lives on a working farm, it is easy to forget how absolutely necessary are those who grow the food. Although the stock market is now often taken as an indicator of wealth, in the high Middle Ages wealth was measured in land, specifically agricultural land, and in the number of people whom one commanded.

Valuable land, such as that constituting a gift to a church, was typically specified as "fields, pastures, meadows, vineyards, woods, and running water," that is, the kind of land suitable for cultivation or resource exploitation and indeed already so used. Fishing rights in the stream and a mill were often mentioned as well. Close behind arable land in value was woodland, which the peasants used for building materials, fuel, pasturage, and occasional wild foodstuffs. The woods (*sylva*) were not trackless forests but

---

8. See also Judith M. Bennett, *A Medieval Life: Cecelia Penifader and the World of English Peasants before the Plague*, 2nd ed. (Philadelphia, 2021), pp. 1–2; Paul Freedman, *Images of the Medieval Peasant* (Stanford, 1999), pp. 9–10; and Barbara A. Hanawalt, *The Ties that Bound: Peasant Families in Medieval England* (Oxford, 1986), pp. 5–6.

woodlots and places where pigs could be pastured and honey and wild fruits and nuts gathered.[9] But the land would have had little worth without those who lived and worked on it. Monks and secular lords either needed to have peasants to cultivate their land or else, as Bernard of Clairvaux famously did, go out and hoe their own turnip fields.

For that reason gifts of land to the church usually specified the workers who came with it. Agricultural land at that time was almost always identified by its peasant inhabitants as much as by its geographic borders. Property was often referenced by the name of its cultivator, or described by its size given in the number of days it would take to plow it. The standard unit of agricultural land was the mansus, the amount of property that would theoretically support a peasant family. The exact size of a mansus varied enormously with time and place, and a mansus could consist of contiguous land or smaller pieces scattered among others' holdings. It would be impossible to put the size of a mansus into modern units of measurement, and that is the point: it was described by the people it supported.

The variations in what constituted a mansus and the role of individual peasants in defining a measure of land are illustrated by a document from Autun. In the middle of the tenth century Bishop Hervé of Autun, fearing that he was dying, decided to make a gift to his cathedral chapter, to establish anniversary observances for his soul.[10] His gift consisted of four mansi, identified by the name of the man or men who held each. Two, located in the village of Bray, were each held by one man, respectively Constantius and Adalerus, matching the normal assumption that a mansus would support one peasant family. The other two, however, located in the village of Monthelon, had three men associated with each mansus, in one case brothers. Was the farming better at Monthelon, so that the same amount of land could support more people? Or, as seems more likely, was a mansus larger there? We do not know, and although this sort of question has been of great interest to economic historians, it is not the issue here. Rather, it should be stressed that the property the bishop was giving his canons for his soul was defined by the peasants who lived there. They were not an incidental add-on to the property. Rather, they were what made the property valuable.

The importance of peasants was here fully recognized. The bishop found it appropriate to name them in his charter, so that over a millennium later

---

9. For pigs' role in the medieval economy, see Jamie Kreiner, *Legions of Pigs in the Early Medieval West* (New Haven, Conn., 2020).

10. *Cartulaire de l'église d'Autun*, ed. A[natole] de Charmasse (Paris, 1865), p. 59, no. 1.37.

we know their names and where they lived. Using documents like this, one can learn a great deal about peasants, their goals, agenda, and determination, as well as about the attitudes of the more powerful, who saw peasants as individuals who had to be negotiated with, placated, even sometimes feared. Legal rulings and the documents produced for every purpose from recording a sale to spelling out the settlement of a quarrel to memorializing a pious gift refer frequently to peasants as a matter of course. These documents indicate that those who drew them up found it entirely natural for peasants to have their own identities and to speak and argue with those far more powerful than they. They were a necessary part of the context for most acts. Contemporaries all recognized this. Modern scholars need to do so as well.

Peasants in Medieval Scholarship

It may perhaps be surprising to suggest medieval French peasants as a relatively unstudied group. After all, every textbook or popular overview of "life in the Middle Ages" mentions peasants, sometimes as an aspect of what is called the feudal system, sometimes in a section about the medieval economy. A sketch of a supposedly typical manor and a picture of an ox are almost mandatory. Ninth-century polyptyques are full of peasants, or at least full of lists of people with notations of what they owed their lords, and scholars have spent a great deal of effort working out the meanings of terms used to characterize peasants in them (a polyptyque is a survey of an estate's land and dues, typically done in the ninth century).[11] Late medieval manorial records and parish records (fourteenth–fifteenth centuries) include plenty of people of low social status, living in the countryside rather than in towns, engaged full-time in agriculture, often in service to someone far more powerful, and these records have been broadly read and analyzed.

The English peasantry especially have been closely studied for the period after the year 1250 or, more commonly, after the year 1300. Much has been discovered about lower-status English women in this late medieval period and the structure of families then.[12] Some regions of late medieval France

---

11. For recent work on polyptyques, see Alice Rio, *Slavery after Rome, 500–1100* (Oxford, 2017), pp. 186–94; and Constance Brittain Bouchard, *Rewriting Saints and Ancestors: Memory and Forgetting in France, 500–1200* (Philadelphia, 2015), pp. 53–62. See also *The Cartulary of Montier-en-Der, 666–1129*, ed. Constance Brittain Bouchard, Medieval Academy Books 108 (Toronto, 2004), pp. 25–30.

12. Nonetheless, it has been argued that scholarship on medieval English manors has tended to focus on lords more than peasants; Phillipp R. Schofield, *Peasants and Historians: Debating the*

produced the equivalent of the contemporary English manorial rolls, making possible comparable studies of peasant life in the fourteenth and fifteenth centuries.[13] And yet documentary historians have for the most part not given the same attention to the peasants of the eleventh and twelfth centuries.

Scholars from other disciplines or other branches of history have, however, analyzed the effects of peasant activity for the entire medieval millennium, including those of the high Middle Ages. Archaeology has brought into view much of the material culture of peasant life, from village structure and mills and forges to pottery and patterns of land clearance, as well as evidence of the diets of all medieval people.[14] Related are environmental history and the history of technology, including developments in farming techniques; such studies provide a great deal of information on the context in which peasants lived and worked as well as their impact on the world around them.[15]

Medieval English Peasantry (Manchester, Eng., 2016), pp. 117–47. The classic work on late medieval English rural society is that of P. Vinogradoff, *The Growth of the Manor* (London, 1905). More recent works include those of Bruce M. S. Campbell, *English Seigniorial Agriculture, 1250–1450* (Cambridge, 2000); M. M. Postan, *Essays on Medieval Agriculture and General Problems of the Medieval Economy* (Cambridge, 1973); Hanawalt, *The Ties that Bound*; Katherine L. French, *The Good Women of the Parish: Gender and Religion after the Black Death* (Philadelphia, 2008); Bennett, *A Medieval Life*; and J. A. Raftis, *Peasant Economic Development within the English Manorial System* (Montreal, 1996). Raftis argued that peasants (or customary tenants as he called them) amassed capital and thus should be seen as playing a major role in England's economic development, a role usually treated as restricted to the landlord.

13. For example, Nicolas Carrier, *La vie montagnarde en Faucigny à la fin du moyen-âge: Économie et société, fin XIIIe – début XVIe siècle* (Paris, 2001). Historians of rural France in the Middle Ages lagged well behind their British counterparts, as Marc Bloch first noted, in his own work designed to show the great variety of French agrarian approaches; *Les caractères originaux de l'histoire rurale française*, new ed. (Paris, 1999; rpt. 2006); originally published in 1931.

14. Examples include Christopher Loveluck, *Northwest Europe in the Early Middle Ages, c. AD 600–1150: A Comparative Archaeology* (Cambridge, 2013); Robin Fleming, *Britain after Rome: The Fall and Rise, 400 to 1070* (London, 2010); and Fleming, *The Material Fall of Roman Britain, 300–525 CE* (Philadelphia, 2021). For an overview of French archaeology by one of its deans, see Joëlle Burnouf et al., *Manuel d'archéologie médiévale et moderne*, 2nd ed. (Paris, 2020). In spite of its title, this book is not a how-to manual but a synthesis of recent findings.

15. Ellen F. Arnold, *Negotiating the Landscape: Environment and Monastic Identity in the Medieval Ardennes* (Philadelphia, 2013); Richard C. Hoffmann, *An Environmental History of Medieval Europe* (Cambridge, 2014). Hoffmann argues that developments in medieval society can best be understood through the interaction between the social-cultural and natural worlds. For plows and draft animals, see John Langdon, *Horses, Oxen and Technological Innovation: The Use of Draught Animals in English Farming, 1066–1500* (Cambridge, 1986). For mills, see Mathieu Arnoux, *Le temps des laboureurs: Travail, ordre social et croissance en Europe (XIe XIVe siècle)* (Paris, 2012), pp. 291 336. Historians of agricultural techniques have at their disposal the many late medieval copies of treatises on the topic; Lisa H Cooper, "Agronomy and Affect in Duke Humphrey's *On Husbondrie*," *Speculum* 95 (2020), 36–38.

Yet most of these works by necessity treat the high medieval peasantry as a largely anonymous group, where it is impossible to learn how and why individuals acted or made decisions. In studies of the rural world of the eleventh and twelfth centuries, peasants generally remain part of the background, as inhabiting a rather a timeless world of subsistence farming and oppression.[16] When they do appear in the scholarship, it is usually not as actors. Rather they are treated rather impersonally, not as people with a say in their own lives.

The original *Cambridge Medieval History* (eight volumes, 1911–36) included no discussion of medieval French peasants at all. At most there are a few pages on peasant life on an English manor in a chapter called "Feudalism," in a volume entitled *Germany and the Western Empire* (1936). Peasants' absence was typical at a time when historians focused on governmental institutions and broad economic trends, rather than on people, especially not on people considered powerless.[17] The situation has improved in *The New Cambridge Medieval History* (seven volumes, 1995–2005), where both the volume on the long tenth century and the first (of two) on the eleventh and twelfth centuries begin with articles on agriculture and peasants, with a nod to Georges Duby.[18] Yet interestingly, peasants as actors are essentially absent from these articles, which focus instead on legal servile-free distinctions, farming methods, and manorial lords. Some sixty years after the original publication of Duby's magisterial *Rural Economy and Country Life*, which portrayed itself as a preliminary assay of a crucial topic, no one else has produced anything as broad.[19] It is still in print, in handy paperback format for classroom use, indicating how little the field has advanced.

The debate over the supposed feudal revolution of the year 1000 was always more about lordship, especially their supposed imposition of new

16. The eminent social and economic historian Léopold Genicot, in his overview of medieval peasant communities, discussed village structure, expansion of the arable, the power of landlords, and the establishment of parish churches, but the peasants in this work remain oddly unseen; *Rural Communities in the Medieval West* (Baltimore, 1990).

17. See also Schofield, *Peasants and Historians*, pp. 2–4. An exception at the time was Eileen Power, whose *Medieval People* (London, 1924) began with an imaginative reconstruction of the life of the ninth-century peasant Bodo.

18. Robert Fossier, "Rural Economy and Country Life," in *The New Cambridge Medieval History*, vol. 3, ed. Timothy Reuter (Cambridge, 1999), pp. 27–63. Fossier, "The Rural Economy and Demographic Growth," in *The New Cambridge Medieval History*, vol. 4, pt. 1, ed. David Luscombe and Jonathan Riley-Smith (Cambridge, 2004), pp. 11–46.

19. Georges Duby, *Rural Economy and Country Life in the Medieval West*, trans. Cynthia Postan (Columbia, S.C., 1968); originally published in French in 1962.

obligations, than about peasants themselves.[20] Similarly, the dozens of excellent French regional studies of the second half of the twentieth century, designed to illuminate medieval French society, have had much more to say about seigneurial authority than about peasant life. Duby's *Three Orders* has as a constant subtext the failure of political schemas of the eleventh and twelfth centuries to account properly for peasants in the Third Estate.[21]

Medieval peasant women in particular have been studied primarily for their legal status and for the kinds of work that they did, not for any ability they might have had to shape their lives. French peasant women especially have been overlooked, treated as silent beings about whom scholars are unlikely to learn anything useful.[22] In all of this, the principal scholarly approach to peasants of the eleventh and twelfth centuries has been to treat them as nearly unknowable, to be pitied at best, with the assumption that we might discover the attitudes the powerful had toward them, their legal status, even (through archaeology) the kinds of crops they cultivated or tools they used, but little if anything of their own actions.[23]

Those who have set out deliberately to study the marginal and the downtrodden in recent years have focused much more on cities than on the countryside.[24] Paul Freedman, whose own scholarship focuses on the peasantry of Catalonia and France, is one of the few to analyze medieval peasants as actors, rather than as abstract economic factors.[25] The only situations where peasants are generally assumed to have agency are peasant revolts, especially during the late Middle Ages, where the inevitable crushing of these revolts

---

20. For example, Fossier, "Rural Economy and Country Life," pp. 33–39; and Bisson, *The Crisis of the Twelfth Century*. Arnoux notes the same scholarly tendency; *Le temps des laboureurs*, pp. 33–34.

21. Georges Duby, *The Three Orders: Feudal Society Imagined*, trans. Arthur Goldhammer (Chicago, 1980); originally published in French in 1978. For this work's impact, see Arnoux, *Le temps des laboureurs*, pp. 37–48.

22. As Sharon Hubbs Wright points out, medieval peasant women have been relegated to the margins even more than have their male counterparts; "Medieval European Peasant Women: A Fragmented Historiography," *History Compass* 18, no. 6 (2020), https://doi.org/10.1111/hic3.12615. That Wright is able to summarize forty years of French, German, Italian, and Spanish scholarship on peasant women in twelve pages indicates how very little work has been done.

23. Poly and Bournazel say regretfully that a "true history" of peasants has not been written, meaning one from the peasants' perspective; *The Feudal Transformation*, p. 119. They make no attempt to fill the gap themselves.

24. For example, Sharon Farmer, *Surviving Poverty in Medieval Paris: Gender, Ideology, and the Daily Lives of the Poor* (Ithaca, N.Y., 2002).

25. Paul Freedman, *The Origins of Peasant Servitude in Medieval Catalonia* (Cambridge, 1991); Freedman, *Images of the Medieval Peasant*; Freedman, "Peasants, the Seigneurial Regime, and Serfdom in the Eleventh to Thirteenth Centuries," in *European Transformations: The Long Twelfth Century*, ed. Thomas F. X. Noble and John Van Engen (Notre Dame, Ind., 2012), pp. 259–78.

was often followed by at least some improvement in their situation.[26] For the high Middle Ages, peasants are sometimes described as resisting, but only in response to new impositions, not as having the initiative to carry out plans and programs of their own.[27] Lords' control over peasant families, their marriages, their transactions, their inheritance, is given much more attention than the many records in which peasants themselves chose their spouses, bought and sold, or inherited.[28]

Peasants were depicted as recently as the 1970s as backward and superstitious, in short the opposite of the educated, thoughtful people considered worthy of study.[29] Yet such characterization of peasants as ill-informed brutes is belied by the experience of anyone who has farmed, an occupation that requires a tremendous technical knowledge of crop plants, tools, and techniques, as well as daily planning, assessment, judgment, and dedication. Medieval peasants were not worked in chain gangs, indeed did not answer to an overseer while they were growing their own food on their own lands, and thus had to rely on their own initiative and their own understanding of the consequences in heading out each day for this very hard labor.

Although Duby, interestingly enough, found plenty of examples of high medieval peasants taking the lead in such areas as opening up new lands for cultivation, planting vineyards, or draining marshes,[30] the more common approach has been to focus on their subjugation. The rise of castellan lordship in the high Middle Ages has been described as resulting in the coercion and violent domination of the peasantry, with no indication that they might have been able to resist. A recent textbook by an eminent economic historian describes peasant status using such terms as "imposition," "humiliation,"

---

26. The classic study of the fourteenth-century English peasant revolt is by Rodney Hilton, *Bond Men Made Free: Medieval Peasant Movements and the English Rising of 1381* (New York, 1973). The fourteenth-century French Jacquerie is much less studied than the English uprising; Justine Firnhaber-Baker, "The Social Constituency of the Jacquerie Revolt of 1358," *Speculum* 95 (2020), 690–91. See also Ghislain Brunel and Serge Brunet, eds., *Les luttes anti-seigneuriales: Dans l'Europe médiévale et moderne* (Toulouse, 2009); and Schofield, *Peasants and Historians*, pp. 91–108.

27. Werner Rösener, *Peasants in the Middle Ages*, trans. Alexander Stützer (Urbana, 1992), pp. 237–51.

28. See also Eleanor Searle, "Seigneurial Control of Women's Marriage: The Antecedents and Function of Merchet in England," *Past and Present* 82 (1979), 5–6.

29. For example, Eugen Weber drew a distinction between the "undeveloped," indeed "savage," rural France of the nineteenth century and the "modern world" of civilization; *Peasants into Frenchmen: The Modernization of Rural France, 1870–1914* (Stanford, 1976), pp. x, 3.

30. Duby, *Rural Economy*, pp. 69–72, 113–15, 170. A similar nod to the role of medieval peasants in agricultural expansion is made in the classic work of N. J. G. Pounds, *An Economic History of Medieval Europe* (New York, 1974), pp. 164–222.

"subjection," and "beatings."[31] Indeed, the agricultural advances of the high Middle Ages have even been assumed to have required the subjugation and impoverishment of the peasantry.[32]

Agrarian history has always focused more on geography, type of crops, and farming techniques than on the farmers themselves, and even so agrarian history has become much less studied in the last forty years than it once was.[33] Peasants are too often treated as passive recipients of economic and social change, rather than as drivers of that change. For example, a standard account of peasant life notes the population growth, expansion of the arable, new settlements in eastern Europe, agricultural developments, and increases in trade and productivity of the tenth through twelfth centuries, but only says that these "left their imprint" on the peasants, rather than noting that these were *driven* by peasant initiative.[34]

Without in any way idealizing the life of a medieval peasant, it is in fact possible with careful examination of the sources to see peasants as having at least some control of their situation and scope for maneuver. In discussing medieval peasant agency, I shall remain focused on peasants as individual actors, rather than more generically as part of a system of food production. Far from being invisible, medieval French peasants are right there in the written sources, indeed all over the place, with a real ability to speak up against what they considered injustice, make bargains with the powerful, and determine at least some of their own fate.

Peasants in Narrative Sources

Compared to the documentary sources, narrative sources of the high Middle Ages have relatively little to say about the activities of medieval peasants. Indeed, their infrequent appearance in such sources may be part of the reason why peasant initiative is not more widely appreciated. The romances and epics the powerful enjoyed scarcely mentioned peasants, for a tournament or a shocking betrayal was always more interesting than the grain harvest.

---

31. Bisson, *The Crisis of the Twelfth Century*, pp. 40–53. Steven A. Epstein, *An Economic and Social History of Later Medieval Europe, 1000–1500* (Cambridge, 2009), pp. 50–51.

32. Moore, *The First European Revolution*, pp. 52–55. Chris Wickham states, "The wealth of lords—whether royal, ecclesiastical, or aristocratic—thus came from what they could extract from the peasantry. They did so by force, and by the threat of force"; *Medieval Europe* (New Haven, Conn., 2016), p. 14.

33. Freedman, "Peasants, the Seigneurial Regime, and Serfdom," p. 260.

34. Rösener, *Peasants in the Middle Ages*, pp. 22–23. The assumption that the economy affected peasants rather than the other way around has long been standard; Schofield, *Peasants and Historians*, pp. 39–42.

Aristocrats' histories of their glorious predecessors rarely refer even glanc-
ingly to peasants. Monastic chroniclers included a good deal on the dealings
of their own houses and their relations with their secular neighbors, but they
barely noted those who provided their food. Overall, the narrative sources
tended to treat peasants as weak and helpless if mentioning them at all. Yet
literature and theological or political treatises from the time can provide
glimpses of attitudes toward peasants from the more powerful.[35] Although
most of the following chapters concern charters, it is worth spending a little
time here on these attitudes as seen in narrative sources.

Peasants were most commonly characterized as part of "the poor," a
large and rather amorphous group that also included the urban poor of the
growing twelfth-century cities. These impoverished people were typically
described as at least the potential victims of the powerful and the violent, to
say nothing of the depredations of weather (hail, drought) and accompanying famine. They appeared in narrative sources most frequently as opportunities for the wealthy to demonstrate their piety and generosity, as when
Count Charles the Good of Flanders saved both peasants and townspeople
from starvation.[36] Galbert of Bruges's account of the count's murder in 1127
specified that he was simultaneously praying, singing psalms, and distribut-
ing pennies to the poor at the very moment of his killing, making the act
even more despicable, and also drawing an equation between relieving poverty and holiness.[37]

Galbert of Bruges was not alone in seeing generosity toward "the poor,"
including peasants, as an important obligation of the rich and powerful.[38]
Many great lords specified gifts to the poor as well as to churches in their
wills in the late twelfth and thirteenth centuries. The thirteenth century was
a time when great lords founded hospitals that served the poor.[39] Yet in all
this generosity to the poor the peasants involved remain somewhat faceless.
They were pitied, they were given alms, they became an opportunity for a

---

35. Those who have studied such attitudes include Arnoux, *Le temps des laboureurs*, and Freedman,
Images of the Medieval Peasant.

36. Galbert of Bruges, *Histoire du meurtre de Charles le Bon, comte de Flandre*, ed. Henri Pirenne
(Paris, 1891), cap. 2–3, pp. 5–7. *The Murder of Charles the Good*, trans. James Bruce Ross (New York,
1959; rpt. Toronto, 1982), pp. 85–89. For Galbert, see Jeff Rider, *God's Scribe: The Historiographical
Art of Galbert of Bruges* (Washington, D.C., 2001); and Jeff Rider and Alan V. Murray, eds., *Galbert of
Bruges and the Historiography of Medieval Flanders* (Washington, D.C., 2009).

37. Galbert of Bruges, *Histoire du meurtre de Charles le Bon*, cap. 12, p. 21. *The Murder of Charles
the Good*, p. 112.

38. Michel Mollat, *The Poor in the Middle Ages*, trans. Arthur Goldhammer (New Haven, Conn.,
1986), pp. 96–97.

39. Adam J. Davis, *The Medieval Economy of Salvation: Charity, Commerce, and the Rise of the Hospital* (Ithaca, N.Y., 2019).

rich man to demonstrate that he was not like the rich man in the biblical story of Dives and Lazarus (much retold in the Middle Ages) who turned the poor man from his gate and ended up in hell. The poor peasants in these stories *had* to be helped by the powerful because they were so weak.

In the eleventh century, with the spread of the Peace of God movement, peasants were singled out as a group that, along with churches and merchants, were vulnerable to the kind of knightly violence the Peace was supposed to prevent. Indeed, knightly warfare throughout the Middle Ages was always devastating to the peasantry, so the idea that they needed protection was more than theoretical.[40] Specifically, those who bore *arma saecularia* promised at the first Peace council held in Burgundy (Verdun-sur-le-Doubs, c. 1020) not to attack any church or churchman or to seize anyone's "ox, cow, pig, sheep, lamb, goat, or ass." These were the animals of country farmers, *agricolae*, the peasantry.[41] The knights who attended the Peace councils promised to protect the weak and the helpless as an act of religious charity, rather than to protect the farmers and merchants as an aid to the economy. But peasants' designation as those who needed protection both helped define them and provided a marker for what was considered suitable knightly behavior in the following centuries.[42]

The twelfth-century abbot and royal biographer Suger described peasants as victims, worthy of mention chiefly because of the virtue displayed by those who protected them. The early pages of his *Deeds of Louis VI* celebrate the young king as someone who overcame tyrants who preyed on the poor, starting with Louis's coronation ceremony, which symbolized his "defense of churches and the poor."[43] Peasant weakness was taken for granted; Suger used the analogy of Louis destroying a castle tower as easily as he could have destroyed a peasant hut (*rusticanum turgurium*) as an indication of the king's great military strength, while underscoring peasant helplessness.[44] In addition, the poor, which included peasants, were to Suger

---

40. Richard W. Kaeuper, *Medieval Chivalry* (Cambridge, 2016), pp. 181–205.

41. The listing of animals that were not to be seized went back to the first Peace council, held at Charroux in 989. Charles-Joseph Hefele, *Histoire des conciles*, trans. and aug. H. Leclercq, 10 vols. (Paris, 1907–38), vol. 4, pt. 2:1409–10. The best modern treatment of the Peace of God remains that of Thomas Head and Richard Landes, eds., *The Peace of God: Social Violence and Religious Response in France around the Year 1000* (Ithaca, N.Y., 1992). See also Duby, *The Three Orders*, pp. 134–39; and Moore, *The First European Revolution*, pp. 7–10.

42. Raoul Glaber's account of the Peace movement, however, stresses protecting churchmen rather than peasants; "Historia" 4.5, in *Opera*, ed. John France et al. (Oxford, 1989), pp. 194–96. See also Mollat, *The Poor in the Middle Ages*, pp. 71–72.

43. Suger, *Vie de Louis VI le Gros*, ed. Henry Waquet (Paris, 1964), cap. 14, p. 80. *The Deeds of Louis the Fat*, trans. Richard C. Cusimano and John Moorhead (Washington, D.C., 1992), p. 63.

44. Suger, *Vie de Louis VI le Gros*, cap. 24, p. 176. *The Deeds of Louis the Fat*, p. 107.

a group touched with the holy, because the group also included ecclesiastics, described biblically as the "poor in spirit."

This group of victims was poor not only in material wealth but in the ability to defend themselves and thus both needed and deserved a protector. Suger's account of Louis's struggles to overcome and discipline the castellans of the Île de France who were attacking both peasants and merchants has usually been read as a marker of how weak the French monarchy was at the beginning of the twelfth century. But more significantly it demonstrates Suger's assumption, one with which he expected his readers to agree, that peasants needed to be protected, for the good of the realm as well as for the good of the protector's soul.

The epic poem *Aliscans*, part of the twelfth-century William of Orange cycle, similarly depicted peasants as weak people who should be protected as a Christian duty. Here a "poor man" (*povres hom*) appears to beg help against the Saracens, who are the default enemies in these epics. They had laid waste his bean field, destroying the crop. The poor man explains that he had hoped to sell the beans to buy bread for his family, but now they have nothing to eat. Even though the peasant (*vilains*) had dug and plowed and planted the beans himself, hoping for a "small profit," the Saracens had eaten up whatever they did not destroy. Our heroes, however, quickly rout the malefactors, killing them all and giving their horses and equipment to the peasant in compensation.[45] The poor man then leaves the story, not to be seen again, having fulfilled his role: he has given the heroes a chance to prove that they support the cause of "justice" by helping the poor and defenseless, especially against enemies of Christianity.

The presumed poverty of peasants put them in a somewhat ambivalent position. Poverty had been equated with holiness, at least intermittently, for over a century before Francis of Assisi's radical rejection of property. In a time of economic growth and even (relative) prosperity, poverty took on a mantle of holiness it had not had in the early Middle Ages, when wealth had been very unusual and hence admirable.[46] Monks had always been expected to give up personal possessions. The Cistercians of the twelfth century additionally rejected anything that gave even the appearance of wealth and comfort. Peasants, who were routinely described as poor (even if in practice a few were well-to-do), thus had at least some claim to being holy.

---

45. *Aliscans*, ed. Erich Wienbeck, Wilhelm Hartnacke, and Paul Rasch (Halle, 1903), lines 7375–7490, pp. 456–64. *Guillaume d'Orange: Four Twelfth-Century Epics*, trans. Joan M. Ferrante (New York, 1974), pp. 265–67.

46. Lester K. Little, *Religious Poverty and the Profit Economy in Medieval Europe* (Ithaca, N.Y., 1978). Mollat, *The Poor in the Middle Ages*, pp. 57–113.

But poverty, admirable poverty as understood in the twelfth century, was supposed to be *voluntary*. Spiritual poverty was something one adopted, rather than something for which one had no recourse. Because peasants could not control their economic status, they were not characterized as holy simply because of that status. In addition, the laboring peasant was not perceived as destitute—he was productive.[47] As a result, peasants of the High Middle Ages could be described either as rightly subordinate to their superiors or, on the other hand, as closer to God than those who were superior by worldly standards—or they could even be described as both simultaneously. Peasants alternated between being pitied and being despised.[48]

For much narrative literature was dismissive of peasants. They were illiterate, they were dirty, they did not know the proper way to behave. Andreas Capellanus, in his satirical "On Love," indicated that it was not worth trying to woo a peasant woman with flattery and persuasive arguments; she would respond only to being taken by force.[49] As clearly inferior, coarse and ugly as well as lacking all refined sentiment, peasants could be scorned, as other supposedly inferior beings were scorned: lepers, heretics, Jews, and the strange foreign people who appeared in fabulous travelers' tales.

Inherent in this attitude was the justification of the lowly status of peasants. The early eleventh-century bishop Adalbero of Laon, who argued in his famous *Carmen* to King Robert that society was divided into three orders, characterized a peasant (*rusticus*) as "lazy, deformed, and completely vile," and depicted serfs (*servi*) as subject to everyone else according to divine law. These serfs, Adalbero continued, who were supposed to be chaste and sober, worked ceaselessly, sighing and weeping copiously—someone would be hard-pressed, he said, even with an abacus, to count up all their different labors. But Adalbero did more than suggest the difficult life of a serf. He fully recognized their necessity for the rest of society. No treasure or even food and clothing could be accumulated without them, he said, so that no free man could function without serfs. Even kings and bishops must depend on them.[50] Their unceasing hard work was therefore required for everyone else to function.

---

47. Mollat, *The Poor in the Middle Ages*, pp. 103–4. Freedman, *Images of the Medieval Peasant*, pp. 11–12.

48. For the prevalence of such paradoxes in medieval thought, see, more broadly, Constance Brittain Bouchard, *"Every Valley Shall Be Exalted": The Discourse of Opposites in Twelfth-Century Thought* (Ithaca, N.Y., 2003).

49. Andreas Capellanus, *On Love*, 1.11, ed. P. G. Walsh (London, 1982), p. 222. See also Bouchard, *"Every Valley Shall Be Exalted,"* pp. 141–43.

50. Adalbero of Laon, *Poème au roi Robert*, ed. Claude Carozzi (Paris, 1979), ll. 37, 285–94, pp. 4, 20–22. See also Pierre Bonnassie, *From Slavery to Feudalism in South-Western Europe*, trans. Jean Birrell

Since medieval theologians routinely credited Adam's sin as the source of human misery in general and hard agricultural labor in particular (Genesis 3:17–18), peasants' condition could easily be interpreted as a sign of their sinfulness.[51] And yet lowliness in general as well as poverty specifically were markers of the good Christian. Jesus after all was described as lowly himself and as associating with poor or marginalized people, and monks emulated the peasantry in clothing and diet. And high medieval peasants were indeed Christian, which gave them a distinct advantage over the Jews, Muslims, and purported pagans of the imagined East.[52]

The dispute over the appearance and activities of Robert of Arbrissel, who founded the monastery of Fontevraud at the beginning of the twelfth century, reveals these conflicted attitudes. Bishop Marbode of Rennes wrote an extremely harsh letter to Robert, saying he was dirty, unshaven, sloppily dressed, barelegged and barefoot, lacking only a club to complete the image of a lunatic. Although Marbode did not explicitly say that Robert looked like a peasant (or village idiot), that was certainly the message he wished to convey, for he claimed that Robert had tried to justify his appearance by saying that it gave him authority among the "simple folk" (*simplices*).[53] It was easy to look down on such a person. And yet peasants' very simplicity and failure to observe, much less understand, more exalted society's norms could be seen as admirable, indeed a criticism of the more worldly. In the first *vita* of Robert of Arbrissel, written by Bishop Baudri of Dol, Baudri defended Robert's rough clothing and bare feet as a sign of his humility and religiosity.[54] Indeed, parts of Baudri's *vita* seem designed specifically to refute Marbode's criticism, to make appearing like a peasant a virtue, not a failing.

A similar ambivalence about the peasantry may be seen in the eleventh-century "Book of Miracles" of Saint Foy. The author, Bernard of Angers, said that he originally mocked the reliquaries both of Foy and of other saints. He said they looked like pagan icons, suitable for the worship of Jupiter or

---

(Cambridge, 1991), pp. 288, 294. Bonnassie does not note Adalbero's stress on the rest of society's dependence on peasants.

51. Michel Lauwers, "Le 'travail' sans la domination?" in *Penser la paysannerie médiévale, un défi impossible?*, ed. Alain Dierkens, Nicolas Schroeder, and Alexis Wilkin (Paris, 2017); Kindle edition.

52. Freedman, *Images of the Medieval Peasant*, pp. 1–3.

53. Johannes von Walter, ed., *Die ersten Wanderprediger Frankreichs*, vol. 1 (Leipzig, 1903), p. 186. *Robert of Arbrissel: A Medieval Religious Life*, trans. Bruce L. Venarde (Washington, D.C., 2003), pp. 96–97. The coarse, dirty, ill-dressed peasant was a common trope in literature at the time; Freedman, *Images of the Medieval Peasant*, pp. 139–40.

54. Baudri of Dol, "Vita B. Roberti de Arbrissello," cap. 18, PL 162:1052. *Robert of Arbrissel: A Medieval Religious Life*, p. 16.

Mars, and he joked about the "superstitious" practice of displaying such reliquaries and about the peasants (*rustici*) who admired them. But eventually, persuaded by the account of Foy punishing a doubter, he had to admit that he had been foolish (*stultus*), and that the simple, unlearned people he had looked down on had a better appreciation of the holy than did he.[55]

Peasants then could be both simple, which was admirable, and gullible, which was not. Guibert of Nogent described the peasantry (*agrarii*) in the region around Laon as coming every Saturday into town from their country villages to buy food, being tricked by the unscrupulous merchants of the town into bending *way* over a chest that was then slammed shut on them, and being held captive until they paid a ransom.[56] Nobles, local merchants, and clergy alike in Laon, he said, welcomed chaos, allowed rampant crime, and even stole the king's horses. But his chief example of the evil nature of these citizens of Laon was their treatment of peasants.

This story appears unlikely in several ways. To begin, Guibert states that the peasants came into Laon to buy wheat and vegetables, whereas it is far more likely that they came to sell their produce than to buy. In addition, it is implausible that having once been fooled like this, the country folk would continue to attend the weekly markets as Guibert said they did, repeatedly being fooled and held captive. As someone who had been born in a castle and lived since his youth in a monastery, he had only the vaguest idea of how an urban farmers market would have operated.

His description of how the peasants reacted to extortion at the hands of the clergy and aristocrats appears just as confused as his following assertion that these extortionists at Laon offered to sell the peasants the rights to a commune (*communio*) for a high price. Now in fact communes were granted to self-organized villages or towns, as discussed in chapter 4, not to peasants from what Guibert described as widely scattered villages. As he continued his description of the commune, it appears (more plausibly) that the citizens of Laon proclaimed their own commune, against the bishop's wishes. In addition, there was far more involved in a commune than reducing the dues of its servile members to one annual payment, as he stated in a comment that has worried and confused modern scholars.[57] But the key point here

---

55. *Liber miraculorum Sancte Fidis*, ed. Auguste Bouillet (Paris, 1897), cap. 1.13, pp. 46–49. *The Book of Sainte Foy*, trans. Pamela Sheingorn (Philadelphia, 1995), pp. 77–79.

56. Guibert of Nogent, *Autobiographie*, ed. Edmond René Labande, Les Classiques de l'histoire de France au moyen âge 34 (Paris, 1981), cap. 3.7, pp. 316–20. *A Monk's Confession: The Memoirs of Guibert of Nogent*, trans. Paul J. Archambault (University Park, Penn., 1996), pp. 145–46. For Guibert, see Jay Rubenstein, *Guibert of Nogent: Portrait of a Medieval Mind* (New York, 2002).

57. Guibert of Nogent, *Autobiographie*, cap. 3.7, p. 320. *A Monk's Confession*, p. 146.

is that, in Guibert's account, peasants were uninformed, easily tricked, and ready to spend money in exchange for false promises. Their simplicity was not that of the innocent child but of the half-wit.

The narrative sources, then, give an ambivalent picture of the peasantry. On the one hand they were to be pitied and protected, both because they produced the food everyone ate and, perhaps more importantly for some medieval authors, because helping them was a charitable and worthy activity. On the other hand, they could become disturbing if they strayed outside what the powerful considered their proper place. On the one hand, their poverty made them at least reminiscent of those following a holy life of renunciation. On the other hand, their lack of decent clothing, housing, or education made them despicable, something to be avoided if at all possible—or better yet, to be conveniently ignored.

Most of those writing histories and works of literature dealt with these ambiguities by depicting a world in which the peasantry barely existed. No one wrote epics or romances in which peasants adopted a charter of liberty inspired by the Customs of Lorris, or were moved by genuine religiosity to try to protect each other from brigands, or opened new fields to cultivation without first asking permission from those fields' lord, or went to the highest court of their region to lodge a complaint against an oppressor, or insisted that they must formally assent to being transferred, along with their land, to a new landlord. Yet as the following chapters will show, high medieval peasants routinely did all these things.

Peasants thus posed a special challenge to medieval elites, simultaneously creatures to be pitied and assisted, because of their naïveté, their poverty, and their weakness, yet also potentially dangerous people who constituted by far the majority of the population yet could not be counted on to stay in their properly subservient position. These impoverished, unlearned peasants were an ill-defined group. The categorization of society as divided into three interdependent orders was proposed at the beginning of the eleventh century, but the concept of three distinct orders never gained much attention in the following two or three hundred years. These categories were institutionalized only in the Estates General of the fourteenth century. And even so, while nobles and churchmen were clearly defined, peasants were assigned to a rather amorphous group of "other"—which however essentially ignored them, preferring well-to-do townsmen for the Third Estate.[58] Even a political

---

58. Duby, *The Three Orders*. Curiously, this book is often misread as suggesting that medieval society really was divided into three distinct orders. Also curiously, Duby stops in the early thirteenth century, a hundred years before the creation of the Estates General.

body in which peasants might have been expected to have a voice left them, poor and voiceless, in the background.

But the charters from the high Middle Ages tell a different story.

Peasants in Medieval Records

This study focuses on the Burgundy-Champagne region, the classic territory "between the Rhine and the Loire" that is often treated as the center of all medieval developments, from monasticism to so-called feudalism. The region is rich in ecclesiastical documents from the eleventh and twelfth centuries, which compromise the bulk of the sources used here. Although most serious scholarship on medieval peasants has focused on the fourteenth and fifteenth centuries, with their manorial rolls and parish records, there are enough documents, especially in monastic archives, for ample evidence of the active peasants of the high Middle Ages.

Specifically the documents used in this book are drawn from some two dozen charter collections and cartularies from northern France, including documents from Benedictine, Cluniac, and Cistercian monasteries, bishoprics, and houses of Augustinian canons. Most of these are charter collections that have been little studied in the past. One cannot give exact figures, and the records of different houses varied considerably, but in the collections with which I am most familiar peasants are mentioned in somewhere between 20 percent and 35 percent of the surviving charters. The bulk of these documents are known now only because churchmen saw fit to copy them into books, cartularies, that have survived time and disaster better than did the piles of loose parchment leaves from which they were copied.[59]

In documents primarily recounting gifts to monasteries and the settlement of quarrels between monks and their secular neighbors, peasants routinely appear, going about their business. The following examples illustrate some of the diverse ways that peasants might appear in a document ostentatiously having little to do with lower-status people. These particular examples do not all show peasants making their own decisions, unlike most

---

59. For the composition of cartularies, see Constance Brittain Bouchard, *Holy Entrepreneurs: Cistercians, Knights, and Economic Exchange in Twelfth-Century Burgundy* (Ithaca, N.Y., 1991), pp. 16–18; and Bouchard, *Rewriting Saints and Ancestors*, pp. 9–52. The classic reference is Olivier Guyotjeannin, Laurent Morelle, and Michel Parisse, eds., *Les cartulaires*, Mémoires et documents de l'École des chartes 39 (Paris, 1993). For a discussion of cartularies' composition and purpose, see, most recently, Joanna Tucker, *Reading and Shaping Medieval Cartularies: Multi-Scribe Manuscripts and Their Patterns of Growth* (Woodbridge, Suff., 2020), pp. 4–33.

of the examples that will be seen in the following chapters, but they do demonstrate the central position they occupied in everything from pious gifts to quarrel settlements. Peasants were valuable, peasants were recognized as individuals, and hence they routinely appeared in the sources.

I begin with a charter from around 1160. It was issued by the archbishop of Sens and recorded the settlement of a quarrel between the cathedral chapter of Sens and the viscount of Sens.[60] This quarrel, involving the leading political and ecclesiastical figures of the Senonais, was according to the charter prolonged and contentious and only settled "due to the mercy of God." It concerned the two parties' authority over some peasants, named as the descendants of one Richelinus. His descendants do not seem to have had much actual say in the outcome, but all parties still had to take them seriously.

The two sides ended up dividing the peasants between them, each side formally noting that they had "freed" (liberos quidem et absolutos) those men and women who were to be dependent on the other. The family tree of Richelinus's descendants and the names of individuals were given in detail, down to his great-granddaughter, indicating that these were not just generic peasants but specific individuals, people so worth arguing about that their ultimate disposition required a formal settlement, with witnesses, seals, and copies of the charter (cyrographs) for all the principals. There would not have been a quarrel, much less a quarrel settlement, had not both parties found members of a single peasant family valuable, worth a dispute.

Around the same time, another heated dispute between secular and ecclesiastical authorities also involved peasants, again indicating how significant peasants were to the powerful. Here the noble lord Stephen of Pierre-Pertuis quarreled with the canons regular of St.-Marien of Auxerre over peasants (homines) who were clearing and cultivating land near one of the canons' granges. The dispute, over which ones would owe tithes to St.-Marien, was finally settled by members of the cathedral chapter of Auxerre and sealed by two bishops and the count.[61]

The charter took for granted that peasants were moving around and opening up new lands for cultivation and could not be forced to follow any particular settlement patterns. The question was how to collect revenues from people who had moved elsewhere. The settlement eventually spelled

---

60. *Cartulaire général de l'Yonne*, ed. Maximilien Quantin, 2 vols. (Auxerre, 1854–60), 2:110–11, no. 102.

61. *Cartulaire général de l'Yonne*, 2:162–63, no. 147. For Stephen and his family, see Constance Brittain Bouchard, *Sword, Miter, and Cloister: Nobility and the Church in Burgundy, 980–1198* (Ithaca, N.Y., 1987), pp. 354–57. For tithes, see also Arnoux, *Le temps des laboureurs*, pp. 237–55.

out a requirement to pay tithes depending on where the peasants lived and worked, which might not be where they had started. Such quarrels over peasants and their labor and dues were serious and hard to resolve because they were so central to the concerns of both churches and lay aristocrats. As this charter suggests, in many cases the most powerful had to make agreements and compromises among themselves to account for what the peasants had already done.

Indeed, many other documents that appear on the face to concern only great lords, both secular and ecclesiastical, may on closer examination prove to be about peasants. Raoul Glaber underscored the value of the peasantry when he described a quarrel between the archbishop of Tours and the count of Anjou early in the eleventh century. The archbishop refused to consecrate a monastery the count had built because, according to Raoul, he believed he should not appear before the Lord acting together with a count who had "stolen property and serfs" (*predia et mancipia*) from his own church.[62] The archbishop in Raoul's account found serfs worth a major quarrel with the most powerful secular lord of the region, indeed a dispute that God required of him.

One particularly telling example of the value of peasants comes from a charter of the nunnery of Marcigny, dating from the first decade of the twelfth century.[63] In it a husband and wife, Hugh and Maria, both entered the cloister, he at Paray-le-Monial and she at Marcigny. As their entry gift, they offered a mansus, according to the attesting charter. This mansus appears to have been unusually rich. It paid annually, according to the charter, a pig worth six solidi, six setiers of wine, four large loaves, four bushels of oats, and four pennies. In addition, the mansus provided labor dues and carting, though the details were not provided. The property was described as consisting of "meadows, woods, waters, vineyards, and revenue." Valuable as this land was, its value could not have been realized without the peasants who lived and worked on it: those who raised the pigs, grew the grain, did the labor, provided the cart, and had enough income of their own to pay a rent in coin.

Agricultural land complete with the peasants working it was thus the object both of many quarrels and also of pious gifts because both monks and their secular neighbors saw it as the basis of wealth. In a typical quarrel settlement around 1145, Guichard, the nephew of the dean of Chalon cathedral, said that he gave up his claims to a piece of land belonging to the monks of La Ferté and, with the land, those who lived there, the brothers Aimo and John, identified as sons of one Amicus. Guichard received thirty solidi

---

62. Raoul Glaber, "Historia" 2.3, p. 62.

63. *Le cartulaire de Marcigny-sur-Loire (1045–1144): Essai de reconstitution d'un manuscrit disparu*, ed. Jean Richard (Dijon, 1957), pp. 84–85, no. 115.

(that is, a pound and a half) as part of this settlement. A separate gift by his uncle the dean to La Ferté at almost the same time suggests that Guichard may have been under family (and ecclesiastical) pressure to end his quarrel.[64]

The point here is that the quarrel was not just over land but over people, significant enough people to be specifically named. The land had value because of the peasants who were on it. Unused land, vacant land, waste land was without value; the new monastic orders embracing poverty and humility deliberately sought out waste land for their new houses because it reflected their search for poverty and isolation, but they quickly put it under cultivation.[65] Arable land, agricultural land constituted wealth, and the foundation of that wealth consisted of the peasant men and women who lived on and worked the land.

Peasant Agency

It should not be surprising that peasants were successful, at least some of the time, in making their own decisions and directing their own lives. After all, a premodern society had no way for a small minority to determine the behavior of everyone else. If back under the slaveholding Roman Empire men had sometimes worried that their slaves might recognize how many of them they were, medieval peasants had no trouble recognizing that they constituted the bulk of the population, indeed virtually everybody outside the cities. Although they did not develop what would now be called class consciousness before the fourteenth century, and did not see peasants in other areas as their natural allies, they certainly recognized that when they worked together with their neighbors they had a great deal of opportunity to shape their own experiences. They may have been burdened with obligations and very hard work and lived in conditions that were always difficult and sometimes brutal, but they were never helpless victims.

Peasants acted with what I call agency, that is, the ability of individuals or groups of individuals to be social agents, to influence and modify both their society and their position in it. Although it is sometimes assumed that a marker of modernity is the ability of adult members of society to make major decisions about their own situation or to resist oppression, with the corollary that most premodern people would have lacked such agency,[66]

---

64. *Recueil des pancartes de l'abbaye de La Ferté-sur-Grosne, 1113–1178*, ed. Georges Duby (Paris, 1953), p. 135, nos. 154–55.

65. Bouchard, *Holy Entrepreneurs*, pp. 97–106.

66. Ionut Epuresco-Pascovici argues on the contrary for medieval people's agency laying the foundation of modern society, although his discussion encompasses only those of more elevated

I shall demonstrate that medieval peasants could and did work to shape their own lives. They were capable of remarkable initiative and resilience and had networks and strategies that made it possible for them to modify their position or negotiate for better conditions. These were a constant; even if they were not always successful in obtaining their goals, one cannot assume that it was from a lack of effort. This book uses then the lens of peasant agency to argue that common assumptions about these people need to be reexamined, and that they need to be much more widely studied and appreciated.

All humans of course have agency, the ability even in the worst circumstances to strive for at least some amelioration. Recently scholars who study marginalized people in the modern world have begun analyzing the ways that low-status people can successfully resist in small ways, without resorting to open revolt against the powerful. As James Scott put it in his classic study of rural villagers in twentieth-century Malaysia, the weapons of the weak are "foot dragging, dissimulation, desertion, false compliance, pilfering, feigned ignorance, slander, arson, sabotage, and so on."[67] All of these were certainly tools known to and used by medieval peasants.

But the agency I shall be discussing here was not limited to such efforts, for medieval peasants were able to seek and indeed achieve far more than minor amelioration of their situation. I would argue that one should not see the peasantry of the high Middle Ages merely as finding ways to circumvent those who constantly demanded food, labor, and dues from them. The coercive abilities of medieval lords were far more limited than those of the powerful in the modern era. And yet scholars have been slow to recognize peasant action, self-determination, or resistance.[68] The peasants of the eleventh and twelfth centuries often took the initiative in improving their

---

status than peasants; *Human Agency in Medieval Society, 1100–1450* (Woodbridge, Suff., 2021). His introduction provides a useful discussion of the concept of agency.

67. James C. Scott, *Weapons of the Weak: Everyday Forms of Peasant Resistance* (New Haven, Conn., 1985), p. xvi. He gives a nod to Marc Bloch and his statement that the only check on lordly abuse of power was peasants' "capacity for passive resistance"; Bloch, *Feudal Society*, trans. L. A. Manyon (Chicago, 1961), p. 249.

68. For example, Bisson states that the "agrarian masses" needed "protection from the noxious forces of a fallen world in exchange for customary services and payments" owed to castellan lords, being incapable of protecting themselves. He adds that the "exploited" peasants experienced lordship as "a willful domination to be suffered in patience"; *The Crisis of the Twelfth Century*, p. 40. Similarly, Vincent Corriol refers to peasants playing a "passive role" in the documents, "unnamed" and "voiceless"; "Nommer les serfs dans la terre de Saint-Claude (Jura—début XIIIe–début XVIe siècle)," in Paul Freedman and Monique Bourin, eds., *Forms of Servitude in Northern and Central Europe: Decline, Resistance, and Expansion* (Turnhout, 2005), pp. 61–62.

position, without reference to any lord who might have forced them to do something different. This is the agency that pervades this book.

In the following pages the reader will find a great many examples of peasant agency. This is neither an exhaustive list nor a scientific sample, but rather an analysis of representative cases that demonstrate the various ways that peasants could make serious decisions about their own lives. Once one begins to look for active peasants in the records one finds that, like medieval women, they were everywhere.

I begin with an extended discussion of peasant status, including the meaning of servitude. Following that I take up the nature of peasant dues and obligations, including the extent to which these were negotiated. Next I address the question of the relationship between peasants and the church, because peasants are too frequently seen as half pagan and living in a world separate from the issues of religion and church governance that concerned the rest of their society. Peasant collective action and readiness both to fight and to negotiate is evident in their participation in "new towns" and communes, the subject of the next chapter. These chapters lay the groundwork for the culminating chapter on peasant agency. Medieval peasants' ability to take control of their own situation is especially evident in their ability to fight back, surprisingly successfully, against what they saw as oppression, through determined resistance, through negotiation, and through taking their cases to court. Peasants may not now be the most obvious or powerful players in their society, but they were as much a part of it as any monk or knight (or nun or lady).

CHAPTER 1

Peasant Status and the Meanings of Serfdom

So far I have spoken of medieval peasants without necessarily trying to define them. The word "peasant" is ours, from the French *paysan*, meaning simply a person of the countryside (*pays*). At the most basic level a peasant is indistinguishable from a farmer, but medieval farmers are now almost always referred to as peasants, a word that also carries unfortunate overtones of dependency and lack of sophistication. In fact the term can work fairly well as a broad term to designate those who lived in a rural setting, primarily engaged in agriculture, which is why I continue to use it, but one must always keep in mind that it is our category, not theirs.

The term "peasants" in this book includes shepherds and herdsmen as well as agricultural workers, most of whom would have lived in villages in the Middle Ages, rather than the isolated farmsteads typical in North America. The term also includes a fairly wide selection of skilled occupations including wheelwright, miller, brewer, or blacksmith, all of which would have been important in village economy.[1] The distinction between a farming village and a small town of one thousand or so inhabitants, where some of the population would have made their living as artisans or in trade, can

---

1. See also Phillipp R. Schofield, *Peasants and Historians: Debating the Medieval English Peasantry* (Manchester, Eng., 2016), pp. 21–23.

never have been distinct. Some agricultural workers and others engaged in the rural economy were serfs, legally unfree, but certainly not all of them.

The exact proportion of peasants in overall medieval society is unknowable, although the figure of 90 percent is often seen. This estimate is based on informed guesses as to how many agricultural workers with premodern technology it would have taken to raise enough food beyond their own needs to feed those not engaged directly in farming: aristocrats, ecclesiastics, people in the skilled trades, and the population of the growing cities. Peasants were at any rate by far the largest segment of the population, a segment that appeared in the records much less often than their numbers alone would have justified. The peasants on which this book focuses were one part of a somewhat larger though also (partially) invisible group that included household servants on the one hand and petty landowners on the other, the latter people who might or might not have tilled the soil themselves but who at any rate had no castles or noble titles.[2] Invisible? Written records are of course created by and for the literate, that is, the elite, but the great mass of the population can still be glimpsed in those records.

A serf, a villager, a rustic, a farmer, a tenant, one of "those who work," someone who was simply called a "man" or "woman," all of these were medieval designations for someone who might now be called a peasant, but they were not synonyms.[3] Status and obligations were not the same across regions or across the centuries. Ninth-century documents were especially rich in terms for peasants, such as *hospes, collibertus, ingenuus, mancipius, colonus,* or *famulus,* and scholars have yet to reach consensus on what all these words meant. Those who described peasant status in charters and treatises at the time appear to have had fairly clear ideas of what they intended by the terms they used, but they rarely attempted to define what to them were self-evident words.

The *servi* and *ancillae* of the tenth and eleventh centuries, characterized using words that went back to Roman law, may confidently be said to be unfree serfs (respectively male and female), but the status of those designated *homines* and *feminae* in the twelfth century are not as immediately obvious. Even without all the confusing mix of terms for serfs and peasants found in the polyptyques of the ninth century, it is difficult to pin down the meaning of terms used for lower-status country people in the high Middle

2. Christopher Loveluck, *Northwest Europe in the Early Middle Ages, c. AD 600–1150: A Comparative Archaeology* (Cambridge, 2013), pp. 33–56.

3. See also Michel Parisse, "Histoire et sémantique: De *servus* à *homo*," in Paul Freedman and Monique Bourin, eds., *Forms of Servitude in Northern and Central Europe: Decline, Resistance, and Expansion* (Turnhout, 2005), pp. 43–45.

Ages. A *rusticus* lived in the countryside, but nothing further can be said for certain about him. An *agricola* was a farmer, designated by the classical Latin word, but this usage was rare in the Middle Ages—*agrarius* was even rarer. A *villanus* lived in a village, but did that mean he was a peasant? Or should we call him a villager or perhaps a villein? And was *villicus* simply a synonym for *villanus* or, as a number of documents suggest, was a *villicus* the head man of a village?[4] And should we even translate *villa* as village or perhaps as manor or estate, thus changing our definition of who lived there?[5]

Describing peasants is further complicated by the appropriation of the term by modern sociology and anthropology, where those called peasants are always assumed to labor to support a class of landowners and overlords. That is, peasants are defined not by what they themselves do but how they support the wealthy and powerful.[6] This modern definition does not, however, work for the Middle Ages. Medieval peasants might indeed work for landowners and overlords, but they were just as likely to work only for themselves and their families.[7]

The conditions under which medieval peasants lived were never uniform. Charlemagne's c. 800 pronouncement on what royal manors were supposed to include (right down to the varieties of apple to be grown) was clearly prescriptive, that is, a model or goal, not descriptive of what his manors were all like. Nor can the small number of existing polyptyques of great ninth-century monastic estates (there are fewer than a dozen) be taken as representative of a typical rural manor. And polyptyques would normally list only a small number of dependent families in a particular village, even though the village might be noted as supporting a church, a mill, and a brewery/bakehouse, indicating a much more substantial local population than the dozen or twenty families enumerated.[8] The peasants who can be glimpsed were part of a much larger number of rural dwellers, whose situation can only be inferred. Even these descriptions of estates in the ninth century have

---

4. Robert F. Berkhofer III identifies a *villicus* as a bailiff or estate manager; "Marriage, Lordship and the 'Greater Unfree' in Twelfth-Century France," *Past and Present* 173 (2001), 4.

5. Léopold Genicot, *Rural Communities in the Medieval West* (Baltimore, 1990), pp. 12–29.

6. Eric R. Wolf, *Peasants* (Englewood Cliffs, N.J., 1966), p. 11. "It is only . . . when the cultivator becomes subject to the demands and sanctions of power-holders outside his social stratum that we can appropriately speak of peasantry." This book, still in print for classroom use, remains one of the few anthropological efforts to define peasantry. James C. Scott's ethnographic study of rural villagers in twentieth-century Malaysia uses "peasant" in this sense as an unproblematic term; *Weapons of the Weak: Everyday Forms of Peasant Resistance* (New Haven, Conn., 1985).

7. See also Bruce M. S. Campbell, *English Seigniorial Agriculture, 1250–1450* (Cambridge, 2000), pp. 1–3.

8. "Capitulare de villis," MGH Capit. 1 (1883; rpt. 1984), pp. 82–91. Constance B. Bouchard, "Peasants and Polyptyques in the Ninth Century: The Peasant Hermod," *Medieval People* 36 (2022), 1–22.

no parallels for the eleventh and twelfth centuries, yet peasant appearance in the charters of the high Middle Ages makes it possible to discover much about them.

Varieties of Peasant Status

Rural agricultural workers might be variously designated by legal status, that is, whether they were servile or free, although here it is important to note that many, indeed most peasants were not serfs in the eleventh and twelfth centuries. They also varied by economic and social status, as some peasants were allodists, that is, they owned their property outright, and others were tenants, being required to pay rent for the land where they lived and on which they raised food.[9] Whether allodists or tenants, they might be relatively well-to-do or might be desperately poor. These categories regularly overlapped; for example, enough tenants also owned some property of their own that the categories were more theoretical than real.

Most of Europe's medieval population was neither rich nor powerful, but they were far from an undifferentiated mass. High medieval charters name a number of individuals without explicitly indicating their status, and yet hint that some might have been well-to-do peasants. The very difficulty of categorizing such people is an indication that there were no clear economic or social markers for a peasant. The petty landowners who appear frequently, making gifts of small pieces of land to churches, are particularly hard to place. It would be too easy to assume that they must have been noble (or at least of knightly status) to be in a position to donate land, but this would be circular reasoning. Equally true of course one should not assume that any donors who appear without any indication of status must have been peasants. But there are far too many such donors for them all to be great lords, especially since their gifts were small and they often disappear into documentary silence after appearing just long enough to make a gift to the monks. Evidently these were at least moderately well-to-do people, indicating that peasant status did not necessarily denote poverty, and those peasants who were (figuratively) breaking their backs in unrewarding agriculture lived surrounded by better-off but still low-status landowners.

The cartularies of the twelfth-century Cistercians are full of donations by people identified simply by their names, not as knights, not as lords of anything, just named individuals, Jotzald or Ulric or Bertram or a hundred

9. Pierre Bonnassie, *From Slavery to Feudalism in South-Western Europe*, trans. Jean Birrell (Cambridge, 1991), pp. 296–98.

other names, with their wives, brothers, and children, giving a meadow or half a vineyard or a piece of arable land.[10] This lack of stated status stands in contrast to many of the people who confirmed or witnessed the gifts, the bishop and castellan lords and knights, identified by title. The donors were certainly country people because they were making gifts of country property, and undoubtedly allodists because they did not have to ask anyone else's permission to make these gifts. They knew who they were, and the scribes who recorded their names and their gifts knew who they were.

It is difficult to determine how much social separation existed between such donors and the tenants who were said to inhabit a mansus and who accompanied that mansus when a knight or cathedral canon gave it to a monastery. One of the earliest surviving charters for Clairvaux is an 1135 pancarte issued by the bishop of Langres, summarizing and confirming gifts to the monks from people identified only by their names. These gifts were small, usually consisting of "whatever we have" in a certain village or territory.[11] Certainly many, even most peasants would have been too destitute to make a pious gift, but clearly the wider rural population, whether we call them peasants or not, included men and women who owned little pieces of land that could be turned into appropriate donations.

Even individuals who can be studied in more detail are often difficult to characterize. A charter from Montier-en-Der from the mid-eleventh century shows a man, Arnulf of Soulaines, who might be considered either a knight or a serf or a small peasant landowner depending on which characteristics one stresses. He appears in the monastery's charters as a "faithful man" (*vir fidelis*) of the monastery, which could suggest that he was a knight. His appearance with a loconym (*de Sufflanna*, "of Soulaines") might also suggest elevated social status. And yet the charter in which he appears is a record of him offering himself to the monastery as a serf.[12]

The charter states that he requested to be associated with the monastery both spiritually (*spiritaliter*), due to the monks' charity, and physically (*carnaliter*), through the service he was offering (*pro sua servitute*). The monks granted him some land and revenues and a third of the tithes at a hamlet near Soulaines but specified that they would not give him anything else, unless he needed to be relieved of desperate hunger or ransomed if captured.

---

10. The pancartes of La Ferté, Cîteaux's first daughter house, have many such donations. *Recueil des pancartes de l'abbaye de La Ferté-sur-Grosne, 1113–1178*, ed. Georges Duby (Paris, 1953).

11. *Recueil des chartes de l'abbaye de Clairvaux*, ed. Jean Waquet et al. (Troyes, 1950–82), pp. 8–14, no. 6.

12. *The Cartulary of Montier-en-Der, 666–1129*, ed. Constance Brittain Bouchard, Medieval Academy Books 108 (Toronto, 2004), pp. 157–58, no. 58.

The concern that he might be captured suggests someone potentially engaged in war, again raising the possibility that he was a knight, but he is never so called. Instead, the charter merely stresses the "service" that Arnulf would be providing, perhaps protecting Der's property around Soulaines.

Arnulf is mentioned again in the charters of Montier-en-Der a generation or so later, toward the end of the eleventh century, when his son, Gui of Soulaines, asked the monks for everything his late father had held. The monks granted the land with its income to Gui and his wife, specifying that they did so for their lifetimes only. Gui and Hildegarde, his wife, gave the monks eight pounds "out of devotion," made the monks their heirs, and specified that they would be buried at Montier-en-Der.[13] In this charter, Gui appears less like a stereotypical peasant (or what one would now consider a peasant) and more like a small-scale landowner. His expectation of being buried at the monastery certainly suggests relatively elite status. And yet his father had offered himself, as a serf, in return for the original grant he received from the monastery. This example then indicates how difficult it is to define exactly the social and economic status of a peasant—and, more importantly, how useless it would be to try to do so.

Even having property labeled a fief (*feudum*) in the documents was not always enough to distinguish a peasant from someone of more elevated status.[14] In spite of historians' laudable efforts to separate peasants with tenancies (manorialism) from knights with fiefs (feudalism),[15] there are examples of what appears to be peasant tenancies called fiefs. A document from Bèze from around 1100 refers to the *foedum* of one of the monks' tenants, *villicus noster*, perhaps a village headsman. He held fields and meadows from the monks and owed them a rent in grain. This man was undeniably involved in agriculture, as his holdings and his rents indicate, despite receiving what was called a fief. In another document from Bèze from around the same time, a man who was acting as secular provost for the monks gave them what the attesting document called his *fedum*, which consisted of two mansi—what scholars always assume are peasant tenancies—saying he did so for his soul. As well as spiritual benefits, the provost received two measures of grain and a cow from the monastery.[16]

---

13. *The Cartulary of Montier-en-Der*, pp. 248–49, no. 117.

14. Fiefs have become much more problematic since the work of Susan Reynolds, *Fiefs and Vassals: The Medieval Evidence Reinterpreted* (Oxford, 1994).

15. I have done this myself; *"Strong of Body, Brave and Noble": Chivalry and Society in Medieval France* (Ithaca, N.Y., 1998), pp. 35–46.

16. *The Cartulary-Chronicle of St.-Pierre of Bèze*, ed. Constance Brittain Bouchard, Medieval Academy Books 116 (Toronto, 2019), pp. 282–83, 298, nos. 234, 246. The countergift of the cow indicates

Peasants with what were called fiefs are also found in other regions. At Marmoutier, outside of Tours, the monks' "Book of Serfs" includes a revelatory charter from the end of the eleventh century. Here the abbot confirmed to a man named Benedict the vineyard he had held "in fief" (*in fevo*) for his lifetime, and then granted him a second vineyard in return for him agreeing to become the *servus* of the monastery.[17] Benedict, the charter said, had been free (*ingenuus*) before becoming a dependent (*famulus*). Here a "fief" appears to have meant simply a lifetime grant, as of course it also meant for the knights who received fiefs from their lords. The monks retained ultimate authority over the vineyards, so that Benedict was not supposed to sell what he had received from them. The only exception was if he became ill or fell into poverty, and even then he would be required to sell only to the monks or their men. In this case the monks showed no concern for whether a fief was appropriate for someone of a certain legal or social status; all that mattered was that the grant was for the recipient's lifetime only.

Given such examples, there appears to have been a continuum of social status, from the highest nobility to the most abjectly dependent serf. Although it is tempting to draw a sharp line between "those who work" and "those who fight," the documents suggest that these were not sharply defined categories. Great lords, knights, small landowners, well-to-do farmers, merchants, artisans, skilled workers, hired laborers, tenants who rented their land from others, and serfs were not necessarily distinct, because the same person might have attributes that could be considered to place him or her in more than one category. Even servile status, which one might have considered the clearest category legally and the lowest, was heavily nuanced in the high Middle Ages.

Servile and Free

Serfs were peasants who were legally unfree, considered "bound in the body" for life to a lord, with restrictions on their ability to act independently; the status was assumed to be hereditary. Because legally they were considered bound to their lord's will, they were not supposed to sue in court or take orders in the church—although there are many examples of them doing so. A century ago scholars assumed that all agricultural workers were serfs

---

the provost had some land, which would have been needed for pasturage, besides that which he held as a *fedum*.

17. *Le livre des serfs de Marmoutier*, ed. André Salmon (Tours, 1864), p. 112, no. 120. See also Dominique Barthélemy, *The Serf, the Knight, and the Historian*, trans. Graham Robert Edwards (Ithaca, N.Y., 2009), p. 55.

in the Middle Ages, but regional studies have made clear that serfs were a subgroup of all peasants in the high Middle Ages, indeed a minority: there were always free peasants, including some who rented their land and others who owned it outright.[18] And servile status essentially disappeared from the records in northern France in the first decades of the twelfth century.

In legal treatises, at least by the thirteenth century, serf and free were binary categories, meaning that a peasant might have servile status, that is, be subject to all sorts of restrictions on everything from marriage to giving testimony, or else he or she might be a free person. But when high medieval peasants became active participants in the decisions that affected them, the line between free and servile was far less clear. In practice there were many gradations in the high Middle Ages between outright servitude, nearly indistinguishable from slavery, and free status.

The distinction between servile and free went back to Roman law.[19] Here the categories were sharp: one was either a slave, without any sort of what would now be called human rights, or else a free man or woman. Although medieval jurists never really broke with Roman definitions, in practice slavery declined rapidly in the early Middle Ages, especially during the plague and climatic disasters of the sixth century.[20] In part large slave-worked plantations became unsustainable during the economic collapse of late antiquity, and it became more viable for landlords to give their slaves a certain amount of self-determination, including the expectation that they feed themselves. In part the spread of Christianity made freeing one's slaves a good deed, and free Christians were not supposed to be enslaved. In part runaway slaves, who could not easily be replaced once the Roman Empire stopped expanding and bringing back new captives, reduced the overall number of slaves, at the same time as the breakdown of Roman central state authority made

---

18. Theodore Evergates, *Feudal Society in the Bailliage of Troyes under the Counts of Champagne, 1152–1284* (Baltimore, 1975), pp. 15–30. Paul Freedman and Monique Bourin, "Introduction," in Freedman and Bourin, eds., *Forms of Servitude*, pp. 1–2. Paul Freedman, "Peasants, the Seigneurial Regime, and Serfdom in the Eleventh to Thirteenth Centuries," in *European Transformations: The Long Twelfth Century*, ed. Thomas F. X. Noble and John Van Engen (Notre Dame, Ind., 2012), pp. 267–68.

19. Alice Rio provides a close analysis of early medieval slavery and serfdom, from the clear legal definitions of Roman antiquity to the medieval revival of chattel slavery, involving, at least theoretically, only religious outsiders; *Slavery after Rome, 500–1100* (Oxford, 2017). For an overview of recent scholarship on Roman and medieval slavery, see Samuel S. Sutherland, "The Study of Slavery in the Early and Central Middle Ages: Old Problems and New Approaches," *History Compass* 18, no. 10 (2020), https://doi.org/10.1111/hic3.12633.

20. For the sixth-century plague, see William Rosen, *Justinian's Flea: The First Great Plague and the End of the Roman Empire* (London, 2008).

suppression of slave rebellions more difficult.[21] Servile status continued, however, even though there is little evidence of outright slavery in northern France after the eighth century, other than the occasional household slave.[22]

The word for serf in medieval Latin was *servus*, the same as the Latin for slave, which is why medieval jurists often conflated the two—the feminine form was *ancilla*, the "handmaiden" of the Vulgate Bible. Yet in practice, even serfs were capable of a good deal of autonomy. Slaves had no rights at all; serfs, in contrast, were granted access to what would now be called rights (marriage, inheritance, property) if they were willing to pay their lords for them.[23]

There was also great variation in the exact requirements under which a serf functioned, and in the records of the ninth and tenth centuries serfs are more commonly referred to by such terms as *hospes* or *colonus*, terms that appear to have designated free tenants in late antiquity, rather than *servus*. Interestingly, *servus* and *ancilla* reappeared in the late tenth century as the standard terms for a serf,[24] and the break in terminology may be indicative of the gulf between the slaves of the Roman Empire at its height and the serfs of the high Middle Ages. The latter made their own decisions in ways the former could not have dreamed.

Medieval serfs may have been descended from slaves of earlier centuries, or may have willingly taken on servile status in return for what they perceived as benefits, or may have been coerced into servitude. They might work the land for their lord of the body or might serve in other ways. They typically owed heavy burdens of labor dues and rent, paid in produce or coin, but so did many free peasants, and some serfs owed very little on a regular basis. They were at any rate expected to be obedient, as Raoul Glaber indicated in the mid-eleventh century, when he used the phrase "more obedient than a serf" to indicate how readily someone obeyed.[25] They might demonstrate their servile status through annual ceremonies or specific fees or just have it preserved in oral memory. All these variations meant an absence of

---

21. A Marxist reading of this transition is provided by Chris Wickham, *Land and Power: Studies in Italian and European Social History, 400–1200* (London, 1994), pp. 9–42.

22. Nonetheless, eastern Europe and the Mediterranean continued an active slave trade in the following centuries—the very word "slave" comes from "Slav." Indeed, Michael McCormick posits that Europe paid in the late eighth and ninth centuries for the spices and silks imported from the east with captured slaves; "New Light on the 'Dark Ages': How the Slave Trade Fueled the Carolingian Economy," *Past and Present* 177 (2002), 40–51.

23. This is Rio's definition of serfdom; *Slavery after Rome*, p. 14. See also Jean-Pierre Poly and Eric Bournazel, *The Feudal Transformation, 900–1200*, trans. Caroline Higgitt (New York, 1991), pp. 120–22.

24. Parisse, "Histoire et sémantique," pp. 25, 40.

25. Raoul Glaber, "Historia" 3.9, in *Opera*, ed. John France et al. (Oxford, 1989), p. 152.

clear demarcations, especially since serfs' obligations were often referred to laconically in charters where the actual topic was something different.

Scholars have often sought to distinguish free peasants in the records from serfs by means of certain markers,[26] but these were never standard or uniform. A ritual in which the serf placed pennies on his head unambiguously indicated subjection, but it appears in only a small number of monastic cartularies. The arbitrary requirement that a peasant work whenever or wherever a lord required, rather than providing a set amount of labor, might distinguish serfs from free tenants, but in practice this was far from universal. Other so-called markers of serfdom have been reified into clearly defined fees, given French names derived from medieval Latin. Most commonly one now sees reference to *mainmorte*, a requirement that a serf's heirs pay an inheritance tax if not living at home when a parent died (also sometimes called *heriot*), and *formariage*, that is, restrictions on whom a serf might marry (also sometimes called *merchet*). The "head tax," where someone places pennies on his head, is termed *chevage*.

One of the apparently clearest indications of servile status and obligations appears in the late eleventh-century "Book of Serfs" of the monastery of Marmoutier, which has provided scholars with what have come to be considered the classic markers of serfdom.[27] Here were copied charters from the late tenth and the eleventh centuries in which serfs were given as gifts to Marmoutier or, in some cases, offered themselves as serfs to the monks. The monks called this collection of documents *De servis*, indicating that they themselves considered *servus* an unambiguous category. Curiously, little scholarly attention has been paid to the details about the peasants described in this book, beyond creating modern definitions of what serfdom entailed.[28]

---

26. For example, Parisse, "Histoire et sémantique," pp. 26–34. See also Vincent Corriol, "Nommer les serfs dans la terre de Saint-Claude (Jura—début XIIIe–début XVIe siècle)," in Freedman and Bourin, eds., *Forms of Servitude*, pp. 59–60.

27. R. W. Southern used documents from Marmoutier to illustrate the nature of serfdom, giving generations of budding medievalists their first definitions of what the status entailed; *The Making of the Middle Ages* (New Haven, Conn., 1953), pp. 98–107.

28. One of the few to utilize this source is Dominique Barthélemy, who uses it to argue against a feudal revolution, saying instead that Marmoutier's records show a continuity of serfdom rather than a new eleventh-century form; *The Serf, the Knight, and the Historian*, pp. 37–67. See also Rio, *Slavery after Rome*, pp. 108–9. Paul Fouracre uses this "Book" not to discuss peasants but rather to argue about the extent that political power did or did not collapse in the eleventh century; "Marmoutier and Its Serfs in the Eleventh Century," *Transactions of the Royal Historical Society* 15 (2005), 29–49. Two important studies of society and memory in the Touraine, based heavily on the records of Marmoutier, oddly omit any discussion of Marmoutier's "Book of Serfs": Stephen D. White, *Custom, Kinship, and Gifts to Saints: The "Laudatio parentum" in Western France, 1050–1150* (Chapel Hill, N.C., 1988); and Sharon Farmer, *Communities of Saint Martin: Legend and Ritual in Medieval Tours* (Ithaca, N.Y., 1991).

Yet the documents the Marmoutier scribes copied did not use nearly as tidy distinctions between serf and free as have been attributed to them. The first document in the volume records the local viscount's donation of a *colliberta* named Ermengarda to Marmoutier.[29] Scholars have generally agreed that a *collibertus* (or here *colliberta*) was not strictly the same as a serf, having as the name suggests at least a hint of liberty about him (or her). Yet the late eleventh-century monks of Marmoutier saw no problem equating this woman's status to that of a serf, as the document's leading position in their "Book of Serfs" indicates.

In addition, the document itself suggests that more was at stake here than the transfer of lordship over one downtrodden peasant woman to the monastery. The donation charter was not merely issued by the viscount himself but rather by the counts of Anjou and Vendôme, the most powerful lords of the region. Anyone who tries to undercut this donation, the charter threatens, will have to pay a fine of thirty pounds of gold, a startlingly large sum. The gift of the *colliberta* Ermengarda, a gift framed with the same biblical language as accompanied major gifts of property at the time,[30] issued by men of exalted status, and accompanied by threats of a serious fine, all indicate that the woman herself had great significance: her presence required the agreement of the powerful, a detailed donation charter, and a copying of that charter several generations after Ermengarda was dead.

The Marmoutier documents further complicate the definition of serf and peasant because those accepting servile status in the monastery were not necessarily agricultural workers. That is, the line between servile and free did not always follow the same line as between farmer and artisan or tradesman. The men and women who were given to the monks or who made themselves the servile dependents of the monastery appear in the documents not only as agricultural workers but often with designations such as blacksmith, cook, carpenter, seamstress, or shepherd. For example, around the middle of the eleventh century a blacksmith named Girard gave himself into servitude to Saint Martin and the monks, along with his wife and children and descendants in perpetuity, saying he did so moved by divine love.[31] Here, an artisan or skilled tradesman becoming the monastery's serf acquired a steady

---

29. *Le livre des serfs*, pp. 1–3, no. 1.

30. For this language, see Constance Brittain Bouchard, *Sword, Miter, and Cloister: Nobility and the Church in Burgundy, 980–1198* (Ithaca, N.Y., 1987), pp. 225–28.

31. *Le livre des serfs*, p. 33, no. 33. See also Barthélemy, who suggests implausibly that *none* of the serfs who gave themselves to Marmoutier may have been agricultural workers; *The Serf, the Knight, and the Historian*, pp. 51–54.

market for his services, while the monks now had a dependable person to produce what they and their dependents needed.

The Marmoutier documents include far more instances of someone voluntarily taking on servitude than do the records of other monasteries, doubtless because the monks of Marmoutier are the only ones known to have compiled a volume specifically to record such events, but such voluntarily submission is also found elsewhere. The Burgundian sources support the evidence from Marmoutier that ecclesiastical serfs were not simply the downtrodden.

For example, in the early decades of the eleventh century four men who already were tenants of Montier-en-Der (*homines nostri*) said they offered themselves in servitude (*servitium*) in return for a piece of land at Effincourt, where they lived. The document specified that they and their descendants would work this land and pay the monks three solidi a year.[32] Given that Effincourt was nearly forty kilometers from the monastery, thus inconveniently distant for regular interactions, it seems fairly evident that the men's offer to take on servile status was less an acceptance of new burdens and more a way to secure some new property for themselves. One may also note that the monks' holdings at Effincourt were nothing like the great manors of the polyptyques, consisting rather of a few mansi there. The three solidi the men offered to pay to Der each year was the most important aspect of the transaction, for the charter specified the penalties if this *censum* were not paid. The men's offer of servitude could have potentially generated requirements for additional labor or payments, but when they made it, its principal effect was making it possible for them to obtain a piece of land for what appears to have been a bargain price.

A quite different case of someone voluntarily becoming a serf in the eleventh century involves a woman named Manna. She had been gravely ill, but after she credited the Virgin and other saints at Soissons for healing her, she offered herself and all her descendants to the cathedral in gratitude. As an indication of her new servile status, she specified that she and her family would all come to the church each year with four pennies on everyone's head. In 1115 Bishop Lisiard of Soissons confirmed her gift of herself, a century or more after the gift was made, detailing Manna's *genealogia* with the names of all her descendants over the next six generations. Making her whole family serfs was the culmination of what the bishop described as many "good

---

32. *The Cartulary of Montier-en-Der*, pp. 139–49, no. 45.

works and alms" already offered to the cathedral; her own body was the most precious thing she could give.[33]

From a modern perspective it may seem strange that someone would choose to become a serf. The usual explanation has been that in the face of famine, Vikings, or other disasters, free peasants would be so desperate that they were willing to give up their freedom for protection, yet the documents do not indicate desperation. Records of northern France in the eleventh century suggest it was a period of growth and spiritual reform, with barbarian raids well in the past.[34] Indeed, the religious ferment of the time may well have been a motivator for those who made themselves the serfs of monasteries such as Marmoutier, as discussed further in chapter 3.

Even being a serf did not necessarily mean that one had no status or possessions. In a charter from the Burgundian monastery of Bèze, probably dating from the late tenth century, the monks received a serf (*servus*) from one Gautsonius and his wife, given to them as a gift.[35] Nothing about this seems different from the usual model of servitude until one realizes that the donor Gautsonius himself was a serf! Married, having a serf dependent on him by legal right (*juris sui*), he was still identified as a servile dependent of the monastery, *colonus Sancti Petri*. The term *colonus* has been debated,[36] but in this context there can be no doubt that it signified serfdom, for the serf (*servus*) who was given was specified as remaining a *colonus*, just like the man who gave him (*sicut et ipse Gautsonius*). Donor and gift thus shared the same legal status. Being a serf did not impede Gautsonius and his wife from having a serf of their own, one they were able to give as a pious gift to the monastery.

Serfs then were a far from uniform group. Indeed, servile status itself was malleable, something that did not keep determined peasants from negotiating their position and status. In spite of restrictions their lords imposed on them, serfs were especially persistent in choosing themselves whom they would marry. In an example dating to the middle of the eleventh century, a serf named Aimeric wanted to marry a woman named Wilburga. Her brothers, however, were said to be reluctant to allow the marriage, noting

---

33. Paris, BnF, Coll. Picardie 281, no. 2. Printed by Parisse, "Histoire et sémantique," pp. 54–55.

34. Barthélemy, *The Serf, the Knight, and the Historian*, pp. 38–40. Fouracre, "Marmoutier and Its Serfs," p. 36.

35. *The Cartulary-Chronicle of Bèze*, p. 108, no. 32.

36. Adriaan Verhulst, "Quelques remarques à propos des corvées de colons à l'époque du Bas-Empire et du Haut Moyen Age," in *D'une déposition à un couronnement, 476–800: Rupture ou continuité dans la naissance de l'Occident médiéval*, ed. Institut des Hautes études de Belgique (Brussels, 1975), pp. 89–95.

that Aimeric owed service (*servicium*) to Lord Narduin of Chaffois. In other words, Wilburga's brothers did not want to allow her to marry someone of servile status. But Aimeric was not deterred.

According to the attesting charter, he "did not wish to desist from his proposal" and went to Narduin, his lord, to ask that Narduin give him to the monastery of Romainmôtier. Lord Narduin agreed, giving Aimeric and his future children to that house on the condition that the monks give him two pennies' worth of wax a year.[37] This was an extremely low annual payment, so it is most likely that Narduin also considered this gift as for the good of his soul, although the charter does not so specify. The important point is that Aimeric, in spite of his servile status, was able to make his own choice of marriage partner and negotiate his status to make it possible. If he had to pay *formariage* or other fee, the document does not record it. He was able to use Lord Narduin's apparent desire to save his soul as a means of bettering his own position. He might still have been considered a serf, but his success in ultimately marrying Wilburga indicates that being a monastic serf was preferable to being the serf of the lord of Chaffois.

In a similar case also from Romainmôtier from the end of the eleventh century, a serf dependent on that house was able to determine his children's status.[38] According to the attesting charter, drawn up appreciably later, the serf, named Mainer, married a woman named Gerlendis, an *ancilla*. The difficulty was that Gerlendis was dependent on a knight, and he held her in fief (*in beneficio*) from the count of Burgundy. Here everyone seems to have assumed that the children of Mainer and Gerlendis would, like her, be the knight's serfs.

But Mainer had a different idea. He, like Aimeric, clearly considered being a serf of Romainmôtier preferable to being the serf of a layman. When he married Gerlendis he approached her knightly lord with an offer. For sixty solidi, he asked the knight to agree that half of their children would be serfs of Romainmôtier, as he was, rather than the knight's. This offer, which demonstrates Mainer's determination to shape the lives of at least some of his children, was accepted. The monks recorded the agreement in their cartulary and named the two children (Tedaldus and Heldihardis, a boy and a girl) who would be their serfs. In addition, they noted, the knight gave a third child, a boy named Hunald, to the monks. Mainer himself was one of those who signed the attesting charter, indicating that he may have had at least a

---

37. *Le cartulaire de Romainmôtier (XIIe siècle)*, ed. Alexandre Pahud, Cahiers lausannois d'histoire médiévale 21 (Lausanne, 1998), pp. 160–61, no. 52.

38. *Le cartulaire de Romainmôtier*, pp. 165–66, no. 57.

minimal education as well as the means to obtain sixty solidi. He had not attained freedom for his family, for they all continued to be serfs, but he had negotiated what he considered an improved condition for at least some of them.

As these examples suggest, lords' attempts to regulate the status and marriages of their dependents should not be seen merely as a marker of servile status, but rather as burdens that peasants attempted to work around through negotiation. Peasants frequently appear to have made their own decisions about whom to marry, regardless of their lords' preference. The count of Joigny and the canons of St.-Marien of Auxerre came to an agreement in 1208 over what should happen when the men and women of a village dependent on the count married the men and women dependent on the monastery, as had been happening. The two parties agreed that they would share any such couples between them, regardless of their "law or condition," and divide up their property, death taxes, and children equally.[39] The attesting document focused on the agreement reached between the count and the monastery, but such an agreement would not have been necessary if the peasants had not been determined to choose their own spouses. They made their own decisions, without consulting those from whom they depended, and these lords were forced to find ways to adjust to what their peasants had done.

Peasant marriages were thus consequential not only for the parties involved but for their children. Although scholars usually conclude that servile status was automatically bestowed at birth, a charter from Bèze, dating to the beginning of the twelfth century, suggests that this was not true in all cases.[40] The modern discussion has generally centered on whether servile status was inherited through the paternal or maternal lines; usually the documents do not say, although what evidence exists suggests that the mother's status was more important. But this kind of ambiguity could be used to the peasants' advantage. It could open the way for some individuals or their offspring to reject servile status, requiring their monastic lords to try to find measures to deal with such issues.

In this charter from Bèze, three men and their brothers from nearby Bourberain received some land from the monastery on which to establish a vineyard. These men already held their houses from the monks as tenants. But the monks clearly worried that these men or their descendants might

---

39. *Recueil de pièces pour faire suite au Cartulaire général de l'Yonne*, ed. Maximilien Quantin (Auxerre, 1873), pp. 32–33, no. 70.

40. *The Cartulary-Chronicle of Bèze*, pp. 303–4, no. 254.

become too independent. If any of these men's sons married a female serf (*ancilla*) of Bèze, the abbot specified, they should continue to serve the monastery and would keep their house and land. But if such a son rejected such service, the house and land would revert to the monastery upon his death. The children of the *ancilla* would not be able to claim the tenancy if their father had failed to accept servile status with its obligations. One must note here the monks' recognition that the sons of a female serf might refuse to recognize that they themselves were serfs, and that the monks lacked the means to enforce this status on them, other than by threatening to keep them from inheriting.

Interestingly, this agreement between the monks and the three men of Bourberain did not specify what happened to the daughters, only to their sons. Yet another charter from slightly later, involving the same families, suggests that the girls took on servile status without necessarily being bound to the monastery.[41] In this case the daughter of one of these three men, here called an *ancilla*, had married a man of Fontaine-Française, six kilometers further from Bèze than Bourberain. Thus she, like her mother, was considered a serf, but notably not a serf of Bèze. A local landowner indeed made a gift of her to that monastery, saying he did so for the soul of his late father, and this transaction could not have been considered a gift if she already served the monks. The donor may have thought this young woman an appropriate gift because her close relatives were already serfs of the monastery, but the point is that she herself was not. In connection with the earlier charter that specified that the men of Bourberain should continue to serve the monks if they married Bèze's female serfs, this particular case indicates that even when someone was born to a female serf, with one's father having voluntarily taken up servile status, one was not necessarily attached to that "lord of the body." Servile status, choice of marriage partner, and inheritance were topics on which the peasants could, at least potentially, negotiate.

It also should be noted that the agreement between the abbot of Bèze and the men of Bourberain was seen as necessary to be spelled out and recorded in the cartulary. The monks were concerned lest the children of their serfs stop behaving as serfs and felt compelled to institute penalties to prevent this from happening. Their concern is highlighted in another charter from around the same time. Here one Odo, a nephew of the late Abbot Odo of Bèze (d. c. 1065) made a similar arrangement to what the three men had made in order to obtain some land for a vineyard.[42] He was granted

---

41. *The Cartulary-Chronicle of Bèze*, p. 307, no. 259.
42. *The Cartulary-Chronicle of Bèze*, p. 305, no. 256.

the land and a house for his lifetime, in return for service and fidelity to the monastery. This service, it was specified, was to be carried out "as that of a freeman" (*sicut liber*), and indeed with an abbot as his paternal uncle he was doubtless of fairly high status anyway. Nonetheless, it was expected, according to the charter, that he would marry a female serf of the monastery and that their children would take up the house and land. If he did not, the charter further specified, he could not expect to pass the property on to any other heirs, but would see it revert to the monastery. Yet even here, and perhaps in recognition of his status, the charter specified that the reversion of the property would be treated as a gift for his soul. This case, and the similar case of the men of Bourberain, suggests that free and servile status were not absolutes, and that lords were concerned about slippage of the service they expected.

Whatever their status, the peasants of the eleventh and twelfth centuries unsurprisingly preferred freedom from the onerous expectations that accompanied serfdom. A charter from Molesme from around the middle of the twelfth century indicates how much control a determined peasant might sometimes have in asserting free status.[43] Here a woman (*mulier*) was claimed as his dependent by an aristocrat. She, however, did not accept this. According to the attesting charter, she herself went to his house and there, before a number of witnesses, put forward a legal argument against his claim (*legitime derationavit*). The lord and his son were forced to accept that she was indeed free (*libera*). If freedom and servitude were legal categories, then peasants themselves were able to make a legal case for the category in which they believed they belonged.

Another twelfth-century case from Molesme underlines the lack of precision in these legal categories. A long charter details how the monks obtained a share in some mills from one Walannus.[44] That he owned a share of mills itself would seem to suggest aristocratic status, reinforced by the detail that his mother had earlier made the monks the pious gift of half a house. His status seems assured by the fact that he drew a sword on a monk who had irritated him, "fearing neither God nor man." Someone with a sword would seem to the modern eye indubitably a knight, the kind of man whose violence threatened peasants. When he repented of injuring the monk and gave what he owned in the mills to Molesme for the good of his soul, he confirmed his gift by putting a book, a high-status object, on the monastery altar,

43. *Cartulaires de l'abbaye de Molesme*, ed. Jacques Laurent, vol. 2, *Texte* (Paris, 1911), p. 175, no. 1.194.

44. *Cartulaires de Molesme*, 2:248–49, no. 1.268.

and the monks signaled the value of his gift by making him the countergift of the half house his mother had originally given.[45] In addition, the monks wrote up the agreement in a cyrograph, a double-charter in which each party would receive an identical copy, indicating that Walannus had easy access to someone who could read, if indeed he were not literate himself.

And yet all the markers of his position appear undercut by the fact that he was married to a female serf (*ancilla*) belonging to the monastery. Her servile status is mentioned not once but twice in the charter, allowing no ambiguity. Her children, one would anticipate, would also be serfs, with little or no rights to anything of their own, yet the monks specified that the half house they had given Walannus would pass to his children as their *hereditas*. The lines between knight, free peasant, and serf seem thoroughly blurred in this charter, and yet the monks were unconcerned by such blurring. Their only concern, according to the charter, was making sure that the *memoria* of how the monastery had ended up with Walannus's portion of the mills be preserved for both the present and posterity. If knights and peasants, two different categories in the paradigm of "three orders," could marry each other and arrange for their children's inheritance, then perhaps these categories were not as sharply distinguished as has been assumed.

Mainmorte

Mainmorte, a death tax levied when the heirs were not living at home, was once taken as an especially clear marker of servile status in the high Middle Ages.[46] And yet the standard scholarly description of *mainmorte* is based on sources from the thirteenth century, from settlements *ending* the practice, not from the eleventh or twelfth century.[47] One should not assume that an agreement to end this particular fee can be taken as indicative of normal practice in the preceding years.[48] *Mainmorte* can be analyzed as a case study of the challenges in defining medieval serfdom and also as an indication of the ability of peasants to improve their position.

---

45. For countergifts, see Constance Brittain Bouchard, *Holy Entrepreneurs: Cistercians, Knights, and Economic Exchange in Twelfth-Century Burgundy* (Ithaca, N.Y., 1991), pp. 66–94.

46. Marc Bloch, *Feudal Society*, trans. L. A. Manyon (Chicago, 1961), p. 263. William Chester Jordan adopts this categorization uncritically; *From Servitude to Freedom: Manumission in the Senonais in the Thirteenth Century* (Philadelphia, 1986), pp. 20–23.

47. See Marc Bloch, *Slavery and Serfdom in the Middle Ages*, trans. William R. Beer (Berkeley, 1975), pp. 42–43, and pp. 208–9 nn. 49–50.

48. Indeed, Parisse noted that in the eleventh and twelfth centuries the sparse mentions of *mainmorte* suggest it was simply an inheritance tax; "Histoire et sémantique," pp. 31–32.

A mid-thirteenth-century charter from the bishop of Auxerre contains an unusually clear description of the obligations *mainmorte* entailed, but it needs to be read in the context of its own time, not as descriptive of twelfth-century practice. In this document the bishop and the villagers of nearby Appoigny reached a negotiated settlement by which they would no longer pay *mainmorte* (*manus mortua*).[49] This very long, very complex charter—it fills eight closely written pages in the bishops' cartulary—spells out concessions that the villagers said they made freely in return for the end of *mainmorte*.

In this charter nothing other than *mainmorte* itself suggests that the peasants were bound by any other aspects of servitude, such as restrictions on choice of marriage partner or appearance in court, and any legal disability they might or might not have had did not keep them from negotiating with the highest spiritual authority of the region. In the charter, all the male villagers are listed by name, all fifty-four of them, and are said to be accompanied by their wives and ill-defined "other" men. The charter is in the first person plural, "we" the bishop of Auxerre and "we" the villagers. The villagers begin by saying that they recognize that they have not been paying the tithes they owe the bishop on their crops. The document goes on to detail which specific crops and animals (i.e., lambs, piglets) should be tithed. The villagers also specify that they will allow the bishop to exercise the wine-ban, that is, the period when the new wine has just come in and he alone can sell, for six weeks rather than the customary one month.

In return, the bishop says that he will now remit the custom known as *manus mortua*. No longer, he promises, when any of his men of Appoigny die will their heirs suffer any "difficulty or perturbation," but will be able to take over the parental house at once, getting both mobile and immobile goods. Even if someone dies without an obvious heir at hand, the bishop continues, if an heir appears within a year and a day, he could take up the property without paying a fine. In addition, the bishop remits the so-called March taille to the villagers (a requirement for agricultural work on his land in early spring), in return for an annual payment of eight pounds each. In all of this, both sides made concessions, working out a mutually agreeable solution to problems—whether nonpayment of tithes or seemingly arbitrary levying of inheritance dues—that had become a major irritant. The charter is phrased as a settlement reached between equals.

The men of Appoigny may have been eager to negotiate their way out of the *mainmorte* owed to the bishop of Auxerre because a number of lords

---

49. *Three Cartularies from Thirteenth-Century Auxerre*, ed. Constance Brittain Bouchard, Medieval Academy Books 113 (Toronto, 2012), pp. 81–90, no. 39.

in the region, both secular and ecclesiastical, had already freed their tenants from this obligation earlier in the century.[50] Peasants were eager to dispense with a burden that the lords themselves found not worth retaining—at least if their dependents made them an attractive offer. For example, all those dependent on the cathedral chapter of Auxerre (as opposed to the bishop) had already negotiated their freedom from *mainmorte*. In that case, the peasants and villagers of the region together raised the rather startlingly large sum of six hundred pounds, which the canons of the cathedral chapter agreed to accept in return for freeing them permanently from *mainmorte*.

Much of the attesting charter, drawn up by the dean of the chapter, details the peasants' own efforts to raise this sum; if someone did not contribute, it specified, the community, and *not* the canons, would seize his property.[51] Here the peasants organized themselves and raised money, collected they said by "good men," to end a practice they found excessively burdensome. Far from being an indicator of continuing servile status, these negotiations to end *mainmorte* in the Auxerrois reveal peasant initiative and determination, and churchmen treated them as worthy men with whom to negotiate.

Secular lords of the region also freed their peasants from *mainmorte* around the same time. A notable example of a powerful lord doing so is provided by Count Peter of Auxerre and Tonnerre. He freed the "men and women" (*homines, femine*) who lived by his castle of Tonnerre from this obligation in 1211. Henceforth if someone died without an heir on hand, their house and goods would be taken in charge by the other inhabitants of Tonnerre, and only if no heir appeared within a year would the count take over the property. He specified that he made this concession out of "love" (*amore*) for the local men and women, rather than stating that they had made any concessions in return, although it seems most likely that they had.[52] The count's use of the word "love" was certainly intended to suggest that the agreement, whatever it had entailed, was reached amicably.

---

50. Jordan counts nearly fifty thirteenth-century examples of freedom from *mainmorte* being granted just in the Senonais, the area surrounding Auxerre's archbishopric; *From Servitude to Freedom*, p. 27.

51. Abbé Lebeuf, *Mémoires concernant l'histoire civile et ecclésiastique d'Auxerre et de son ancien diocèse*, new ed. by A[mbrose] Challe and M[aximilien] Quantin, vol. 4, *Recueil de monuments, chartes, titres et autres pièces inédites* (Auxerre, 1855), pp. 67–68, no. 99. A few years earlier the bishop had freed the villagers of Varzy from *mainmorte*, in return for five solidi a year per household and an agreement to start paying their tithes. In the *vita* of the bishop the villagers are called *incolae*, but in the bishop's own charter *burgenses*. *Les gestes des évêques d'Auxerre*, ed. Guy Lobrichon et al., vol. 2 (Paris, 2006), p. 165, no. 58; GC 12, instr. col. 146, no. 62.

52. *Recueil de pièces pour faire suite au Cartulaire de l'Yonne*, pp. 47–48, no. 105. Two years later, Lord Ascelin of Merry similarly granted a number of villagers freedom from *mainmorte*, again without noting any real concessions on their part; ibid., pp. 62–63, no. 126.

Serfdom then was a status that, in practice, was only loosely defined. As the examples above indicate, serfs found many ways to negotiate their way out of unfavorable obligations, such as that they only marry certain people, or fees like *mainmorte*. The ceremony of putting pennies on one's head appears to have been far from universal, and arbitrary labor obligations might be demanded of free peasants as well as serfs. Some serfs owned serfs of their own, while others advanced to some wealth or to positions of authority in spite of servile status. Peasants for the most part still preferred not to be legally unfree, or at least not to be serfs dependent on secular lords. But in the eleventh century, as best documented at Marmoutier and Romainmôtier, peasants might find being a serf offered certain advantages, at least if it meant being the serf of a monastery. But whether serfdom was imposed or voluntarily adopted, it was a status that varied enough and was open enough to interpretation that serfs, even those without legal capacity, could find room to maneuver and negotiate their way to at least a somewhat improved condition.

The Retreat of Serfdom in the High Middle Ages

The above discussion has hinted at but not directly addressed one important issue, the disappearance of the terminology of serfdom from twelfth-century charters in northern France. When did serfs manage to shake off their servile status and become not *servi* and *ancillae* but just men and women? And were they actually doing so, or did merely the words used in charters change? As in so many other issues involving the peasantry, categories are not as clear or tidy in practice as one might anticipate.

The men of Appoigny freeing themselves from *mainmorte* look like free peasants in every respect other than having owed what has generally been assumed to be an unambiguous marker of servitude. The term "manumission," which had originally been used for freeing slaves and then serfs, might be used somewhat differently, such as for the yielding of an unjust claim to a monastery's dependent peasants,[53] further complicating the picture. But a change in how peasants were described, an abandonment of legal terms that went back to late antiquity, certainly suggests an important change. Those writing legal treatises in the thirteenth century, inspired by Roman law on slavery, may indeed have been trying, without notable success, to impose a

---

53. It is used this way in a document from Bèze from around 1130; *The Cartulary-Chronicle of Bèze*, pp. 351–52, no. 309.

reified definition of servile status on a peasantry capable of manipulating definitions for their own benefit.

An example of a serf moving himself and his family into freedom comes from Montier-en-Der in the late eleventh century. It involves a priest named Herbert, born a serf—his mother indeed was still of servile status when he was an adult—but who had clearly not been kept from taking orders because of this birth. Herbert decided to redeem, as the document put it, both his mother and his sister from the servitude that he appears to have escaped in becoming a priest (*redimens matrem et sororem suam*). It took enterprise, determination, and a fair amount of money to do so. He paid Erlebald, whose serfs they were, thirty-one solidi, and also made smaller payments to several knights, with their wives and mothers, who agreed and witnessed the transaction. The record of Herbert redeeming his mother and sister ended up in Montier-en-Der's cartulary because he then said that he was placing them under the dominion of Saint Peter, the monastery's patron saint.[54] The mother and sister were still subject to someone other than themselves, but clearly being subject to a saint was vastly preferable to being subject to a knight.

Herbert was not alone in overcoming servile birth. Many peasants could and did rise from servitude to positions of authority. An example is Robert, who began as a serf subject to the monastery of Bèze but who became lay provost for the monks, responsible for a great deal of their property. According to a document from around 1140, drawn up after Robert had taken the monastic habit and died, he had been born to a *servus* and an *ancilla*.[55] The document said that he had been raised, *exaltatus*, to his office. He wielded real power as provost, and, according to the document's account, he used his office as an excuse for fire, rapine, and lawsuits, before finally repenting of his evil ways.

When he retired as provost and became a monk, several people tried unsuccessfully to claim that they, as his heirs, should take over as provost. Robert himself vigorously denied their claims, which they raised again after his death. This time the self-proclaimed heirs, who one would have to conclude were also of peasant stock, took their case to the court of the duke of Burgundy. They lost here, but it is certainly significant that a group of villagers could and did argue their case before the most powerful lord of the region. It is also significant that in the document of 1140, none of the claimants are said to be servile. Two generations earlier, in the time of Robert's

---

54. *The Cartulary of Montier-en-Der*, pp. 244–45, no. 115.
55. *The Cartulary-Chronicle of Bèze*, pp. 356–57, no. 311.

parents, the terms *servus* and *ancilla* had been common, but no longer. The duke ruled against Robert's heirs not because they were serfs but because the monks persuaded him that the office of provost was not hereditary.

Provost Robert died at a time, the third or fourth decade of the twelfth century, when my reading of the documents from Burgundy / Champagne indicates that servile status disappeared from the records. Both Georges Duby and Theodore Evergates noted something similar in their own studies of the region, and Michel Parisse's semantic study of the word *servus* in French charters more broadly suggests its disappearance not long after the year 1100.[56] Those who might earlier have been described using servile terms were now called simply *homo* and *femina*. At most the terms *servus* and *ancilla* might appear in a formulaic statement intended to indicate all peasants of a region, "whether free or servile men, or free or servile women" (*præter servos seu liberos, et ancillas vel liberas*).[57]

Burgundy and Champagne were not alone. A number of French regional studies have suggested that serfdom was "slow" in coming to their regions since it is not regularly found in twelfth-century records, not recognizing that this may have been the standard pattern. For example, in the Jura and the Verdunois, as in Burgundy / Champagne, there is little evidence of serfdom before the middle decades of the thirteenth century. Similarly, the Paris basin has been noted as a center of peasant freedom in the eleventh and twelfth centuries, in spite of revolts by serfs against harsh exactions in the late thirteenth and fourteenth centuries.[58]

Here the murder of Count Charles the Good of Flanders is significant. The plot against the count began, according to Galbert of Bruges, because a serf who had risen to a position of power was afraid of having his servile origins discovered.[59] Although this explanation does not entirely make sense,

---

56. Georges Duby, *Rural Economy and Country Life in the Medieval West*, trans. Cynthia Postan (Columbia, S.C., 1968), pp. 187–90. Duby, *La société aux XIe et XIIe siècles dans la région mâconnaise*, 2nd ed. (Paris, 1971), pp. 201–4. Evergates, *Feudal Society in the Bailliage of Troyes*, pp. 16–17. Parisse, "Histoire et sémantique," pp. 45–46. Similarly, Marmoutier recorded its final example of someone becoming a serf there at the very beginning of the twelfth century; *Le livre des serfs*, pp. 30–31. Bloch postulated the end of the status of *collibertus* between 1100 and 1140; *Slavery and Serfdom*, p. 94. See also Poly and Bournazel, *The Feudal Transformation*, pp. 131–32.

57. This formula is found in an 1153 charter of the count of Nevers; *Cartulaire général de l'Yonne*, ed. Maximilien Quantin, 2 vols. (Auxerre, 1854–60), 1:507–8, no. 350.

58. Corriol, "Nommer les serfs," pp. 59–62 and n. 1. Ghislain Brunel, "Les hommes de corps du chapitre cathédral de Laon (1200–1460): Continuité et crises de la servitude dans une seigneurie ecclésiastique," in Freedman and Bourin, eds., *Forms of Servitude*, pp. 134–36.

59. Galbert of Bruges, *Histoire du meurtre de Charles le Bon, comte de Flandre*, ed. Henri Pirenne (Paris, 1891), cap. 7–8, pp. 12–14. *The Murder of Charles the Good*, trans. James Bruce Ross (New York, 1959; rpt. Toronto, 1982), pp. 100–101. See also Jeff Rider, *God's Scribe: The Historiographical Art of*

it is surely indicative of Galbert's views of the changes in his society. He saw all around him people born into servile status interacting with those of free status, indeed having no discernible difference between them. Galbert disagreed with what he saw, but he was witnessing a change taking place right around the one-quarter mark of the twelfth century, where serfs were able to rise to positions of power and pass as free.

Northern France in the twelfth century of course is not medieval Europe, much as it sometimes seems that way to social historians. But in other areas as well, there is little evidence of serfdom in the twelfth century. Indeed, it has been suggested that a "new" (or "second" or "reimposed") serfdom appeared in many parts of Europe in the thirteenth century, when it became increasingly common and more stringently enforced.[60] In England, true legal unfreedom appeared only in the thirteenth century, as landlords began demanding increased labor from their tenants. The development of common law then made free (rather than servile) status an important criterion for having one's case heard in court, meaning that serfs had more difficulty in passing for free.[61] In German territories, servile terms are rare in the documents before the thirteenth century, and most scholarship on serfs has focused on the end of the Middle Ages. In high and late medieval Austria serfdom continued as a legal category, even while serf-knights, *ministeriales*, became the de facto rulers in their regions.[62] In Catalonia, serfdom appeared for the first time only in the late twelfth and especially thirteenth centuries.[63]

If peasants were indeed freer in the twelfth century than either earlier or later, that is, that more than just the terminology changed, how did this happen? The records strongly suggest that peasants took the initiative in freeing

Galbert of Bruges (Washington, D.C., 2001), pp. 11–15. Suger made a similar connection in his own account of Charles's death. Suger, *Vie de Louis VI le Gros*, ed. Henry Waquet (Paris, 1964), cap. 30, p. 242. *The Deeds of Louis the Fat*, trans. Richard C. Cusimano and John Moorhead (Washington, D.C., 1992), p. 138. Thomas Bisson downplays the servile origins of the plotters, seeing the murder instead as despicable in contemporary eyes because it broke oaths of fidelity; *The Crisis of the Twelfth Century: Power, Lordship, and the Origins of European Government* (Princeton, 2009), pp. 261–62.

60. Freedman, "Peasants, the Seigneurial Regime, and Serfdom," pp. 269–70. Freedman and Bourin, "Introduction," pp. 4–8.

61. Christopher Dyer, "Villeins, Bondmen, Neifs, and Serfs: New Serfdom in England, 1200–1600," in Freedman and Bourin, eds., *Forms of Servitude*, pp. 419–35. Campbell, *English Seigniorial Agriculture*. Paul R. Hyams, *Kings, Lords, and Peasants in Medieval England: The Common Law of Villeinage in the Twelfth and Thirteenth Centuries* (Oxford, 1980).

62. Kurt Andermann, "Leibeigenschaft in der Markgrafschaft Baden an der Wende vom Mittelalter zur Neuzeit," in Freedman and Bourin, eds., *Forms of Servitude*, pp. 197–211. John B. Freed, *Noble Bondsmen: Ministerial Marriages in the Archdiocese of Salzburg, 1100–1343* (Ithaca, N.Y., 1995).

63. Paul Freedman, *The Origins of Peasant Servitude in Medieval Catalonia* (Cambridge, 1991).

themselves. In part they may have succeeded because enforcing servitude was not worth it to the powerful. During the eleventh century, castellan lords increasingly asserted their authority over all men and women of a region, both servile and free, in what is known as banal lordship. Indeed, some scholars have gone so far as to suggest that serfs who had barely emerged from the slavery of Roman antiquity at the end of the tenth century were now put under new forms of "feudal" servitude.[64] Yet as both free and unfree became subject to the justice and dues of the local lord in this period, the distinction between them was broken down, giving rise to new opportunities for the unfree.[65] It may not have been in the interest of a lord to try to keep track of who was and was not a serf, especially as the four pennies a year of head tax one occasionally finds in the charters would have been trivial; all that mattered was that everyone, whether free or serf, paid their rent and labor dues.

But most of the decline in serfdom must be attributed to the peasants themselves, even if they maneuvered to use whatever their lords sought to their own advantage. They offered lords sums of money for a change in status. They arranged for the replacement of arbitrary labor demands by regular payments, as in the agreement between the bishop of Auxerre and the men of Appoigny. Some managed to shift from dependence on a secular lord to the more desirable dependence on a monastic lord. Couples could maneuver to marry in spite of lordly restrictions designed to keep control of their offspring. In addition, if a particular fee (*mainmorte, formariage*) was not levied in a particular generation, it would have been easy to forget (or "forget") the status these were supposed to indicate. And in the expanding economy of the twelfth century there were plenty of opportunities for serfs to move away, to a growing city or new town (discussed in chapter 4) or to the new settlements off in central Europe, in any case to somewhere they would not be recognized as servile.

For serfs did move, creating awkward and confusing situations, when their lords had trouble keeping track of them even if the serfs did not actively seek to escape servitude. Around 1120 the cathedral of Basel and the monastery of Romainmôtier made an agreement, that if any of the cathedral's serfs (*servi* and *ancillae*) moved into the monks' territory, they would become the monks' serfs. The reciprocal arrangement was made for the monks' serfs moving to Basel.[66] The agreement was phrased as simply an understanding

---

64. Most notably Bonnassie, *From Slavery to Feudalism*, pp. 288–313.

65. Freedman, "Peasants, the Seigneurial Regime, and Serfdom," pp. 264–68. Poly and Bournazel, *The Feudal Transformation*, pp. 28–34.

66. *Le cartulaire de Romainmôtier*, pp. 118–19, no. 25.

between the bishop and the monastery's prior, but the principals fully accepted that peasants, including servile peasants, were likely to make their own decisions about where to live. Rather than trying, unsuccessfully, to force them to remain where they did not want to be, it was more feasible in effect to trade them. But note that the ecclesiastical lords themselves did not initiate any such trade. Rather, the peasants decided to move, and the ecclesiastical lords made the best of it.

Whatever the cause and whatever the process, northern France had very few people called serfs by the second quarter of the twelfth century. The absence of the word *servus* of course did not mean the absence of servitude. But I would argue that many peasants were able to free themselves during the twelfth century, during a period of economic growth and societal transformation. Most significantly, the effective absence of serfdom as a legal category in northern France in the twelfth century has to be considered as due in large part to peasant agency.

Still, the disappearance of certain obligations or certain terms in the documents cannot be treated as a final end to serfdom, as the thirteenth-century revival or new imposition of servile restrictions suggests. Even though *mainmorte* was widely ended at this time, other markers of serfdom appear to have been on the ascendance. For example, the dependents who had been called simply *homines* for five decades or more began increasingly to be called *homines de corpore*, men of the body. In 1213 a knight released (*quitavi*) two of his "men of the body" from their service to him (*servagium*) and presented them to the Premonstratensian church of Douchy.[67] These two men, brothers, though of servile status, were still given the dignity of their own names in the attesting charter, Laurent Passart and Simon. But the term "man of the body" suggests a new interest by lords in the thirteenth century in enforcing their personal authority over their peasants.

As noted above, it is sometimes suggested that the rise of banal lordship after the year 1000 led to new servile impositions that must have become even harsher in the twelfth century. On the other hand, the demands put on peasants in the late thirteenth and fourteenth centuries have sometimes been assumed to have been prevalent in the twelfth century as well. But in focusing on the eleventh and twelfth centuries, filling a lacuna in the scholarship,

---

67. Soissons, Bibliothèque municipale, MS 7, fol. 83v. An edition of the cartulary of Prémontré is being prepared by Yvonne Seale and Heather Wacha; see Seale and Wacha, "The Cartulary of Prémontré: People, Places, and Networks from Medieval to Digital," *Medieval People* 36 (2022), 353–71.

I would argue that this was a period in which many serfs were able to free themselves from the worst of legal servitude.

The reasons why serfdom may have reappeared (or appeared for the first time) in the thirteenth century are beyond the scope of this book, though the slowing of economic growth may have provided peasants less room for maneuver, while making lords even more stringent in their demands. But as the following chapters further demonstrate, high medieval peasants actively sought to control key aspects of their lives—and succeeded surprisingly often. The harshness of the demands put on them only increased their efforts to improve their position. Being a serf did not mean that someone was helpless, but this status clearly presented challenges, which was why peasants were eager to escape it. The economic expansion of the eleventh and twelfth centuries presented the serfs of northern France the opportunity, even if only temporarily, to negotiate and to act like free men and women.

CHAPTER 2

Peasants, Property, and Payments

Whether serf or free tenant, peasants were highly valuable. The inherent value of peasants to medieval society lies in the fact that they were the ones who cleared the land, pastured the animals, and grew the food. Without them, townspeople, lords, ecclesiastics, and their households either would not have had anything to eat or would have had to produce it themselves. Agricultural land would have been worthless without peasant labor. Peasants produced food for their own families, sold food to the population of the growing towns, and, through their rents and dues, supported their lords. Just as peasant status and social position varied widely, so too did their obligations and the payments they made to those in authority over them.

The Value of Peasants

Part of the reason the value of peasants may now be overlooked is because they normally appeared in the sources not in their own charters but in the charters of the powerful. Those who had charters drawn up might focus on what they considered an important issue, so that in these charters peasants appear almost as an afterthought. Or the powerful might be recorded as doing something *to* peasants. But even such records suggest that peasants had real value, although the subject of a record might appear to be something quite different.

For example, a charter might record the settlement of a quarrel between two lords, but partway through it would become clear that the topic of their quarrel was rights over certain peasants. The nuns of St.-Julien of Auxerre and the counts of Joigny quarreled extensively in the late twelfth century over four men whom both sides claimed; the quarrel lasted twenty years and was ultimately settled only by order of the pope.[1] Or a charter might attest to a pious gift, focusing on the spiritual benefits the gift would entail, but the gift consisted of subject men and women. For example, when Countess Ida of Nevers wanted to establish an altar at the cathedral of Auxerre where masses would be said for the soul of her dying son, she gave the bishop some thirty families in 1175, all her villagers at Varzy, a gift confirmed by King Louis VII.[2] In other cases, a document might detail the transfer of a piece of land with its accompanying tenants in terms little different from how a charter might describe another piece of land and an accompanying fish weir. A typical charter is found in the cartulary of Montier-en-Der, where in the third quarter of the eleventh century a priest gave the monastery three mansi along with three *servi*, with the stipulation that he would be accepted into the monks' *societas*.[3] The serfs themselves are referred to here as one would refer to any piece of property. Peasants' frequent appearance as objects of the actions of others does much to explain their standard characterization as passive.

Even so, they were neither faceless nor nameless. Rather, even the most powerful treated them as individuals. When they were given to a church as a pious gift, they were typically listed by name. These people were equal to the powerful in the eyes of God according to Christian theology. Even if the powerful would have had trouble accepting them as their social equals, they certainly treated them as fully human in the high Middle Ages. At a time of relative underpopulation, wealth was assumed to reside at least in part in how many people were under one's authority. Peasants were considered to make good gifts not because they were disposable but because they were valuable. That the monks of Marmoutier at the end of the eleventh

---

1. *Three Cartularies from Thirteenth-Century Auxerre*, ed. Constance Brittain Bouchard, Medieval Academy Books 113 (Toronto, 2012), pp. 193–95, nos. 5–6.

2. *Three Cartularies from Auxerre*, pp. 33–35, no. 5.

3. *The Cartulary of Montier-en-Der, 666–1129*, ed. Constance Brittain Bouchard, Medieval Academy Books 108 (Toronto, 2004), pp. 219–20, no. 93.

century felt it appropriate to create a cartulary just of donations (including self-donations) of serfs indicates that here was an important category of monastic property.

Peasants were valuable not merely collectively but as individuals. Even serfs had to be treated as individual people when they appeared in land transactions. In 1100 one Hubert Dalmace, acting with his wife and brother, gave the Cluniac nunnery of Marcigny some agricultural land, specifying that all the serfs (*servi* and *ancillae*) who lived there were part of the gift. But it was not enough to say this in general terms. The names of the serfs were all given in the charter, to avoid any ambiguity.[4] In addition, Hubert Dalmace named eight more male and female serfs, with their children, whom he had claimed from Marcigny but who he now granted to the nuns. As this example makes clear, the people who worked the land were at least as crucial a part of a donation as the land itself.

Indeed, the land was often identified specifically by the names of the tenants who lived there. When a knight made his daughter a nun at the house of Pomeraie in 1153, his entry gift for her was composed of several pieces of land, each identified by the man or woman who worked or rented that land. His gift, according to his donation charter, included the nut-tree orchard of the late Otbert; Peter's farmstead; Joscelin's holding; and the three pennies a year paid by Phyllis, wife of Richard.[5] Similarly, when Letbald of Nanton made a gift to the Cistercians of La Ferté a decade or so later, the property was identified as the vineyard that Marcel of Laives worked and a field for which the Brutinange family paid a rent of a setier of wine and twelve pennies a year.[6]

When Bishop Walter of Laon settled his quarrels with the canons of Prémontré in the middle of the twelfth century, confirming what his episcopal predecessors had granted or confirmed to them over the previous three decades, he spelled out all the fields and vineyards and orchards in question, not merely by locating them in their proper villages but by giving the names of the men and women who lived and worked there: Otbert, Petronilla the mother of Gui, Rengard, Robert the son of Adelaide, and so on and so on. In

---

4. *Le cartulaire de Marcigny-sur-Loire (1045–1144): Essai de reconstitution d'un manuscrit disparu*, ed. Jean Richard (Dijon, 1957), pp. 70–71, no. 98. The cartulary scribe, writing when these serfs were most likely all dead, abbreviated the list down to the first name and *et cetera*, just as scribes routinely abbreviated witness lists of the powerful.

5. *Cartulaire général de l'Yonne*, ed. Maximilien Quantin, 2 vols. (Auxerre, 1854–60), 1:516–17, no. 358.

6. *Recueil des pancartes de l'abbaye de La Ferté-sur-Grosne, 1113–1178*, ed. Georges Duby (Paris, 1953), pp. 132–33, no. 150.

many cases the document specified how much these people owed in annual rent, in coin and produce. Several times Bishop Walter noted the original donor of property, some of whom had held high positions in northern France, such as Thomas of Marle, but the name of the donor would clearly have been insufficient without more explicit indication.[7]

This settlement was not simply of local concern, for the attesting document said that Bishop Walter acted at the urging of King Louis VII and of the papal legate, and the agreement was mediated by the bishops of Noyon and Soissons and the abbots of the neighboring monasteries. It was not enough to settle a quarrel over property. The property had to be specified, and the only ready way to do so was by the names of the inhabitants. Long before street addresses or numbered parcels of land, property was best defined by the people who lived there, and most of these people were peasants.

The Cistercians, who wanted uninhabited land that would be worked by their *conversi* if not indeed by the monks themselves, were unusual, unusual enough that donors, failing to grasp that this was not what the monks wanted, kept on making them gifts of inhabited land. More typically religious houses wanted the specification in charters that land included inhabitants, as in the 1113 agreement between the duke of Burgundy and the bishop and cathedral chapter of Autun. In the long, detailed charter recording the settlement of a quarrel between two of the most important entities in Burgundy, the land in dispute was always described as inhabited.[8] Property that was worth a quarrel lasting months, involving some of the other major Burgundian political figures as mediators, and that led to recriminations and accusations by both sides, was clearly valuable property. The repeated stipulation that inhabitants came with the property is a clear indication that the peasant tenants were an integral part of the land's value.

Moreover, when land was donated to a church, it was crucial that the tenants of that land be identified. When Lord Geoffrey II of Semur, who had helped found the nunnery of Marcigny, made a gift of land to that house around 1070 on the occasion of his daughter Lucia taking the veil there, he specified the names of the three men who cultivated the three mansi that constituted his gift.[9] Such identifications both made it explicit which mansi were in question and also told the nuns that the donated land was profitable, as empty agricultural land would not have been. The importance of this gift of three (inhabited) mansi was underscored by Lord Geoffrey having his

---

7. Soissons, Bibliothèque municipale, MS 7, fol. 19r–v.

8. *Cartulaire de l'église d'Autun*, ed. A[natole] de Charmasse (Paris, 1865), pp. 19–21, no. 1.12.

9. *Le cartulaire de Marcigny*, p. 8, no. 6.

family members and neighbors confirm and issuing a curse against any who tried to claim the land.[10]

Another document from the cathedral chapter of Autun is even clearer on the significance of the peasants who worked the land. In 1112 one Walo Besort gave up to the canons his claim to three brothers who lived at the village of Corcelle. This was more than a simple end to a quarrel, for Walo said that he was doing so for the good of his soul and his ancestors', indicating that the brothers had real value. They were specifically named in the attesting charter, Avin, William, and Robert, as was their nephew Girard. All of their sons and daughters, the charter continued, and any male or female members of this lineage, would be subject in perpetuity to the canons, not to Walo or his descendants. These were certainly peasants, possibly even serfs although they were not identified as such, for the charter said that they would be subject to the *potestas* and *dominium* of the canons.[11]

The value both Walo and the canons saw in this family is further indicated by the fact that he had members of his own family confirm. Additionally, a long list of castellans, knights, and other locals all witnessed the charter, which was formally drawn up and dated by the year of the incarnation, the month, the phase of the moon, the indiction, the epact and concurrent, and the reigns of the king, bishop, and duke. Far from being insignificant or interchangeable, these three peasant brothers and their families were as crucial to the canons, whose land at Corcelle they worked, as to the man who hoped that in giving up his claim to them he might help save his soul: they could not be left nameless or faceless.

One of the documents from Marmoutier is equally revelatory of how important the gift of serfs might be.[12] In the middle of the eleventh century one Bernard gave Marmoutier two *colliberti*, brothers, specifying their parents and where they came from. The monks gave Bernard twenty solidi as a countergift and also gave his son a horse worth fifteen solidi, for agreeing to his father's gift. But this was not all. Bernard had, it turned out, held the *colliberti* in fief (*in faevum*) from a knight, who also had to agree to the gift. Bernard and the knight between them had to oppose the "false claim" of

<hr />

10. When Adelaide of Sertines entered Marcigny as a nun, around the same time as Lucia of Semur did so, she similarly specified the name of the man who worked the land she gave to the house; *Le cartulaire de Marcigny*, pp. 17–18, no. 17.

11. *Cartulaire de l'église d'Autun*, pp. 89–90, no. 2.4.

12. *Le livre des serfs de Marmoutier*, ed. André Salmon (Tours, 1864), pp. 5–6, no. 4. For another case from Marmoutier from around the same time, where a family of knights fought over two generations to hold onto a female serf and her descendants, see Paul Fouracre, "Marmoutier and Its Serfs in the Eleventh Century," *Transactions of the Royal Historical Society* 15 (2005), 41–43.

Bernard's son-in-law, who claimed that the *colliberti* had been given to *him* as the dowry of Bernard's daughter. Once everyone had agreed to the gift and received suitable countergifts, the gift had to be witnessed by some twenty-five people of standing, including the principal officers and functionaries of the monastery. Human capital was just as valuable as land.

A similarly elaborate charter concerning serfs comes from the Cluniac priory of St.-Marcel of Chalon. In this charter from 1104, the duke of Burgundy, Hugh II, gave up his claims to some serfs living at Fleurey-sur-Ouche, serfs who were subject to St.-Marcel. Fleurey was located nearly sixty kilometers from Chalon, but it was very important to the monks, as the emperor Louis the Pious had given them the church there. Indeed, they remembered (and had a forged document to prove) that they had originally received Fleurey back in the sixth century from the Merovingian king Guntram, whom they honored as their founder. A council had more recently confirmed the church at Fleurey to St.-Marcel. Fleurey was an equally significant place for the duke, for his ancestor Duke Robert had died there some thirty years earlier.[13]

With Fleurey's significance to both parties, it is not surprising that a quarrel over it should only be ended with the intervention of two archbishops, two bishops, two Cluniac abbots, and some of the most powerful laymen of the region. What might seem surprising is that the quarrel was principally over serfs. Or, more accurately, serfs and salvation. The duke finally gave up what was characterized as a false claim (*calumnia*) for the remission of his and his father's sins, according to the attesting charter. The monks established an anniversary remembrance for the duke's recently deceased father, as well as giving the duke a countergift of two hundred solidi and a palfrey. Although the duke's chief concern was his father's soul, he did not overlook the individuality of the actual serfs involved. The ten men involved were all named, including noting which ones were brothers. They, along with their (specified but unnamed) wives and sisters and their progeny, were crucial to the agreement. Collectively, these men and women constituted the value of Fleurey; the village and its church would not have been worth arguing over without them.

The value that peasants gave to land when it was donated or became the basis of a quarrel was often made explicit when a charter spelled out what they owed. A late eleventh-century charter from the nunnery of Marcigny suggests the complexity of such arrangements. Two wealthy men,

13. *The Cartulary of St.-Marcel-lès-Chalon, 779–1126*, ed. Constance Brittain Bouchard, Medieval Academy Books 102 (Cambridge, Mass., 1998), pp. 24–27, 31–32, 63–69, nos. 4, 7, 35–37.

probably brothers, gave a large amount of land in Aquitaine to Marcigny, a gift substantial enough that a Cluniac priory was subsequently established there.[14] This gift of land, the donors specified, came with all of the customary dues (*consuetudines*) they had been collecting there, excepting only half the pasture fees they charged the local *rustici* for pasturing sheep. They agreed not to sell or pawn their reserved fees to anyone other than the monks, and in addition promised that they would not charge the monks such fees if they pastured sheep there. As well as exercising pasture rights, they had been exercising control over the woods, for they went on to specify that both the monks and the local inhabitants would be able to collect wood for building and for fuel. Any dues the inhabitants had been paying for woods usage, or, according to the document, for anything else, were henceforth to go to the monks. This gift, which was said to be made for the souls of the donors and their parents, was confirmed by the count of Angoulême, their lord.

This document seemed to take for granted the magnitude and varieties of rents that tenants might pay for their land. But peasants, the *rustici* of the charter, did not simply pay rent. They gathered wood and pastured their animals, and they needed to go beyond their own property to do so. The brothers had been exercising what have come to be called banal rights over all their territory, apparently charging these *consuetudines* on everyone who lived in the region, whether or not they were their tenants, as suggested by the document's phrase, "all the men who wish to live in that area" (*hominibus vero qui in ipsis terris manere voluerint*). Even peasants who were not someone's tenants could be a valuable resource.

Rents and dues then, whether paid in produce or coin or labor on the lord's demesne land, was a large part of what lords gained from their peasants, but certainly not all. A charter from the cathedral chapter of Autun further demonstrates the variety of ways that the powerful relied on the productivity of peasants. In the early twelfth century Count William II of Nevers granted the cathedral canons "all he had" at the village of Marigny.[15] This grant was clearly complicated, for his charter began by spelling out what he was *not* granting to the canons but rather keeping for himself. The charter indicates that he might have given the canons his land at the village, but he retained the valuable rents and service of the local *rustici*.

---

14. *Le cartulaire de Marcigny*, pp. 49–50, no. 65.

15. *Cartulaire de l'église d'Autun*, pp. 91–92, no. 2.6. The editor mistakenly identifies the count as William III rather than William II. For Count William, see Constance Brittain Bouchard, *Sword, Miter, and Cloister: Nobility and the Church in Burgundy, 980–1198* (Ithaca, N.Y., 1987), pp. 346–47.

Each household, he said, would continue to pay him twelve pennies a year and as much grain as they had previously been paying, although he said that he would henceforth reduce the amount by a setier a year. This generalized comment about the amount they had been paying suggests that different households had been paying somewhat different amounts, and that the exact requirements were recorded in memory rather than in writing. Anyone who came to live in the village would be expected to pay the same twelve pennies a year, plus an again unspecified rent in grain. In addition, the *rustici* were to allow pasturage and hay for his marshal's horses and provide carts for transporting the count's wine and, twice a year, for carrying firewood to his castle. The canons of Autun, he specified, were not to allow pasturage of animals in his woods, so keeping the woods for his own purposes was clearly important. He would also continue to call on the *rustici* for service in his armies. He would, he added, continue to exercise high justice in the village, that is, any case where the accused might be put to death or lose a member, although the canons, he conceded, would be able to request mercy.

This long list of peasant obligations that the count was preserving for himself is indicative of the varied ways that peasants could provide resources that the powerful needed: rents, help with transportation, even service in armed conflicts. Exercising justice must have provided some financial reward, as well as demonstrating authority. The count finished his charter by saying that his wife Adelaide agreed and giving a long list of witnesses, both local notables and his own *servientes*: his provost, marshal, butler, vintner, and notary. The officials of the cathedral chapter of Autun also all witnessed and signed, suggesting that they valued gaining clear title to the land, which the count said that he and his ancestors had held "justly or unjustly," but it cannot have been worth as much as it would have been if the peasants there had not been fettered with continuing obligations to Count William.

The canons clearly saw as a problem the skimpiness of peasant obligations to them, rather than to the count of Nevers. A generation later, in 1158, Count William III, at the canons' urging, granted them the right to demand an arbitrary payment, a taille (*tallia*), from the inhabitants of Marigny.[16] These inhabitants included, his charter specified, both his own men of the body, presumably the children or grandchildren of the *rustici* in William II's charter, and also those who had since moved to Marigny and its *potestas*.

William III was, however, chary of letting the canons receive too much from the peasants over whom his father had sought to retain dominion. The taille, he stated, could not be demanded on "just any occasion" (*quibuslibet*

---

16. *Cartulaire de l'église d'Autun*, pp. 96–97, no. 2.11.

occasionibus) but rather only for "manifest necessity." His examples of necessity indicate both the type of event for which a cathedral chapter might suddenly require money and the extent to which peasants were perceived as a resource to cover unexpected expenses. According to the charter, the taille could only be levied if the canons needed to buy land, faced serious hunger, or received a visit from the pope or the king. All of these would have required heavy expenditures, especially housing, feeding, and entertaining a papal or royal retinue. William III's charter, like his father's earlier charter, was signed by multiple witnesses including members of his own family and retinue, as well as by the cathedral officers of Autun.

In spite of the rents he was receiving, the count and the canons both assumed that the inhabitants of Marigny would have enough left to provide for themselves, pay a taille that covered serious expenses at least occasionally, while also being able to provide pasturage for the count's horses, service as needed in his army, and carts to carry his wine and his firewood. These peasants were evidently prospering, with liquid wealth that might be called upon. They themselves doubtless resented any imposition of a taille, but from the point of view of the powerful, the peasantry functioned almost like a living savings account. They took care of themselves with little input, and their cash and their labor could be called on to meet unanticipated needs. These charters then indicate both how much twelfth-century peasants were able to accumulate, in spite of periodic exactions like this taille, and also how valuable peasants were to those under whose authority they lived.

Varieties of Peasant Dues

As the above examples have suggested, the dues that peasants were expected to pay were far from uniform. Just as peasant status and social position varied widely, so too did their obligations and the payments they made to those whom they served. Although it may be tempting to treat a few documents, where the peasants' required payments are spelled out, as normative, there was certainly no standard, and rents, dues, and other obligations might be quite different at different times, in different places, and even for different households in the same place.

Other records in which peasants and their mansi appear also indicate great variation in holdings, requirements, or rents, even though there are overall patterns. Labor, money, and produce or other agricultural products might all be used in payment, but the exact mix was never standardized—some peasants paid only one of these, and some none at all. Most rent amounts stayed the same over the years, not changing with inflation. Churches might expect a percentage of a crop (as opposed to a set amount), in the form of a tithe. Some dues were levied arbitrarily: the taille (*tallia*), money that might be demanded in cases of a lord's sudden need, and the corvée (*corvata* or *corvee*), labor demanded above the normal labor dues (these two terms might also be used interchangeably). Not surprisingly, these latter two were the dues peasants resented the most.

Rents and dues were usually collected on a per-mansus basis, rather than on a per-person basis. Variation between what a mansus might owe varied tremendously, even in the same village. Reasons for the differences between rents at different mansi in various times and places can only be speculated upon. Perhaps heavier rents were established when the person who initially held a mansus was a serf, and the amount stayed the same even when that person's successors became free. Perhaps a mansus was unusually large or small, or more or less productive, leading to higher or lower expectation of revenue. The exact amount owed may well have gone back years, even generations, to an early negotiation between a tenant and a landlord, and the amounts, rarely written down, doubtless were subject to at least some fluctuation or creep with changing understanding and circumstance.

Rents and dues were generally recorded only at turning points, when a new landlord took over or new tenants took up the property. For example, when Atto of La Chapelle gave the Cistercian monastery of La Ferté four mansi in a recently cleared former woodland (*vaura*) in the 1150s, he specified that three of them paid collectively nine loaves of bread, nine setiers of wine, nine measures of grain, and nine solidi in the money of Chalon-sur-Saône; presumably each paid three of each. One could assume that these mansi had been established in the former woodland all at the same time, which was why their rents were the same. But the fourth paid a different rent: one loaf of bread, one measure of grain, and thirty pounds Chalon.[17]

Why such differences? At this distance all we can do is speculate. The fourth mansus may have been composed of slightly different land less suitable for wine grapes, or it might have been cleared at a different time with different priorities, or the original settler there may have been pasturing animals rather than focusing on crops, or several other possibilities—taking account that the associated land must have been very productive, given the high amount of rent. But none of these suggest that the expected rents were

---

17. *Recueil des pancartes La Ferté*, pp. 154–55, no. 185. Similarly, when the Crusader Geoffrey of Dracy gave one mansus to the Cistercian monks of Maizières and pawned another to them, his charter spelled out exactly how much they could expect to receive in dues, in both grain and coin, apparently the first time their dues had ever been recorded in writing. Paris, BnF, MS nouv. acq. fr. 8677, pp. 1–3.

simply due to landlord demands. Even if one cannot explain why rents varied so much in particular cases, one can certainly see that rents were one of the areas in which peasants were able to have at least some predictability in their lives. When these four mansi were given to La Ferté, the rents were recorded in writing. The tenants might not have a say in this case in their homes' transfer to the monks, but at least they need not fear a sudden increase in what they owed.

Another example from La Ferté underscores the diversity of the payments various peasants might owe. In the middle decades of the twelfth century the monks acquired a fair amount of land at the villages of Varennes and St.-Ambreuil, with the support of the count of Chalon. Their pancartes that detailed the gifts and exchanges that made these acquisitions possible also included a list of what the men and women in these villages owed each year, under the heading of *noticia census*.[18] Seven people, both men and women, were listed, each with their name. They each owed a payment in coin, ranging from two *nummos* to three *denarii*. One in addition owed a cartload of grain, and two of them a *pose* of land, which appears to have been some form of labor. This detailing of annual rents was probably the first and perhaps the only time that these peasants had their obligations recorded in writing rather than oral memory.

Here the monks of La Ferté decided it was necessary to write down the obligations of their new tenants once their land became subject to the monastery. Indeed, our most common records of peasant dues were created when peasants and their rents were given to a church. Such was the case when the lady Emeldis Murella gave the nunnery of Marcigny some land in the middle decades of the twelfth century, for the good of her soul; her charter specified exactly how much the two peasant tenants on that land paid as *servitium*. The first, Peter Serge, paid four solidi on the feast of Saint Martin (November 11); three measures of oats, a capon, and two pots of wine in March; and two more pots in August, as well as half a bushel of wheat and some shocks of hay. The second, Otger, paid eighteen pennies, a measure of oats, two pots of wine, half a bushel of wheat, a shock of hay, and a capon; the timing of these payments was not specified.[19]

The differences in the obligations just of these two men who both lived in the same place certainly indicate that there were no standard rents. Even more, it indicates the complexity of the peasant agricultural economy: in this case the two men grew two kinds of grain, raised chickens, tended wine

---

18. *Recueil des pancartes de La Ferté*, p. 93, no. 87.
19. *Le cartulaire de Marcigny*, pp. 128–29, no. 230.

grapes, and sold enough of their produce that money payments were feasible. And yet different tenants paid different amounts, due to reasons (size of
mansus? time of taking up the tenancy? legal status of the tenant?) at which
we can only guess. The occasions when dues were recorded in writing, as
here when the land and the men on it were transferred to Marcigny, must
have been very infrequent. One can assume that the peasants themselves,
eyeing their neighbors' obligations, did their part in keeping them honest.

A quarrel settlement involving the old Benedictine house of Moûtier-St.-
Jean from around the same time suggests more uniform rents but again indicates the variety of agricultural products that peasants (here called *rustici*)
produced.[20] In this case, three knights, one Roger of Ancy and the husbands
of his two sisters, claimed that the households in the monastery's village
of Etivey owed them *salvamentum*. This "safeguard" appears to have been
the dues the monks owed to Roger and his family members as monastic
advocates, protectors of the monks and their property, dues customarily collected from the monastery's tenants. Roger and the others exercised justice
at Etivey and were entitled to regular rents there, but only at that village,
not elsewhere. Here each of the mansi in the village owed essentially the
same amount, although eighteen of the mansi were designated "half" mansi,
which owed only half as much.

The quarrel between Roger and the monastery arose because, according
to the abbot's complaint to the bishop, Roger was demanding more than he
was owed. In relenting, Roger had the bishop spell out exactly what each
mansus owed each year, to be collected by the knights' agents, *ministri*. In
this case, each mansus owed a bushel of barley or oats, two loaves of bread
(for which two pennies could be substituted), two haunches of pork if a pig
was butchered on the mansus, two chickens, and a pot of wine. The wine
could be replaced by its monetary value in the local market. The grain and
wine were to be paid on Saint Martin's day, the bread and pork on the Feast of
the Innocents (December 28). This detailed agreement also specified that if
someone new moved to Etivey and took up one of the half mansi, he should
be given some land outside the village to make his portion up to a full mansus and owe dues accordingly, and if several families shared a mansus, they
should share the appropriate rent between them.

After spelling out the obligations of all the families dependent on Moûtier-
St.-Jean who lived in this village, the agreement went on to specify what
would happen if these obligations were not paid. After one week, the document stated, the knights' *ministri* could make a *clamor* to the abbot. If after

---

20. *Cartulaire général de l'Yonne*, 1:355–57, no. 214.

two more weeks the dues had still not been paid, they could seize what was owed themselves. Clearly Roger and the other knights were concerned that the peasants of Etivey might prove recalcitrant. As the abbot's dependents, they had him as at least a temporary shield between them and knights and *ministri* angry at not receiving what they were owed, in effect a three-week grace period.

Here, in one of the few cases in which peasants' fixed rents were specified, one again sees them producing a varied number of products and having at least some money of their own. Etivey may have been a "new town," which would explain the uniform rents, a place to which someone might want to move, as the document noted might happen (see chapter 4). In a quarrel between three knights and a monastery, peasants and their dues were a valuable commodity, and the abbot wanted assurance there would be no heavy impositions on them unless they were seriously late with their twice-a-year payments.

In another case from around the same time also involving a quarrel over the *salvamentum* that an abbey's tenants owed its advocate, the viscount of St.-Florentin and the monks of St.-Germain of Auxerre came to an agreement mediated by the count of Blois.[21] It was a complicated agreement, because it involved several different villages and several different sets of obligations. At Villiers-Vineux the monks themselves owed the viscount forty solidi a year, which income he had granted to several of his own men,[22] and the tenants owed one measure of grain a year, the actual measure being larger or smaller depending on whether they had any cattle. This relative uniformity in obligations seems to have been a feature of fees owed to an advocate. These could seem like very low rents, but they do not include whatever the peasants might have owed the monastery as its tenants. In addition, each household owed some labor dues, three days of assistance (*bien*) a year, plus two days of plowing and, for those with cattle, three days of *corvee* a year, indicating that more could be expected from these tenants. If for some reason the viscount did not request this assistance in a particular year, the agreement specified, he could not roll the days of service over into the next year. Although the charter portrays this last condition as benefiting St.-Germain, the people who actually benefited would have been the peasants. Nothing indicates their reaction to this ruling, but its inclusion

---

21. *Cartulaire général de l'Yonne*, 1:433–35, no. 281.

22. The following year, the viscount remitted twenty of these solidi to the monks, for his wife's soul, recompensing the man who had held that income from him; *Cartulaire général de l'Yonne*, 1:438–29, no. 285.

suggests that accumulated service days from year to year had been a peasant grievance—now resolved in their favor.

The long charter that the count of Blois produced to cover the details of this agreement went on to specify that these tenants could seek justice either in the viscount's court or with the abbot if they had any quarrel, and that the viscount would handle any case of theft or false measures. This passing reference to judicial issues indicates that these villagers of Villiers-Vineux were capable of having their day in court if they felt aggrieved. Finally, after the monks granted the viscount the right to hunt in some of their woods, and the viscount granted the monks ownership of two mills, the document returned to the peasants. If they left the village and crossed the Armançon river toward St.-Florentin, they would leave the dominion of St.-Germain and become the viscount's men and women (*homines et femine*). The same was specified if they married those who lived beyond the river; they and their children would become the viscount's tenants, rather than merely subject to his justice. The powerful might have wanted to regulate this sort of peasant initiative, but they gave no sign of wanting—or being able—to suppress it.

This settlement might appear to have ended the quarrels, but that was not to be—and peasants continued to be central to the competing claims of monastery and viscount. A short time after the count of Blois issued his charter, a new quarrel arose between St.-Germain and the viscount, primarily over a new oven at St.-Florentin. As part of the agreement, the parties reiterated that those tenants of St.-Germain who married the viscount's dependents would become his as well, but a specific woman and her children were excluded from this overall expectation, with the viscount giving them to the monks.[23] It is impossible to say why she should have been singled out, but the scribe writing up the charter knew and included her father's name and the names of both her husband and her husband's father; she was far from nameless or faceless. Framed as an agreement between a wealthy abbey and a powerful viscount, the agreement nonetheless reveals assumptions about the ability of peasants to bring legal cases, to enrich themselves through raising cattle, to move, and to choose their marriage partners.

Negotiation of Dues and Status

What might seem like arbitrary demands from landlords often appear on closer examination to have been the result of peasant negotiation. Documents from high medieval Burgundy/Champagne indicate that not only

---

23. *Cartulaire général de l'Yonne*, 1:467–68, no. 317.

were dues and obligations very different for different peasants, but these peasants could and did renegotiate them. The best opportunity for such renegotiation was when the land on which they lived was being transferred to a new landlord. Although the document would focus on the donation itself and the spiritual benefit the donor sought, it might also reveal peasants acting to change the terms of their tenure.

When important landowners gave property to a monastery, the documents might note the consent of the men and women who had lived and worked on that land. Such was the case with Rocelina, discussed above at the beginning of the introduction. Most of the documents did not mention such consent, but because the donation itself was the key event that the monks wanted recorded, it may well have been given but not been preserved in writing, or at least not in the sometimes laconic or abbreviated form found in a cartulary. The strongest evidence of how frequent peasant interaction may have been in events that affected them is the utterly matter-of-fact way these people's participation and assent were treated when a document did mention them. Nothing about their role in witnessing and giving consent to a gift that deeply involved them was marked as unusual. Indeed, the casual way that the scribe might note their role indicates it was normal.

For example, around the middle of the eleventh century a knight gave Bèze two mansi for his wife's soul, along with two named peasants and their families. The monks' cartulary spells out that these mansi would pay every year a bushel of wheat and half a bushel of oats, a setier of wine, a piglet worth six pence, five pennies, and the service of an ox and a cart during grape harvest.[24] It would be easy to overlook these details, but they are significant.

Here, in the middle of the eleventh century, when modern descriptions of manorial practice assume all peasant tenants owed regular labor dues, and lords were supposedly imposing more and more such obligations due to the so-called feudal revolution,[25] these peasants owed none—other than helping out during grape harvest. A bushel and a half of grain a year would be trivial. They must have been growing wine grapes of their own to owe any part of their rent in wine.[26] The piglet and the coins, the latter presumably from selling produce, suggest that they had at least a marginally varied diet. These

---

24. *The Cartulary-Chronicle of St.-Pierre of Bèze*, ed. Constance Brittain Bouchard, Medieval Academy Books 116 (Toronto, 2019), pp. 197–98, no. 105.

25. Robert Fossier, "Rural Economy and Country Life," in *The New Cambridge Medieval History*, vol. 3, ed. Timothy Reuter (Cambridge, 1999), pp. 33–39.

26. Although it tells us little about eleventh-century vineyards, it is worth noting that Bèze is in the heart of the Burgundy wine region, and that Evelyn Waugh considered Bèze wine worth special mention in his classic World War II novel, *Brideshead Revisited* (New York, 1944).

were prosperous peasants, and hidden behind the rather laconic account of the gift were surely discussion and negotiation to make sure that the peasants did not object to it, when all the donor wanted was to assure prayers for his late wife's soul. Perhaps most significantly, these peasants were called serfs (*servi*), so their prosperity cannot be explained away as that of free peasants.

Peasants continued to be involved in the gifts of which they formed a part a century later. An example comes from the Cistercian monastery of Pontigny in 1167.[27] One William of Chéu gave the monks, with the consent of his whole family, some land and a house at Auxerre, a fairly sizeable piece of land to judge by the boundaries the charter detailed. It was also significant as land held in fief from the count of Nevers, who confirmed the gift. But there along with the well-to-do family of landowners and the count were two men, *homines*, along with their wives and sons. Everyone was identified by name. These *homines*, the document specified, had worked on the land (*in ipsa terra laboraverant*) and had planted the vineyards there. This whole family group, it was recorded, agreed and confirmed William's gift, *concesserunt et laudaverunt*. Their inclusion in the transaction indicates that peasants who actually worked a piece of land were considered crucial; without their consent it is doubtful that William would have been able to make his gift at all. That is, in order for the land to be given, both the person from whom the donor William held in fief, the count, and those who worked for him had to agree. Documents like this give a glimpse into transactions where both the most and the least powerful were expected to play an active part.

Peasants were not of course always successful in negotiating their position or their dues, but the number of charters that show such negotiations indicate that this was always a possibility. An example from the monastery of Montier-en-Der from the middle of the eleventh century shows that at least a well-to-do peasant might initiate negotiations over the payments required of him. An important villager (*villicus*) named Letaud had leased a mill from the monks, paying them three pounds a year. It was unclear whether Letaud operated it himself or employed a miller, but at any rate he clearly found it economically advantageous to do so.

But it was apparently not advantageous enough. In the attesting charter, he started by asking that the monks free him completely from paying the three pounds. This outrageous request appears to have been intended to start negotiations. The abbot, not surprisingly, refused to stop requiring the payment, but Letaud came back with another proposition. He would return

---

27. *Le premier cartulaire de l'abbaye cistercienne de Pontigny (XIIe–XIIIe siècles)*, ed. Martine Garrigues (Paris, 1981), p. 173, no. 103.

a two-thirds share of the mill to the monks, keeping the rest for his lifetime and that of his son, but for a reduced payment of only one pound a year. In addition, he promised that after his and his son's deaths, their share in the mill would revert to the monastery, presumably to be rented out at a higher rate. The abbot and monks agreed to this new proposal and recorded it, saying they did so lest anyone alter it, by cunning or by force.[28] In this case Letaud was able to arrange for secure lifetime authority over the mill for himself and his son, for a substantially reduced rent. He was treated as an appropriate person with whom to negotiate, someone capable of making proposals, someone with whom the monastery could make a binding agreement. Letaud ended up with a settlement highly advantageous to him, and the monks considered it advantageous enough to them in the long run that they were willing to accept it.

Indeed, a closer look at many charters that mention peasants, taken from a number of different locales in the eleventh and twelfth centuries, demonstrates that the powerful men and women who drew up charters involving peasants often had to take the latter's wishes into account. For example, around the middle of the twelfth century one William of Chalon, dying, gave some land to the Cistercian monks of La Ferté. But apparently he did not consult with Achard, the peasant who was working the land—the document refers to his *labor*. After William's death, his two executors, along with his minor sons, managed to persuade Achard to release the land to the monastery by offering him a large amount of grain a year, in this case reversing what one might expect to be the normal pattern, here payments in grain going *from* the landlord to the peasant, not the other way around. Achard's consent was important enough that it was written up at the monastery and confirmed by the bishop of Chalon.[29]

Although one might wonder whether Achard was unusual, there are enough examples of peasants giving consent to a gift that involved them to suggest that this consent was routinely sought. When the archdeacon of the monastery of Flavigny gave a *homo* named Segnoreth to the cathedral canons of Autun in 1177, he did so, the charter specified, with Segnoreth giving his willing consent, *volente et concedente*.[30] Interestingly, the charter stressed that the archdeacon "gave" and "conceded" Segnoreth to the canons, and that he had "invested" them with this *homo*, but it does not indicate *why* he did so. The probable reason was to establish prayers for his soul. But the peasant's

28. *The Cartulary of Montier-en-Der*, pp. 154–55, no. 56.
29. *Recueil des pancartes de La Ferté*, p. 69, no. 37.
30. *Cartulaire de l'église d'Autun*, p. 108, no. 2.20.

agreement could not be taken for granted, even though the benefit for the archdeacon's soul could be assumed, indeed went without saying. The charter made sure to state that Segnoreth had agreed to becoming the cathedral's man. Clearly his assent was vital.

In these cases, the peasants involved had the ability to have a say in decisions affecting their position and obligations, to the extent that neither monks nor powerful lords could simply coerce them into doing what they wanted. Interactions such as those between Achard and the monks of La Ferté would not have been recorded in the monks' archives had not both the monks themselves and the laymen making them gifts believed the peasants' assent was crucial to the transactions. The same is true of Segnoreth, given by a churchman to the cathedral canons of Autun. In all these cases, peasant assent was important enough that it had to be spelled out, not merely assumed. The implication in these charters is clear: if the peasants involved had *not* agreed to be transferred, the whole transaction would have collapsed.

One of the other areas in which peasants made their own decisions, at least some of the time, was being able to choose their own marriage partners. Scholars often refer to *formariage* or *merchet*, a fine levied on a serf if they sought to marry someone who was not a serf of the same lord, but in fact these terms are rare in twelfth-century sources—although *merchet* became a marker of servile status in thirteenth-century England.[31] The previous chapter discussed the issue of peasant marriage with examples of serfs in the eleventh century and the first years of the twelfth, and by the middle of the twelfth century it became very difficult for lords to make decisions about peasant marriages.

In part, of course, elites had far more on their minds than the question of which person the peasants who paid them rent or labor might decide to marry. As long as nothing about a peasant marriage disturbed the payments, the details were unimportant in the vast majority of cases.[32] An example from late eleventh-century Marmoutier illustrates some of the issues.[33] One Gandelbert, who had earlier become a serf of the monastery (perhaps through offering himself to the monks), married a widowed female serf (*ancilla*) of the region, named Gerberge. She appears, like Gandelbert, to have originally been a free person, but the attesting charter said that she had earlier taken on

---

31. Eleanor Searle, "Seigneurial Control of Women's Marriage: The Antecedents and Function of Merchet in England," *Past and Present* 82 (1979), 5–6.

32. Elisabeth Van Houts, *Married Life in the Middle Ages, 900–1300* (Oxford, 2019), pp. 49–52.

33. *Le livre des serfs*, p. 100, no. 106.

servile status by marrying a serf of Marmoutier. Now, with her first husband dead, she and Gandelbert married and asserted that they were not serfs. It appears that Gerberge's position was that she had only been servile while married to a serf, and that with him gone so was her status as an *ancilla*. Gandelbert in turn appears to have taken the position that if marrying a serf made someone into a serf, then marrying a free woman made him free.

The monks of Marmoutier were not convinced. The prior had Gandelbert dragged back to the monastery and imprisoned him until he agreed he was indeed a serf. He eventually did so, and he and Gerberge came before the monks in their chapter house and swore before witnesses, "so this would not happen again" according to the attesting charter, that they were indeed serfs, and offered the symbolic four pennies on their heads. But it is important to note here that the prior might be able to imprison a serf, but that serf had to give his own assurance of servile status—the prior could not simply assert it.

The charter was witnessed by some twelve men of the monastery, including a fisherman and two cooks. The witnesses were there, according to the charter, "lest he deny it again." The ceremony was very similar to what a knight giving up false claims to monastic property might have undergone, except that a knight would not have had to put pennies on his head, and the witnesses would have been neighboring knights and lords rather than cooks and a fisherman. Gandelbert and Gerberge might have been unable to claim free status, but they had been able to marry without seeking permission or paying a fine, and the monks recognized their capacity to make their own decisions enough to require them to accept servility publicly and in person, recognizing the real possibility that they might "deny it again."[34]

Monks and other landlords were especially interested in the inheritance and marriages of those who provided essential services to their lords.[35] Yet even here they could not simply impose their will on their serfs or other tenants. In another example from Marmoutier from the 1060s, the monks had as *maior* over one of their granges a serf, Otbert. When he died, leaving only a son and a daughter, his widow Maria petitioned the abbot to make the daughter free, so that she could marry a free man. The abbot agreed, although apparently reluctantly, stipulating that both the young woman and her brother would have to leave their father Otbert's land. He had held it, the

34. See also Fouracre, "Marmoutier and Its Serfs," p. 37.

35. Robert F. Berkhofer III, "Marriage, Lordship and the 'Greater Unfree' in Twelfth-Century France," *Past and Present* 173 (2001), 4–8.

attesting document suggested, because he served as *maior*, and the monks wanted to grant it to someone else. Even so, Otbert's son was specified as remaining a serf, and if the young woman did not marry her free husband after all, she was stipulated as returning to servile status.[36]

Here, even while the abbot was attempting to make sure that the office of *maior* not pass to someone who was not the monastery's serf, he made no attempt to choose the young woman's husband for her. Again, the peasant family came to the monks' chapter house, before both the monks themselves and witnesses from their household, and formally accepted the agreement, indicating that their acceptance was required. The charter added the names of the brother and sister, Gausbert and Cecelia, having failed to give them earlier but clearly considering them important. They might have been peasants, indeed serfs, in a difficult personal situation, but they were still people recognized as having the capacity to make their own decisions.

Control over peasant marriages was also made more problematic in the twelfth century by the development within canon law of the centrality of the partners' consent. No one other than the principals, neither lords nor parents, were supposed to have final say over formation of a marriage. Especially in the monasteries from which so much of our information comes, there came to be a clear sense that the law of the church meant that lords could no longer make their dependents' choice of marriage partner for them. Rather, the clergy took the side of the peasants, in arguing for peasant self-determination in choosing marriage partners.

Indeed, in 1155 Pope Hadrian IV issued a ruling, which became a decretal within canon law, that lords could not withhold permission from their *servi* to marry. Around 1180, Alexander III followed up with a ruling of his own, also adopted into canon law, that established the free consent of the principals as required for Christian marriage.[37] Lords were still deeply concerned that the marriages of their peasants might cause them economic harm, but charging fees rather than forbidding such unions was their only viable option within church law. As the above examples suggest, a peasant's marriage, like the transfer of land with its peasants to a monastery, could and did become an opportunity for a tenant to negotiate for lower or less burdensome dues, or for a serf to negotiate for freedom. Just as different peasants might owe very different rents or obligations, so different peasants found different opportunities to negotiate their status or their payments.

---

36. *Le livre des serfs*, p. 73, no. 76. See also Fouracre, "Marmoutier and Its Serfs," p. 38.
37. Berkhofer, "Marriage," pp. 8, 15–21. Van Houts, *Married Life*, pp. 1–2.

The crucial point is that the records repeatedly indicate that they did so, and they were very often successful.

One can thus see a great variety of peasant dues and obligations, just as there was a great variety in peasant status. But several features stand out, principally the value that everyone recognized lay in peasant labor. The dues they paid, whether in coin, produce, or work days, including both regular payments and occasional extra required contributions, provided everyone's food and gave value to the land. The peasants themselves recognized how necessary they were. They were able to use turning points, such as the donation of the land on which they lived to a monastery, to negotiate for better conditions or reduced payments, or at least for consistency in their dues in the future. Their overall acceptance of their position—there were no widespread peasant revolts in the high Middle Ages—should not obscure their ability to make many of their own decisions, including where to live and who to marry. The powerful, needing the peasants, had to be ready to deal with these decisions.

CHAPTER 3

Peasants, Religion, and the Church

In his 1945 memoir, *Christ Stopped at Eboli*, Carlo Levi described as savages the southern Italian peasants among whom he had lived in exile (he called them *my* peasants), people who saw themselves as without religion. "'We're not Christian,' they say. 'Christ stopped short of here, at Eboli.' 'Christian' in their way of speaking means 'human being.' . . . We're not Christians, we're not human beings; we're not thought of as men but simply as beasts, beasts of burden."[1] For Levi, peasants lived in a timeless world, one with neither history nor religion, and medieval peasants have often been presented in the same way.

By far the majority of all medieval documents that survive from before the mid-thirteenth century, including those in which peasants appeared, come from ecclesiastical archives. And yet the relationship between the peasantry and organized religion is often not considered. Most overviews of church history barely mention peasants, while most histories of lower-status

---

1. Carlo Levi, *Christ Stopped at Eboli*, trans. Frances Frenaye (New York, 1947; rpt. 2006), p. 3. See also Paul Freedman, *Images of the Medieval Peasant* (Stanford, 1999), p. 1. One could argue that, if Levi's peasants really said that Christ got no further than Eboli, then they were not so much characterizing themselves as a people without religion as complaining that everyone in authority, even Christ, had abandoned them.

people barely mention the church.[2] Although many scholars (including me) have written extensively on the relationship between the medieval nobility and the church, indicating that the issue is not simply one of focusing on ecclesiastics rather than lay people, the relationship between the peasantry and organized religion has been, at best, underappreciated.

Peasants and Religion

In part the tendency to overlook the relationship between the peasantry and medieval religion is the legacy of a long-standing characterization of peasants as brutes, uncivilized, and half (if not entirely) pagan. Levi was not alone.[3] After all, the very word "pagan" (*paganus*) originally meant a country person, a person of the *pagus*; it came into use in late antiquity as a synonym for *rusticus*, someone crude, unlettered, and unfamiliar with proper religion.[4] Indeed, both "peasant" (*paysan* in French) and "pagan" are derived from *paganus*. Although recently scholars have begun taking the religion of low-status people more seriously, the depiction of peasants as people without religion long lingered. The drive to convert the Anglo-Saxon kings of England in the sixth and seventh centuries, combined with the slow spread of Christianity into Scandinavia and eastern Europe in the following centuries, might suggest a society barely emerged from paganism. Yet given that Gaul had been thoroughly Christian since at least the sixth century, it is counterproductive at best to describe the majority of the French population as non-Christian half a millennium later.[5]

If not actually pagan, peasants have often been depicted as passive recipients of religious practice.[6] Georges Duby, for example, contrasted theology

---

2. For example, Werner Rösener's study of medieval peasants does not mention religion or the church at all; *Peasants in the Middle Ages*, trans. Alexander Stützer (Urbana, 1992). Two influential histories of the medieval church, published in English some seventy years apart and both still in print, fail to mention the peasantry except extremely briefly. Margaret Deanesly, *A History of the Medieval Church, 590–1500* (1925; rpt. London, 1989). Gerd Tellenbach, *The Church in Western Europe from the Tenth to the Early Twelfth Century*, trans. Timothy Reuter (Cambridge, 1993); originally published in German in 1988.

3. This characterization was still accepted late into the twentieth century, as exemplified by Eugen Weber, *Peasants into Frenchmen: The Modernization of Rural France, 1870–1914* (Stanford, 1976). Miscellaneous fun fact: it is well known that the hole in the floor with places for one's feet is called a "Turkish toilet" in France. Less well known is that a nice white porcelain fixture is often called "Christian" in explicit contrast. Christianity equals modern civilization.

4. Freedman, *Images of the Medieval Peasant*, pp. 137–38.

5. A similar point is made by John H. Arnold, *Belief and Unbelief in Medieval Europe* (London, 2005), p. 28.

6. Eric R. Wolf, *Peasants* (Englewood Cliffs, N.J., 1966), pp. 97–106. Joseph H. Lynch, an excellent historian of the church, still treated peasants as receiving religious rituals with little understanding and no engagement; *The Medieval Church: A Brief History* (New York, 1992), pp. 126–29, 190–92.

and "peasant wisdom" (to the detriment of the latter), described medieval peasants as having essentially no access to organized religion, and indicated that relics "dazzled ruffians and peasants" (apparently interchangeable groups).[7] Even if peasants are treated sympathetically, their religiosity has often been seen as at best uninformed, at worst deviant.[8] A treatment of peasant religion may appear solely in discussions of heresy, or heresy itself may be treated primarily as an aspect of "popular" belief, rather than a learned dispute over doctrine.[9]

Those authors who described the Middle Ages as an age of faith tended to exclude the peasantry from this vision. As rural parishes did not really start to appear until the twelfth century, and the 1215 decree that everyone attend church at least once a year was considered an innovation, it was easy to assume that the medieval peasantry had little if any access to institutionalized religion. Yet medieval liturgical books assumed that the sacraments, from baptism to last rites, would be administered to those of all social and economic statuses and frequently mentioned the presence of "the people," that is nonelites, in church. As parish churches became more common in rural areas, priests were concerned with the pastoral care of their parishioners.[10]

Perhaps ironically, parallel to the depiction of peasants as irreligious savages was a long series of suggestions by historians that they were credulous, overawed by the church, dumbly accepting whatever the priests told them, following the precepts of a religion that left them wracked with superstitious fear. Indeed, these supposed semipagan peasants were sometimes credited with any medieval religious practice that historians found distasteful or superstitious, such as miracle stories or relic collections, even though those were central to mainstream Christianity in the Middle Ages. Yet as more

---

7. Georges Duby, *The Age of the Cathedrals: Art and Society 980–1420*, trans. Eleanor Levieux and Barbara Thompson (Chicago, 1981), pp. 46, 75, 159.

8. For example, Malcolm Lambert, *Medieval Heresy: Popular Movements from the Gregorian Reform to the Reformation*, 3rd ed. (Oxford, 2002). Emmanuel Le Roy Ladurie treated fourteenth-century heresy in southern France as a peasant phenomenon; *Montaillou: The Promised Land of Error*, trans. Barbara Bray (New York, 1978). Similarly, Bernard Hamilton's recent treatment of lay religiosity in the twelfth century primarily treats peasants as followers of Bogomil or Cathar heresies; "Religion and the Laity," in *The New Cambridge Medieval History*, vol. 4, pt. 1, ed. David Luscombe and Jonathan Riley-Smith (Cambridge, 2004), pp. 499–533.

9. Norman Cohn's equation of heresy with social revolution by the downtrodden is still influential some sixty-five years after its first publication; *The Pursuit of the Millennium: Revolutionary Millenarians and Mystical Anarchists of the Middle Ages*, 3rd ed. (Oxford, 1970); originally published in 1957. The book remains in print in paperback for classroom adoption.

10. For the ways that the liturgy and pastoral care were brought to the wider medieval population, see the essays in Miri Rubin, ed., *Medieval Christianity in Practice* (Princeton, 2009).

recent scholars have made clear, writing miracle stories and acquiring and testing relics were elite activities, not the province of the unlettered.[11]

Yet just as it would be mistaken to treat as non-Christians people whose ancestors had considered themselves Christians for over twenty generations, so it is equally mistaken to portray them as naïve believers. I would argue that the peasants of the high Middle Ages would have strongly rejected any suggestion that they were not Christians, but that their religious beliefs left plenty of room for questioning ecclesiastical authority. Neither half pagan nor ready to believe whatever the churchmen told them, they followed their own version of what they considered Christianity. Lacking theological nuance, peasants' understanding of religion could be denigrated by their better-educated contemporaries. But it would be difficult to find any medieval sources that described peasants as simply credulous.

Even though it is assumed in modern Western society that well-educated elites are more likely to be skeptics and doubters, and that the "simple folk" are more religious, that assumption was upside down in the Middle Ages. Then, when any formal education was thoroughly imbued with religion, the elites, not the "simple folk," fought against religious doubt and strove (at least intermittently) to assure their salvation. Bernard of Angers, arguing in the mid-eleventh century for the authenticity of the rather startling miracles of Saint Foy, characterized a doubter as "impious," a "depraved liar," a "son of the devil," and a "peasant" (rusticus), as if these all were essentially interchangeable attributes.[12] Unlearned, perhaps even unbaptized, this man ridiculed the saint's miracles as outrageous and unbelievable—a reaction against which Bernard himself sometimes had to fight in his own mind.

When the monks of Laon took their relics on a tour to raise money to restore their ruined church in the early twelfth century, it was the lowborn whom Guibert of Nogent said they feared, doubters who would mock the power of the relics, threaten the monks, refuse them hospitality, and possibly steal the offerings. Guibert certainly did not assume—nor did he think his audience would assume—that lower-status people, including those he

---

11. The pioneering works on this topic were Patrick J. Geary, *Furta Sacra: Thefts of Relics in the Central Middle Ages*, 2nd ed. (Princeton, 1990); and Thomas Head, *Hagiography and the Cult of Saints: The Diocese of Orléans, 800–1200* (Cambridge, 1990). Geary found it necessary to argue against the idea of relics as the product of a simple and irrational folk; *Furta Sacra*, p. 3–4. Duby in contrast characterized reliquaries as "effigies [that] brought alive the anthropomorphic gods which peasant peoples with no history had always venerated"; *The Age of the Cathedrals*, p. 282.

12. *Liber miraculorum Sancte Fidis*, ed. Auguste Bouillet (Paris, 1897), cap. 1.7, p. 31. *The Book of Sainte Foy*, trans. Pamela Sheingorn (Philadelphia, 1995), p. 64.

called "despicable peasants" or "vulgar people," would credulously believe whatever churchmen told them.[13]

The eleventh-century monk Raoul Glaber's description of the heretic Leutard, often depicted as one of the first heretics of the high Middle Ages, has been used as an example of the deviance of peasant beliefs.[14] But a closer examination of the passage in Raoul's "Historia" reveals that Leutard was more complicated than he is now often described. Raoul calls him a heretic, which is the correct term, for Leutard believed that he was acting in accordance with God's will, even though the local churchmen (and Raoul) believed he had completely misinterpreted what God wanted and was instead following Satan. Leutard was clearly a peasant, working in a field (in agro) on what Raoul called a "rural project" when, tired, he decided to take a nap. While he was sleeping, he later claimed, a swarm of bees entered his body. They told him what God supposedly wanted him to do, which was to go into the church and destroy the crucifix. The "feeble minded peasants" (rustici mente labiles) believed him when he said he was obeying a divine revelation.

In spite of Raoul's dismissive attitude toward peasants, he did not treat heresy as a uniquely peasant activity—in fact just the opposite. He spent far more time on a heresy at Orléans that was promulgated by two priests, not unlearned or low-status people.[15] Even more significantly, he assumes (and assumes his audience will agree) that Leutard and the other rustici were church-going Christians. Leutard went into the church feigning an intent to pray, a normal activity for a peasant. Those initially shocked at his behavior thought he must be mad (insanus) to destroy a crucifix, indicating they understood proper Christian behavior. As Leutard started preaching wild sermons and denying the necessity of tithes, he did so with reference to the Bible. He was only stopped when the bishop of Châlons accused him of heresy, that is, of being someone who knew (or ought to know) orthodox Christianity but rejected it. Abandoned by the vulgus populace who listened to the bishop rather than to him, he ended his life by throwing himself down a well. A mad, simple-minded peasant heretic was defined by the Christianity

---

13. Guibert of Nogent, Autobiographie, ed. Edmond-René Labande, Les Classiques de l'histoire de France au moyen âge 34 (Paris, 1981), cap. 3.12–13, pp. 378–88. A Monk's Confession: The Memoirs of Guibert of Nogent, trans. Paul J. Archambault (University Park, Penn., 1996), pp. 173–81. The despicable vulgar people (nequissimo vulgo) were clearly peasants, inhabitants of a rural village; Autobiographie, p. 388.

14. Raoul Glaber, "Historia" 2.11, in Opera, ed. John France et al. (Oxford, 1989), pp. 88–90. Lambert, Medieval Heresy, pp. 35–36.

15. Raoul Glaber, "Historia" 3.8, pp. 138–50.

he knew well even though he rejected it, and his followers were brought back to proper religious practice by the bishop.[16]

One cannot have it both ways. Peasants cannot be treated *both* as pagans and as the progenitors of medieval Christian practices—much less as naïve believers wholly under clerical influence. Of course peasants did not have a sophisticated understanding of theological issues, but neither did most of the aristocracy. The unsophisticated Leutard created his own version of religion, as directed by his bees. The extensive quarrels between the abbot of Vézelay and the peasants and villagers of the region around the abbey, detailed in chapter 4, indicate that peasants were perfectly capable of asserting their rights against their lord, even if that lord were a church, and that neither the abbot nor the collection of powerful laymen and churchmen brought in to settle those quarrels saw anything out of the ordinary in the proceedings.

And there is plenty of evidence of peasants wanting to involve themselves in religious practices in a positive way, not merely in disputes. During the 1130s the villagers of Soupir, near Prémontré, decided to build themselves a church, wishing, according to the attesting document, to act as "good parishioners." For various reasons, "wars and various importunities" the charter continued, their efforts stalled, so they asked Baldwin, their landlord, to petition the abbot of Prémontré to take over (and presumably pay for) the church's construction. The abbot agreed, and the villagers in return gave Prémontré a large tract of land adjacent to what Baldwin had recently given to the monastery.[17]

The bishop confirmed this agreement and stated that the villagers had done so for the good of their souls. He went on to name them individually: some forty families, doubtless the entire village. Two of the families had men identified as a knight, *miles*, but the others appear to have been low-status country people, in short, peasants. For an entire village to seek to associate themselves with the new, highly respected house of Prémontré, making substantial gifts of land in order to have their own parish church, is a clear indication that taking part in the organized religious life was an important goal for at least these peasants.

In another case from three generations later, the villagers of Sormery in Burgundy were accused of taking wood from a forest belonging to the

---

16. Pierre Bonnassie confuses the issue by treating Leutard not as a heretic but as the peasant leader of a rebellion against harsh lordship; *From Slavery to Feudalism in South-Western Europe*, trans. Jean Birrell (Cambridge, 1991), pp. 310–12.

17. Soissons, Bibliothèque municipale, MS 7, fol. 26v.

Cistercian monastery of Pontigny.[18] The villagers asserted that they were entitled to this *usuagium* because they had long taken wood from there to rebuild or repair their parish church. They were supported in this assertion by the abbot of St.-Martin of Troyes and by the lord of Sormery, called both *nobilis* and *miles*, along with his family. The quarrel was settled when their noble lord agreed, for the good of his and his family's souls, to give the parish church of Sormery twenty solidi a year, presumably to buy the wood they needed without having to take anything from Pontigny's forest. Here everyone assumed that taking wood for a church's upkeep was a normal activity for villagers, indicating that the church was important to them. It is also noteworthy that the villagers were able to gain the support of the local lord and of the abbot of the religious house that, it would appear, was responsible for naming the priest of Sormery. The only person to make a concession in the final agreement was this local lord. He managed both to placate the villagers and to make a gift for the good of his soul, but it was the villagers' activity, taking wood to which they had persuaded him they were entitled, that led both to the quarrel and to its eventual settlement.

It is well known that parish churches really only began to be common in the twelfth century, but the corollary may be overlooked: peasants, as well as those who had moved to the growing cities, had their own preferences in parish churches. In Sens in the middle of the twelfth century two parish churches quarreled over the disposition of bodies of parishioners who had died while outside their own parish. The quarrel was settled by the abbot of St.-Pierre-le-Vif of Sens.[19] Although his attesting charter was framed as ending a dispute between two churches, it made clear that the real issue was recognizing the last wishes of dying parishioners. Even the choice of burial location by a low-status person had to be taken seriously enough that this choice could draw well-established churches into serious quarrels. The issue would not even have arisen had not the parishioners in question been deeply involved with the church they considered theirs.

While the exact nature of peasant religious beliefs must remain largely unknown, the documents in many cases do show repeated interactions between peasants and churchmen. Peasants could use churchmen to serve their own purposes or, less cynically, might make pious gifts of their own to churches, suggesting that perhaps we can discern some aspects of their religiosity after all. Neither pagans nor credulous believers, and certainly not the

18. *Recueil de pièces pour faire suite au Cartulaire général de l'Yonne*, ed. Maximilien Quantin (Auxerre, 1873), p. 35, no. 76.

19. *Cartulaire général de l'Yonne*, ed. Maximilien Quantin, 2 vols. (Auxerre, 1854–60), 2:90, no. 83.

creators of the genre of miracle stories, they frequently sought to interact with priests and monks, to bring themselves closer to God through association with churches and monasteries. Peasant invisibility in modern accounts of the medieval church would have seemed very odd both to them and to those who wrote the charters in which they appeared.

The Revolt of the *Capuciati*

Northern France was largely untouched by the dualist heresy that led eventually to the Albigensian Crusade. That heresy of course was not a uniquely peasant phenomenon; the count of Toulouse himself was said to have followed its teachings. But Burgundy had its own late twelfth-century heresy, that of the so-called *capuciati* in the 1180s, that did involve the local peasantry. Even in the high Middle Ages, before the violent peasants' revolts of the fourteenth and fifteenth centuries, peasants were capable of open attacks on those they considered oppressors and of giving such attacks a religious dimension. The revolt of the *capuciati* is well documented in the narrative sources, which described the events less in religious terms and more as examples of the danger and chaos that arose when the weak dared oppose the powerful: indeed the very breakdown of Christian society.[20]

According to the sources, the *capuciati* began as a religious movement, when a peasant had a vision of the Virgin and organized the villagers of the region to stand up to brigands who had been terrorizing the region and hampering trade. They adopted badges with the image of the Virgin and wore white caps or hoods—which gave the group their name. However, the sources continue, the group soon turned from attacking brigands to attacking anyone in the aristocracy whom they considered an oppressor. Their greatest error, according to the bishop of Auxerre's biographer, was their attempt to upend the hierarchy, that is, their rejection of the distinction between the great and the small, described as an ill-founded attempt to appropriate the "liberty" of the Garden of Eden.

At this point the bishop decided to take matters into his own hands. His biographer stated, "The wages of sin are servitude" (a reworking of

---

20. Constance Brittain Bouchard, *Spirituality and Administration: The Role of the Bishop in Twelfth-Century Auxerre*, Speculum Anniversary Monographs 5 (Cambridge, Mass., 1979), pp. 101–3. The principal sources are the *vita* of Bishop Hugh of Auxerre; *Les gestes des évêques d'Auxerre*, ed. Guy Lobrichon et al., vol. 2 (Paris, 2006), pp. 179–83; and the *Chronicon* of Robert of St.-Marien, MGH SS 26:247. This movement is discussed briefly by Michel Mollat, *The Poor in the Middle Ages*, trans. Arthur Goldhammer (New Haven, Conn., 1986), p. 83; the translation mistakenly refers to white *capes* rather than caps. For the context of the movement, see Freedman, *Images of the Medieval Peasant*, pp. 74, 98.

Rom. 6:23 that had begun with Isidore of Seville), asserting that the peasants, whom he called "plebeians," owed their subject status to their own sins. The bishop raised a group of armed men and quickly crushed the "rebellion," not just ending the movement but ordering the *capuciati* not to wear any hats at all to punish them for their distinctive headgear, so that they had to work in their fields in the sun without protection. This warlike bishop was proud, again according to his (not entirely admiring) biographer, for having taught those he called *servi* that they should not rise up against their lords.

Even though this effort at open opposition to those they considered oppressors was briskly put down, the rebellious peasants of the Auxerrois are indicative both of the possibility of peasant action (if not necessarily *successful* action) and of their religiosity. After all, their movement started with a religious vision. The Virgin, the peasants appear to have expected, wanted them to triumph. Now instead the bishop triumphed, but this incident demonstrates the possibilities of collective self-help—as well as its limitations, and as well as the dismissive attitude of the powerful toward those they considered ought to be their inferiors.

Perhaps those who wrote the narrative accounts in which peasants could make token appearances feared their agency. If peasants were weak and pitiable, then there was no reason to anticipate them doing anything that might disturb the existing structures. Alternately, if they might engage in anything from armed rebellion to trying to steal money offered to the saints, then it was better that they not be given the opportunity to act on their own initiative. Peasant action, their efforts to improve their position, may not have been a central concern of either documentary or narrative records, but there are enough examples to establish that such agency was real, and enough ambivalence in the response to suggest that it was frightening to the elite.

Service to Monasteries

When a layman gave a church property, it was almost always agricultural land, which meant that it was or had been cultivated by peasants. In many cases, perhaps most, the peasants now became the tenants of the church, rather than of their former lord. Typical is a gift to the Cluniac priory of Romainmôtier from the first years of the twelfth century. A priest named Fuldrad gave the monks a horse, twelve *jornales* of land, and two serfs. The serfs were specifically named, Robert and Helias. Fuldrad added that anyone who tried to take back this gift should be cursed with anathema maranatha,

indicating how important it was that the serfs not be taken from the monastery.[21] Here, as in scores of other examples from northern French cartularies,
those who donated arable land to a religious house also donated the peasants who lived and worked on it. The fact that they were frequently named
indicates that they were more than an afterthought.

Indeed, the peasants who made up part of a gift of land were frequently
recorded as giving their assent to their transfer to new masters in order to
ensure a smooth transition, as discussed in the previous chapter. The frequency
with which peasant consent was specified certainly suggests that the lack of
such agreement could cast serious doubt on the validity and permanence of
a transfer of property. In addition, from the peasants' point of view, there
appear to have been distinct advantages to becoming the men and women of a
religious house rather than of a secular landowner. The point here is that both
lay donors and the religious houses to which they made their gifts had to be
aware of peasant tenants and make provision for them.

For example, one Geoffrey Flocel gave the nunnery of Marcigny some
land in the 1130s, including a vineyard, saying he did so on the occasion of
his daughters becoming nuns. According to the donation charter, he specified that he had given another vineyard to the farmer (*agricola*) who had held
the vineyard he was now giving to Marcigny; this other vineyard was clearly
intended to replace the one now passing to the nuns.[22] Agricultural land and
the peasants that worked it could not easily be separated from each other,
and hence donors had to be sensitive to the prior tenure of peasants when
planning to make a gift.

In an early eleventh-century example from Romainmôtier, the monks
were very concerned that they receive the service (*servicium*) of a family
living in the nearby village of Bannans. Initially King Rudolph III of Burgundy
and the archbishop of Lyon confirmed, at the request of the abbot of Cluny,
that the seven children of one Martin were the men and women (*homines* and
feminae) of the monastery, to command as the monks wished.[23] It is unclear
what was so special about this family that the abbot should have gone to a
king and an archbishop to gain confirmation of the service of these family
members, but they certainly were important. They were all individually
named in the attesting charter, Eldenard, Willimar, Rainer, Langis, Gisela,
Martina, and Hildegard (the last three were the women).

---

21. *Le cartulaire de Romainmôtier (XIIe siècle)*, ed. Alexandre Pahud, Cahiers lausannois d'histoire
médiévale 21 (Lausanne, 1998), pp. 162–63, no. 54.

22. *Le cartulaire de Marcigny-sur-Loire (1045–1144): Essai de reconstitution d'un manuscrit disparu*, ed.
Jean Richard (Dijon, 1957), pp. 179–80, no. 302.

23. *Le cartulaire de Romainmôtier*, pp. 147–48, no. 43.

A generation or so later, the monks paid the lord of Salins one hundred solidi when he agreed to give up his claims to the "service" of just one of these, Willimar, along with his wife and children.[24] The lord of Salins treated this yielding as important enough that he said that he did so for the good of his soul and added that he should share the fate of Judas if he or any of his relatives ever went against the agreement. Martin and his descendants, never identified as serfs, were neither invisible nor interchangeable, but were known as individuals by the monks of Romainmôtier and highly appreciated for what they did.[25]

But what of the land that some religious houses acquired, especially the Cistercians, who wanted no tenants on their property? As initially stated in the statutes of the first recorded Chapter General meeting, traditionally dated 1134, the monks rejected receiving rents from peasant villagers (*uillanos*) along with revenues from mills, ovens, tithes from others' labor, or ecclesiastical revenues like burial fees, all of which were said to be contrary to "monastic purity."[26] But Cistercian houses had at least some peasant tenants from the order's beginning; Viscount Raynald of Beaune, who gave the monks of Cîteaux some of their original land in 1098, initially retained the service of the three serfs who lived there for himself, but when he died a decade or so later, his sons both confirmed their father's gift of land and added to it the serfs themselves.[27]

Still, the Cistercians preferred to cultivate their land either themselves or with their lay brothers. Thus the monks might specify that property given to them have the tenants removed.[28] In such cases the donation charter might

---

24. *Le cartulaire de Romainmôtier*, pp. 149–50, no. 44.

25. Late in the eleventh century, Lord Peter of Scey, who described himself as most noble and his castle as magnificent, gave Romainmôtier, while dying, a mansus at Bannans, complete with a serf named Theoderic and Theoderic's children and a mill. This gift was important enough that when a knight gave up his claims to the mansus, after "invading" the village according to the attesting charter, the settlement was confirmed by the count of Burgundy; *Le cartulaire de Romainmôtier*, pp. 150–52, no. 45.

26. *Twelfth-Century Statutes from the Cistercian General Chapter*, ed. Chrysogonus Waddell, Cîteaux: Commentarii Cistercienses, Studia et Documenta 12 (Brecht, Belgium, 2002), p. 516, no. 23.

27. *Chartes et documents concernant l'abbaye de Cîteaux*, ed. J. Marilier (Rome, 1961), pp. 49–51, 98, nos. 23, 101. For the date of the sons' confirmation, see Constance Brittain Bouchard, *Holy Entrepreneurs: Cistercians, Knights, and Economic Exchange in Twelfth-Century Burgundy* (Ithaca, N.Y., 1991), p. 120, n. 78.

28. Bouchard, *Holy Entrepreneurs*, pp. 118–21. Constance Hoffman Berman argues implausibly that peasant tenants routinely became lay brothers; *Medieval Agriculture, the Southern French Countryside, and the Early Cistercians: A Study of Forty-three Monasteries*, Transactions of the American Philosophical Society 76.5 (Philadelphia, 1986), pp. 53–60. In fact, *conversi* are not found at Cistercian houses before about 1120, and they were very unusual for the next three decades; Jacques Dubois, "L'institution des convers au XIIe siècle: Forme de vie monastique propre aux laïcs," in

either describe efforts to move the peasant tenants off the land or otherwise deal with their presence. For example, in 1146 one Geoffrey of Moulin had the bishop of Langres confirm that he had given the Cistercian monks of Pontigny all the property he had at Ste.-Procaire (located just three kilometers from the abbey), promising that it would be uncultivated and that none of his men would be living there.[29] It would be easy to conclude that the former inhabitants of Geoffrey's land were simply turned out of their houses without recourse. And indeed such harsh evictions must surely have happened in some cases. But here one detail indicates that Geoffrey's peasants were not left destitute. The donation charter copied into Pontigny's cartulary specified that "for the sake of peace" Geoffrey intended to move (*transferrent*) the inhabitants' houses (*domos*).

Where did he move them? The document does not say, but it cannot have been far from Ste.-Procaire, where they had been living, for Geoffrey's brother was specified as entitled, for his lifetime, to continue to collect the tithes of those "secular men" who had been working the land. Had the men not settled nearby, and had they not been able to find or been granted new land to work, there would have been no tithes to collect. It cannot have been easy for the peasants to be uprooted because their landlord wanted to make a pious gift to a monastery that preferred land without tenants. Their consent was not specified, presumably because they did not consent. But they were still provided houses and land to work. Peasants were too valuable to be treated as expendable.

Ste.-Procaire appears to have had a number of peasants living there before Pontigny began acquiring land in the area, because the question of what to do with them continued. A decade after Geoffrey's gift, in 1156, Count William III of Nevers granted the monks a great deal of property in and around that village, in exchange for a grange of theirs at Lorant that he had wanted and that appears to have been less desirable from their point of view—presumably because it was less conveniently located.[30] The count enumerated those who held property from him at Ste.-Procaire and who wished to donate it to Pontigny, as well as confirming gifts there to the monks from those who owned their land outright (*in dominio*). He noted that the monks

I laici nella "Societas christiana" dei secoli XI et XII, Miscellanea del Centro di studi medioevali 5 (Rome, 1968), pp. 186–91.

29. *Le premier cartulaire de l'abbaye cistercienne de Pontigny (XIIe–XIIIe siècles)*, ed. Martine Garrigues (Paris, 1981), pp. 174–75, no. 105.

30. *Le premier cartulaire de Pontigny*, pp. 154–57, no. 85. For this transaction, see also Martha G. Newman, *The Boundaries of Charity: Cistercian Culture and Ecclesiastical Reform, 1098–1180* (Stanford, 1996), pp. 75–77.

would be removing the *habitatores* of the village from their holdings and therefore promised to pay them *recompensatio*. Although this particular charter did not specify what kind of compensation the peasants would receive, it is clear that all agreed they could not simply be brushed aside—and the peasants themselves must have made this point clear.[31]

Indeed, the Cistercians did accept some agricultural land with the peasants still in residence. Around 1130, that is, before the first documented pronouncement by the Cistercian Chapter General that houses of the order should not accept peasant tenants, one Robert of Buxy and his wife made a gift to the monks of La Ferté, Cîteaux's first daughter. Their gift consisted of the agricultural labor of all the *rustici*, previously their tenants, whom the monks would invite into a newly cleared woodland next to the monastery's own fields. The borders of the territory where these peasants would live and work was carefully delineated. But, Robert added, he did not want to be completely deprived of agricultural labor, and therefore he explicitly excepted those *rustici* who lived in the adjacent village, who would remain under his dominion.[32]

Here one sees the importance of peasants and their efforts, both to the monks, who invited the peasants to help them expand their arable land, and to the donor Robert and his family, who found their labor important enough that to lose it all would be a serious deprivation. The assignment of the peasants to La Ferté and the designation of who would and would not be working for the monks was significant enough that Robert had the lord from whom he held in fief give his consent and had seven men confirm as witnesses, adding that he himself had no children old enough to consent.

Peasants and their labor indeed were crucial enough to any agricultural enterprise that a number of Cistercian houses in Burgundy continued to receive land complete with peasant tenants throughout the twelfth century. Such gifts reached a high point during the 1170s.[33] For example, when the duke's constable was dying in 1170, he gave La Bussière a tenancy that included tenants. Four years later, the lord of Fouvent gave Theuley a *homo* and his *tenementum* for the soul of his late father.[34] Alternately, someone

---

31. This exchange with the count appears to have been sufficient for the monks of Pontigny to finish establishing a grange at Ste.-Procaire, for it was listed among their granges in a papal confirmation of their possessions later that year; *Cartulaire général de l'Yonne*, 1:549–50. no. 384.

32. *Recueil des pancartes de l'abbaye de La Ferté-sur-Grosne, 1113–1178*, ed. Georges Duby (Paris, 1953), pp. 43–44, no. 4.

33. Bouchard, *Holy Entrepreneurs*, p. 119.

34. Paris, BnF, MS nouv. acq. fr. 8664, fol. 56. Vesoul, Archives départementales de la Haute Saône, H 409. For English parallels, see R. A. Donkin, *The Cistercians: Studies in the Geography of Medieval England and Wales* (Toronto, 1978), p. 61.

might give the Cistercians an annual income derived from peasant rents, as when a layman gave Maizières forty solidi a year and specified by name the peasants whose rents would produce this amount.[35] Even Cistercian monasteries, which wanted to avoid the role of landlord, could not easily ignore the peasants who lived on and worked land donated to the monks or paid them dues.

The frequency with which gifts to monasteries, even Cistercian monasteries, consisted of land with its peasant tenants thus indicates the centrality of the peasantry to something as supposedly unworldly as gifts for one's soul. The peasants may not have had much say in the matter, but there are enough cases where their assent was sought, or their relocation was arranged, to demonstrate that their presence had to be taken into account. Indeed there are indications that the peasants often were highly interested in being associated with churches. The villagers who gave land to the Premonstratensians in return for assistance in building their own parish church are an example of this desire to associate with organized religion. Even clearer are the examples of peasants voluntarily becoming serfs of a monastery.

One of the clearest markers of peasant respect for the church is their willingness, indeed eagerness, to become ecclesiastical dependents. As noted in chapter 1, free men and women might voluntarily take on servile status if their new lord were a church. Typical is a charter of Marmoutier from the middle decades of the eleventh century in which one Baldonetus, described as a *famulus* and explicitly said to be born of free parents (*ex parentibus liberis ortus*), made himself a serf of the monastery.[36] Although one might cynically assume that he saw some worldly advantage in doing so, this is not what the document says. Baldonetus gave as his motivation not economic exigency but rather divine love.[37]

He immediately offered what must have been demeaning symbols, putting a cord around his own neck and placing four pennies of head tax on the altar, making it clear that the servitude he was taking on was a form of humiliation. But he was eager to do it and indeed specified that all his descendants would likewise be serfs of the monastery. Baldonetus noted that

---

35. Paris, BnF, MS nouv. acq. fr. 8680, p. 20.

36. *Le livre des serfs de Marmoutier*, ed. André Salmon (Tours, 1864), pp. 3–4, no. 2. There are a number of other examples of a serf giving himself to Marmoutier where the wording of the documents follows the same general model; see Dominique Barthélemy, *The Serf, the Knight, and the Historian*, trans. Graham Robert Edwards (Ithaca, N.Y., 2009), pp. 43–44.

37. R. W. Southern dismisses the religious element of a freeman's subjection of himself to the monks of Marmoutier, saying it was "a mere form of words"; *The Making of the Middle Ages* (New Haven, Conn., 1953), p. 99. Barthélemy similarly characterizes such expressions of religious motivation as "general, conventional, and derivative"; *The Serf, the Knight, and the Historian*, p. 61.

God does not make a distinction of persons but judges all according to their merits, and he must have felt this deeply to make the decision to bring himself closer to God and the saints by becoming Marmoutier's serf. Nothing indicates that he was pressured by layman, churchman, or circumstance. As humiliating as the ceremony purposely was, it is crucial to note that it was Baldonetus's own decision.

This case demonstrates that one of the most valuable gifts a peasant could make was his (or her) own person. Both men and women might voluntarily choose to become dependents of a church. When they did so they were not so much fleeing from danger as moving toward salvation. The many serfs who subjected themselves to Marmoutier in the eleventh century considered a status as the monks' dependents preferable to being anyone else's serf—or for that matter in some cases to being free.

Those peasants who became the serfs of a monastery would often have to negotiate with others besides the monks in order to do so, which demonstrates both their initiative and their ability to make their own choices. In Burgundy in 1019 a serf named Walter gave his master, a knight, one hundred solidi. This was apparently the going price for someone to buy his freedom, for the knight spoke as though Walter becoming free (*ingenuus*) might have been an option: "We do not make him free," he said, "but rather delegate him as a serf of Flavigny." Instead of granting Walter his freedom, the knight gave this *servus* to the saints and the monks, saying he did so for his own soul, and that Walter would henceforth render to them whatever he had previously rendered to his master.[38] Walter evidently preferred his situation as a serf of the monastery to that of serf to a layman—he had after all accumulated the sizeable sum of a hundred solidi to buy his way out of service to his knightly master—and this master was able to make a gift that he believed would help his own soul's salvation while also pocketing the money. Both considered the transaction a benefit.

A cynic might suggest that Walter was deceived, that he had wanted his freedom and ended up losing his money while only being transferred from one state of servile dependency to another. But that is not what the document says. It rather creates an equivalence between freedom and subjection to a monastery. This particular case may be clarified by analogy to a very similar case at Marmoutier, which occurred just a few years earlier. Here not one but two charters were issued, one by a serf named Durand Warin, who gave himself to Marmoutier, and one by the laymen who had been his

---

38. *The Cartulary of Flavigny, 717–1113*, ed. Constance Brittain Bouchard, Medieval Academy Books 99 (Cambridge, Mass., 1991), pp. 116–17, no. 46.

masters, formally donating him to Marmoutier.[39] Durand Warin said explicitly that he had "redeemed" himself and his family from his "secular lords," for a sum not specified, and instead submitted them all to the monks. He further specified that the monks would not give him to any other lord; for him there was a clear distinction between being the monks' serf and anyone else's serf. He would not have composed the Latin of the charter himself, but those who wrote it put it in his voice, indicating the necessity of his agreement to the transaction.

In the charter issued by the laymen from whom Durand Warin had redeemed himself and his family, they said they were making a gift to Marmoutier for the good of their souls. They lost a serf but gained prayers; the initiative, however, was Durand Warin's. One has the distinct impression that rather than the serf being deceived into thinking he was gaining his freedom when he was not, it was the knightly masters who found they were losing a valuable serf and, by turning the loss into a pious gift, tried to make the best of the situation.

From the serf's point of view, this donation of himself *was* a pious donation. And, in the spirit of the New Testament admonition that the last shall be first, serfdom to a church was defined as liberty, a point made in a number of documents from Marmoutier. For example, a charter of 1062 indicates that a baker (*furnerius*) named Lambert "gave himself into servitude to Saint Martin," explicitly so that he "might be given eternal liberty."[40] This document was drawn up by the monks, not by Lambert himself, but he would not have put himself, his wife, and his children and grandchildren into servitude as he did had he not seen doing so as having its reward.

All the above examples are from the eleventh century. At Marmoutier this could be an artifact of their "Book of Serfs" having been composed at the very beginning of the twelfth century, and thus not containing later self-donations. But in fact when serfdom disappeared from Burgundian records in the first half of the twelfth century, as detailed in chapter 1, records of such self-subjugation appear to have died out as well. Peasants, as noted below, could become *conversi* at one of the new, rigorous monasteries, but this was a different process than becoming a dependent: a *conversus* was a brother to the monks, even if of lower status.

One of the last examples of someone donating himself to a monastery comes in an 1124 charter of Prémontré, issued not long after that house

39. *Le livre des serfs*, pp. 11–12, 53, nos. 10, 54. See also Barthélemy, *The Serf, the Knight, and the Historian*, pp. 41–43.

40. *Le livre des serfs*, p. 24, no. 22. For similar examples, see Barthélemy, *The Serf, the Knight, and the Historian*, p. 46.

was founded. The bishop of Soissons attested that one Ivo, his parishioner and a *civis* of that city, had given himself, his wife, and all their progeny and their possessions to the monastery, saying they did so out of love of God and a desire to follow the apostles, complete with biblical quotations.[41] This was a fairly wealthy couple, because they said that they were giving houses, vineyards, and winepresses, but they gave it all up, according to the bishop's charter, to Christ. A generation later, after Ivo's death but while his wife and children were still alive, the then bishop confirmed this donation and gave additional detail, indicating the exact location and extent of these gifts.[42]

Should Ivo and his family be considered peasants? One might call them burghers (or bourgeois) as citizens of the city of Soissons, but northern French cities were just starting to grow in the early twelfth century, and the growth was almost entirely due to country people moving to town. Ivo and his family thus were likely only a generation at most from the rural economy. In fact, they were still involved in it, because they owned vineyards and winepresses. Although for the most part I discuss country people rather than townspeople, in the early twelfth century the distinction was far from clear.

As has already been discussed, of course, not all peasants were desperately poor, so owning property by itself does not disqualify them from being characterized as peasants. Both the original donation charter and the confirmation a generation later referred to this family's "service" to the monastery. The point that this example makes especially clear has already been seen in other contexts, which is that there was enormous variety in wealth and status among the great majority of the medieval population now characterized as peasants. If even those who owned vineyards would consider it spiritually advantageous to give themselves to a monastery, then one should not be surprised that those explicitly called serfs should make such a self-donation.

Peasants were a desirable gift from the recipient church's position because they were just as valuable to ecclesiastics who received their rents and labor as they were to secular lords, and for the same reasons. The monks of Marmoutier would not have gone to the effort of creating a whole cartulary enumerating the donations (or self-donations) of serfs to the monastery if they had not believed their dominion over these serfs worth preserving in memory. Creating a cartulary was a deliberate effort to organize and

---

41. Soissons, Bibliothèque municipale, MS 7, fol. 67r–v.
42. Soissons, Bibliothèque municipale, MS 7, fol. 68r–v.

memorialize material in the archives, not a simple transcription of whatever happened to be there.[43]

Peasants making themselves serfs of the church, like laymen making a gift of such serfs, were donating something important: their labor. But as serfdom disappeared from the records of northern France, such self-donation also vanished. Instead peasants made gifts of property, in many ways indistinguishable (except for the size of the gift) from the pious donations made by the aristocracy.

Gifts to Churches from Peasants

A number of monasteries' documents include records of peasants seeking to save their souls by making gifts. Peasants could and did own property, and, like the more powerful, they could and did make donations of that property. A charter from Bèze from around 1016 provides an example.[44] In this case, two brothers, well-to-do peasants, who had owned some land outright a few kilometers from the monastery, decided to leave the region and move some distance away, to a village near Besançon, saying that they did so because of the "enmity" of their neighbors. When doing so, they gave their allodial land to the monks and also promised to send the house one measure of wax a year. They may have done so hoping for the salvation of their souls, but the one document that records these events, drawn up some fifteen years later, does not so specify. Rather, the document states that the brothers and the monks agreed that, if the brothers decided to return to the region of Bèze, they could have their old hereditary property back—on the condition that they would now hold it from the monks, rather than owning it outright.

In addition, and here the abbot clearly indicated the value he put on these peasants, he now asked the bishops of Besançon, Lyon, Langres, Autun, and Mâcon all to confirm that these were free men and that no one should subject them or their heirs to servitude. If anyone did so, the bishops specified at the abbot's request, that person would be excommunicated. For the abbot to have gone to such trouble for peasants who were no longer living nearby, and who had not even owed rent to the monks for their land before they left, indicates that the personal relationship that had been established was very

---

43. Constance Brittain Bouchard, *Rewriting Saints and Ancestors: Memory and Forgetting in France, 500–1200* (Philadelphia, 2015), pp. 9–21.

44. *The Cartulary-Chronicle of St.-Pierre of Bèze*, ed. Constance Brittain Bouchard, Medieval Academy Books 116 (Toronto, 2019), pp. 138–39, no. 46.

important. These were not generic peasants or even generic rent-payers. The brothers had established a connection with Bèze by the gift of their allodial property, and the monks recruited the most powerful ecclesiastics of the region to assure that these men were not subjected to "violence" and would retain their former liberty.

In another example from Bèze from the middle of the eleventh century, the monastery received a gift from one Berno of Genlis, identified as a *villicus*, the head man in a village. He insisted that the land he gave the monks was his allodial property and symbolically placed a marker of his gift on the altar, just as knights did. He stipulated, however, that he would be able to keep the usufruct of the land for his lifetime.[45] Here everything about the transaction indicates someone who could make his own decisions and set his own terms: it was Berno's own land, and he could decide to keep the produce of the land for his lifetime and still gain spiritual benefits. The only difference between his gift and those from knights, which fill the pages of the cartulary of Bèze, was that Berno was clearly not a knight.

Similarly, around 1170 one Robert, also identified as a *villicus*, gave the Augustinian priory of St.-Étienne of Dijon his share of the tithes of Cussey, acting with his brother.[46] That such villagers should have had control over tithes, a century after French churches began trying to take tithes out of lay hands, indicates the ability even peasants could have to keep what they considered theirs. And just as was often the case with aristocratic donors, their heirs tried to reclaim their parents' gifts.[47] The seriousness of this claim was such that when Robert's heirs gave up their claims, the abbot promised them a new cloak every year and a meal once or twice a year if they stopped by the priory.

In a comparable case from Prémontré, another man named Robert, in this case Robert Fulcherus, became a *conversus* at the house at the end of the twelfth century. Although it is possible that he was aristocratic, the term *conversus* at the time almost always designated a lower-status lay brother, when used as a noun as here. Robert Fulcherus owned enough property to be able to make a fairly generous gift to the canons when he joined: half a house, three vineyards, and a small woods. His gift is known only because his four children disputed it after his death. The bishop of Soissons settled their quarrel in 1206, interestingly returning the donated property to Robert's heirs

---

45. *The Cartulary-Chronicle of Bèze*, p. 210, no. 125.

46. *Chartes de l'abbaye de Saint-Étienne de Dijon de 1155 à 1200*, ed. Georges Valat (Paris, 1907), pp. 56–57, no. 41.

47. Constance Brittain Bouchard, *Sword, Miter, and Cloister: Nobility and the Church in Burgundy, 980–1198* (Ithaca, N.Y., 1987), pp. 209–17.

rather than ruling for Prémontré, while specifying that they would give the canons six barrels of white wine a year. The attesting document spelled out what proportion of this wine each of the four would pay.[48]

The document gives no explicit indication of the status of any of the family members. But the internal evidence suggests they were vintners. Robert Fulcherus may well have helped tend the vines for the canons after he became a *conversus*. His gift was primarily made up of vineyards, which his heirs were eager to reclaim. They made the payment to replace their father's gift in wine, with the source of each one's payment specified by the name of the relevant *clos*. No lord approved their settlement, so they presumably were allodists, owning their vineyards outright. This quarrel settlement thus indicates that those without noble titles or *miles* after their names could and did own property outright and donate that property to a church, and even might prevail in a quarrel with an important religious establishment.

Because a great many documents do not specify the status of the lay people who appear in them, many more peasants may have made their own small gifts to churches than is recognized. Without an explicit statement, such as calling the donor a *rusticus*, it is impossible to be sure, but many of the small donations to twelfth-century Cistercian houses appear to have come from men and women of the countryside, lower on the social scale than the knights whose status was noted. At La Ferté, for example, in the first half of the century, a woman named Odears "Navilleri" (probably indicating she came from Navilly), together with her husband, brother, and son, gave the monks whatever she had in a certain hamlet. In return, she received five solidi and a cheese.[49]

Who was Odears? She never appears again in the documents, so it is impossible to know more about her than the few laconic phrases that identify her as the person who made a gift, with members of her family. The few coins and the cheese she received as a countergift suggest that her gift was small. Nothing was said in the brief summary of the gift that was recorded in the monks' pancarte about prayers or the good of her soul, but surely something of the sort was anticipated. The point is that people with little property or influence made gifts to monasteries, just as did the rich and powerful, and the recipients considered those gifts significant enough to record them in writing and later memorialize them in a cartulary or

---

48. Soissons, Bibliothèque municipale, MS 7, fol. 29r–v.

49. *Recueil des pancartes de La Ferté*, pp. 68–69, no. 36. Duby, as editor, identifies the transaction as a sale, but the document itself calls it a gift, *donum*.

pancarte. Odears is just one example among hundreds. Was she a peasant? She cannot be specifically assigned to any social status, but the only reason *not* to consider her one of the many people we now group under the heading of "peasant" is the modern assumption that peasants would not make pious gifts.

Similarly, one Arnulf of Chablis made a postmortem gift of all his property to the monks of Pontigny in the 1130s.[50] We know that he did so because his brother-in-law Herbert objected, saying he was entitled to half of Arnulf's property during the latter's lifetime and all of it after his death, and the quarrel was recorded by Bishop Hugh of Auxerre, who had been abbot of Pontigny himself before his episcopal election. The quarrel was important enough that it was settled only by a court case that involved the count of Blois, the count of Tonnerre, and the bishop of Auxerre. Herbert claimed that he could bring priests who would swear that Arnulf had granted him the land before he gave it to Pontigny, but his witnesses apparently were insufficient, for the case was settled by compromise. Arnulf was able to keep his land for his lifetime, and the monks were confirmed in whatever he had or would give them on his death, but he agreed to give Herbert six pounds to keep the peace.

Were Arnulf and Herbert peasants? Like Odears, they owned land and were in a position to make pious gifts with that land. Yet again, the only reason *not* to think of them as low-status people is the a priori assumption that such people would never be in a position to make pious gifts or to appear in court cases. Arnulf is identified in the bishop's attesting charter as a *capicerius*, which is usually translated as "vestry keeper," meaning more broadly someone who does jobs to help take care of a church and its furnishings, presumably the church of Chablis. The six pounds he paid to settle the quarrel would not have been considered a major sum in the 1130s. He was at any rate certainly not a knight or someone of similarly high status, for the bishop of Auxerre's charters at this time routinely so identified the *milites* who appeared in them. Herbert, his brother-in-law, was called the *homo* of the count of Tonnerre, but again this term cannot be translated automatically as "knight," for agricultural workers, indisputably peasants, were referred to as *homines* at this time. This example rather suggests the wide variation in wealth and status of the vast majority of the population who were not knights, nobles, ecclesiastics, or townspeople, with some being important enough that the mighty of their region might have to become involved in disputes over their donations.

---

50. *Cartulaire général de l'Yonne*, 1:329–30, no. 191.

Clerical Peasants and Lay Brothers

Although the legal principle was well established that those of servile status could not become clerics, any more than they could swear in court, because their will was not free, in practice peasants, including those legally unfree, could and did join the church. An 1132 example from the monastery of St.-Michel of Tonnerre indicates how normal this could seem.[51] The monks had complained that archbishops and bishops had been advancing the house's *homines* to the priesthood, even those of servile status (*qui servilis condicionis existunt*), and that they had been doing so without the monks' permission. Their complaint reached the ears of Pope Innocent II, who ordered all bishops and archbishops not to do so, unless they had the monastery's permission.

This situation at first glance might suggest that peasants could not join the clergy. But that was not the issue. The pope gave every indication of accepting such men as priests. For him, the issue was that bishops were violating the relationship between the monastery and its dependents, ordaining them without permission. For Innocent, monastic exemption (although his ruling did not use that term) from episcopal heavy-handedness was of great significance, but he took it for granted that, in the right circumstances, even those of servile status might rightfully be ordained.[52] Thus intelligent, ambitious young men from peasant backgrounds could sometimes have careers in the church as a possible path toward upward mobility.

Even if they did not seek ordination, peasants could join the church by becoming lay brothers at a number of twelfth- and thirteenth-century monasteries. Lay brothers, as the name implies, were "brothers" within the monastery but not full monks. They could not become priests or even fully participate in the liturgy because they lacked the necessary Latin education (and in this they were more like laymen than ecclesiastics), but they were very much part of the new monastic orders of the twelfth century. Becoming a lay brother, a *conversus* as it was termed, was a way for a peasant to follow a religious vocation without having to know Latin, or even how to read and write. The institution of lay brothers probably had its origins in the Carthusian order at the end of the eleventh century, but it spread most notably in the twelfth century with the Cistercians.[53]

---

51. *Cartulaire général de l'Yonne*, 1:287–88, no. 166.

52. On monastic exemptions, see, most recently, Kriston R. Rennie, *Freedom and Protection: Monastic Exemption in France, c. 590–1100* (Manchester, Eng., 2018).

53. The fullest recent study is by James France, *Separate but Equal: Cistercian Lay Brothers, 1120–1350* (Collegeville, Minn., 2012). See also Janet Burton and Julie Kerr, *The Cistercians in the Middle Ages* (Woodbridge, Suff., 2011), pp. 149–88, and Didier Panfili, "Les convers cisterciens: Frères ou serfs?" in *Labeur, production et économie monastique*, ed. Michel Lauwers (Turnhout, 2021), pp. 403–56.

In essence, lay brothers were halfway to becoming monks, living in common as monks did although in their own separate structure, eating the same limited diet as the monks, wearing the same coarse clothing, following a life of obedience and frequent prayer. But rather than focusing on reading, writing, and the liturgy, they raised their monastery's food, tended its flocks, ran its mills, and did other labor-heavy chores. A few were from more socially elevated backgrounds, but most appear to have been of peasant stock. They were called *conversi*, those who had converted, because they had adopted a monastic lifestyle. The Cistercians preferred that their houses not have their own serfs or tenant peasants, so lay brothers worked the fields on the monastery's lands, doubtless doing a better job than the young knights who had become monks would have done.[54]

Although by the middle of the twelfth century the term *conversus* was most commonly used to refer to a lay brother, it still retained its broader sense of someone who had left the world for the cloister. Around 1150 one Robert of Grison became a *conversus* at the Cistercian house of La Ferté and gave the monastery "whatever he had" at Neuilly, located not far from La Ferté. His brother, his sister, and his sister's husband all confirmed. This was an important enough gift to be recorded in one of the monks' pancartes and confirmed by the bishop of Chalon.[55] Was Robert a peasant? If so, this document indicates that a peasant was in a position to make a substantial property gift. Or was Robert an aristocrat, even a knight, although the charter does not call him such? The use of a surname, of Grison, might so suggest, except that Grison was not the name of a town or a castle but rather of a stream, a tributary of the River Grosne on which La Ferté was located. As this is Robert's only appearance in the records, it is impossible to determine his origins. The point here is exactly that: peasants and middling-status country people were not sharply distinguished groups, and the term *conversus*, used for a lay brother, retained its original sense of someone voluntarily turning to the religious life, and it was an admirable status for anyone, including a peasant.

In the Cistercian order, all monks were expected to be adult converts, most typically young men from fairly well-to-do backgrounds who decided for religious reasons to give it all up for a life of radical simplicity. The order did not want the child oblates who made up a major proportion of the membership of houses of older orders, but rather adults who had

---

54. France, *Separate but Equal*, pp. 1–27.
55. *Recueil des pancartes de La Ferté*, pp. 146–47, no. 176.

made their own decisions. Everyone, even mature men who felt themselves declining and preferred to reach their final days in a holy setting, underwent a period of strict novitiate.[56] The lay brothers similarly were adult converts, who had made a conscious decision to use their agricultural skills in service to God.

If living at the main monastery, lay brothers would typically have their own house. Cistercian monasteries all had granges in addition, small houses remote from the main church, where both monks and lay brothers would live while the latter carried out agricultural activities. The small number of monks posted to a grange would supervise the lay brothers and perform the liturgy, to which the lay brothers were expected to make a suitable response. Both monks and lay brothers would be rotated between granges and between the granges and the main house.[57]

Just as the life of the monks of the Cistercian order was governed by rules, in particular the Benedictine rule as supplemented by early normative texts, so there were regulations governing the lives of the lay brothers. These rules, the so-called *Usus conversorum*, appear to have first been written within twenty years or so of Cîteaux's foundation. The *Usus* evolved and developed over the course of the twelfth century, before being superseded by a more systematic set of regulations in the thirteenth century. It provided a parallel set of strictures for the lay brothers, including their own weekly chapter meeting, where they would be reminded of their responsibilities and, if necessary, be chided for their lapses and given a chance to amend them.[58]

The *Usus conversorum* took for granted that the lay brothers would be working hard. Indeed, the Prologue to the earliest version stresses that abbots should be as mindful of them as of the regular monks, neither assuming that their capacity for heavy labor meant that little attention needed to be given to their material needs, nor assuming that because of this labor they should be allowed to eat more richly and plentifully than did the monks.[59] Although agricultural work was the main occupation of the *conversi*, they also engaged in other useful trades around the monastery. The *Usus conversorum* provided regulations for cobblers, weavers, millers, skinners, wagoners,

---

56. Bouchard, *Sword, Miter, and Cloister*, pp. 49, 54–55.

57. France, *Separate but Equal*, pp. 88–150.

58. *Cistercian Lay Brothers: Twelfth-Century Usages with Related Texts*, ed. Chrysogonus Waddell, Cîteaux: Commentarii Cistercienses, Studia et Documenta 10 (Brecht, Belgium, 2000).

59. *Cistercian Lay Brothers*, p. 56. See also Burton and Kerr, *The Cistercians*, pp. 156–58.

herdsmen, shepherds, and blacksmiths.[60] In all these cases, the lay brothers were expected to adhere to something close to the full monastic life of simplicity and silence in going about their daily affairs.

The mention of the varied activities in which the lay brothers might take part indicates how much the monks needed these men, to perform tasks that were certainly required at a monastery but which knightly converts might not find easy to pick up. These were skilled trades, as of course is farming, and the monks functioned much better with men who had a background in these trades. The lists of male names found as witnesses at the ends of charters seem often to have included lay brothers, indicating that their voices were wanted in confirming and attesting to important events.

Scholars have long appreciated that even if one adopts the old chestnut of medieval society being divided into "three orders," then the nobility and the church have to be considered closely intertwined. In the same way, the many close relationships between French peasants and the high medieval church need to be appreciated. We do not have anything that peasants wrote themselves describing their religious views, but that is no reason routinely to label them as half pagan or as in superstitious awe of the church, much less to attribute to them any (or every) aspect of medieval Christianity that does not match modern understanding of the religion.

Even without their own words, one can gain an appreciation for peasants' interaction with organized religion through their actions. Some clearly preferred being serfs of a monastery to being serfs of a layman, to the extent that they might give up free status to become a monastic serf in the eleventh century. Peasants who became the serfs of a religious house gave their most valuable possession, their own labor, and even when such willing subjugation was no longer recorded in the twelfth century, they might make gifts of other property—sometimes small, but sometimes quite substantial. They could become ordained priests at least occasionally, and the spread of the new monastic orders that tried to avoid peasant tenants would have been impossible without peasant *conversi*. The Cistercians' strictures against accepting tenants accompanying gifts of land meant that they required a new group of peasants, the *conversi*, internal to the order. These men become in essence half monks and performed the many varieties of agricultural and other skilled labor without which the order could never have grown and prospered.

---

60. *Cistercian Lay Brothers*, pp. 65, 73–74.

Given the large number of medieval churches with which the northern French countryside is still dotted, it should not be surprising that medieval peasants always had to be aware of churches and ecclesiastics. The illiterate who were supposed to learn Bible stories and tales of the saints from the carvings and paintings of rural churches always included peasants.[61] The Christian church played a major role in the society of the high Middle Ages, and the relations between that church and the peasantry have to be part of the period's history.

---

61. Even the educated might need a guide to help them appreciate complex iconography; Conrad Rudolph, "Macro/Microcosm at Vézelay: The Narthex Portal and Non-elite Participation in Elite Spirituality," *Speculum* 96 (2021), 650–61.

CHAPTER 4

Peasants, New Towns, and Communes

One of the clearest markers of peasant initiative is the growth of "new towns" as they were called (*villa nova*), new settlements where landlords lured peasants to unused land with promises of franchises and low rents. These new settlements of the twelfth and thirteenth centuries were not only instrumental in opening up new agricultural land but also granted peasants specific freedoms and rights. They are a marker of population growth, of overall economic growth, and of new opportunities for the peasantry in the high Middle Ages. I intend here to shift attention from the lords who made grants of franchises in new towns to the peasants who demanded them, including the connection to the communes being established at the same time in cities large and small.[1] The economic expansion of this time not only was due to the work of the peasantry, it also made it possible for them to better their position.

---

1. My approach differs here from that of Thomas Bisson, who discusses charters of franchise as an aspect of increased royal authority over local lords and an increasing use of governmental officials; *The Crisis of the Twelfth Century: Power, Lordship, and the Origins of European Government* (Princeton, 2009), pp. 350–58.

New Towns and Charters of Franchise

During the twelfth century a number of northern French villages obtained charters of franchise as they were called, giving the villagers a substantial amount of self-governance, where the powerful formally granted many rights of self-determination. These appeared most frequently at newly established settlements but were also often granted to existing villages. The spread of these charters provides evidence of peasants negotiating for more control over their own lives. The line between those who dwelt in farming villages and those in small towns was fluid, and many of those living in small towns were engaged in agriculture.[2] The peasantry's interest in moving to new towns where charters spelled out privileges for the residents was doubtless influenced by the spread of urban communes, which began to appear around the end of the eleventh century.[3]

For example, Louis VI confirmed the commune of the city of Beauvais, at the citizens' request, shortly after he inherited the crown in 1108, and his charter was repeated and reconfirmed by Louis VII.[4] The *communia* was established through the oaths of all the men living in Beauvais or just outside. The expectations for these men that the royal charter spelled out were brief, but it is noteworthy that these citizens were assumed to be perfectly capable of binding oaths. The men swore to assist any merchant robbed within a league of the Beauvais market and agreed to give the bishop three horses if he and his retinue were traveling to the royal court. In a major gain for the commune, justice was to be administered by the peers of an accused man (*per pares*). The French kings continued to grant communes to cities large and small across their realm; Philip II was especially active in doing so.[5]

Communal arrangements like these, although established in cities rather than in farming villages, indicate a strong desire by those below the level of the aristocracy to organize themselves both politically and economically and

---

2. David M. Nicholas stresses the continuities between cities and rural villages, in both population and governance; *The Growth of the Medieval City: From Late Antiquity to the Early Fourteenth Century* (Harlow, Eng., 1997). See also Derek Keene, "Towns and the Growth of Trade," in *The New Cambridge Medieval History*, vol. 4, pt. 1, ed. David Luscombe and Jonathan Riley-Smith (Cambridge, 2004), pp. 54–56.

3. Susan Reynolds, "Government and Community," in *The New Cambridge Medieval History*, vol. 4, pt. 1:95–100.

4. *Recueil des actes de Louis VI, roi de France (1108–1137)*, ed. Jean Dufour, 3 vols. (Paris, 1992–93), 3:353–56, no. 413.

5. John Baldwin, *The Government of Philip Augustus: Foundations of French Royal Power in the Middle Ages* (Berkeley, 1986), pp. 59–64.

to settle on predictable expectations. Communes were often viewed with suspicion by those in authority, because they recognized that those acting collectively could undercut that authority. Guibert of Nogent famously called the word *communio* "new and evil," even though he described a commune simply as a replacement of the various dues levied on serfs with a single annual head tax. He described the commune established at Laon as a scheme by the clergy and wealthy townspeople to raise money by selling rights to such a commune to the rural populace.[6] Now of course communes involved much more than he suggested, and Laon's commune was designed to benefit the city's inhabitants, not the rural villagers. Moreover, contrary to Guibert's characterization of the peasantry as simple and gullible, they understood and appreciated communes and their promised freedoms very well.[7]

The growing cities may have been the first to seek self-governance for their citizens, but rural villages were not far behind. Charters of franchise for farming villages were closely tied to the clearing of new lands for crops.[8] The expansion of the arable in the high Middle Ages was due in large part to peasants seeking to improve their position without needing direction or even permission from the more powerful. They extended the fields they already had and sought new lands on which to settle and to put under the plow. Lords, in offering them the freedoms found in new towns, sought to turn peasant initiative to their own advantage, even as the peasants themselves were able to use the lords' interest in profit as an opportunity for self-determination.[9]

A document from St.-Michel of Tonnerre from around the middle of the twelfth century provides an example of peasants quietly expanding the land they worked.[10] The purpose of the document was to record an

6. Guibert of Nogent, *Autobiographie*, ed. Edmond-René Labande, Les Classiques de l'histoire de France au moyen âge 34 (Paris, 1981), cap. 3.7, p. 320. *A Monk's Confession: The Memoirs of Guibert of Nogent*, trans. Paul J. Archambault (University Park, Penn., 1996), p. 146.

7. Jacques Foviaux connects the twelfth-century effort to create a commune at Laon with the self-governance of the thirteenth century; "L'organisation d'un *oppidium* devenu *civitas*: L'*institutio pacis*, origine de la commune de Laon?" in *La charte de Beaumont et les franchises municipales entre Loire et Rhin* (Nancy, 1988), pp. 119–47.

8. Charles Higounet, *Défrichements et villeneuves du bassin parisien (XIe–XIVe siècles)* (Paris, 1990). Hubert Collin, "Réflexions sur la carte de repartition des chartes de franchises en Lorraine (XIIe–XIVe siècles)," in *La charte de Beaumont*, pp. 174–75.

9. The counts of Troyes, deeply interested in the economic return of the Champagne fairs, started granting charters of franchise to nearby villages and towns in the 1170s; Theodore Evergates, *Feudal Society in the Bailliage of Troyes under the Counts of Champagne, 1152–1284* (Baltimore, 1975), pp. 41–47.

10. *Cartulaire général de l'Yonne*, ed. Maximilien Quantin, 2 vols. (Auxerre, 1854–60), 1:376–77, no. 233. This document was used by Marc Bloch as an example of the deserted villages that marked an underpopulated medieval landscape; *Les caractères originaux de l'histoire rurale française*, new ed. (Paris, 1999; rpt. 2006), p. 70. He identified the *villa* as Paisson.

agreement between three entities, all of whom shared dominion in an unin-habited *villa*, called "Parson." There the abbey of St.-Michel had half, Lord Milo of Noyers one-third, and the knight Desiderius one-sixth of dominion over the territory. These three agreed to the rents that would be paid by the peasants working that land, and how the rents would be divided. But here the real interest is how a deserted *villa* came to be paying rents.

The men of the neighboring village of Pimelles, dependents of St.-Michel, had been going to the unworked lands and cultivating them, establishing fields and planting crops. They were also taking wood from the forest associ-ated with "Parson" and pasturing their pigs there. The agreement between the monastery, the castellan lord, and the knight acknowledged the villagers' continued right to do so but specified that each of the men would pay two measures of grain a year, one of wheat and one of oats, and be subject to the (arbitrary) corvée. Nothing extra was specified as due from their woods usage. From the point of view of the lords, the important issue was dividing these rents. From the point of view of the peasants of Pimelles, the impor-tant issue was securely obtaining new land on which to raise their crops and pasture their animals, at a very low rent. This expansion of the arable, which benefited the lords both secular and ecclesiastical, would not have been pos-sible without the peasants' initiative.

Here the peasants of Pimelles continued to live where they always had, though cultivating an increased amount of land, but in many other cases an entirely new village would be established. Such a village was founded jointly by the canons of Prémontré and Lord Walter of Guise and Avesnes in 1210. The canons had owned property at nearby Hannape for three generations, but almost no one appears to have been living there; it was called a farm or hamlet (*curtis*), a more insignificant place designation than a *villa*. But presumably as a way to generate revenue from what had been unproductive territory, the canons and Lord Walter agreed on how much land would be granted to anyone who moved there, and what their rents and dues would be. To make moving there attractive, the newly established *villa* was officially designated as having freedom (*libertas*).[11]

Unlike most peasant villages, where nearly everyone owed somewhat dif-ferent amounts, the new village of Hannape was organized with great regu-larity. Each *burgensis* in the village was to receive three units of land (*aissinos*), including some in the village itself, one assumes for a house and yard, and some outside, for growing crops. Collectively these units of land constituted a mansus. Rents were fixed and very low: one measure of oats, one capon,

---

11. Soissons, Bibliothèque municipale, MS 7, fols. 58v–59r.

one loaf of bread, and one penny a year for each of the *aissinos*. In addition, each village family was to pay twelve pennies a year in village tax and an additional four pennies to compensate for freedom from tolls that otherwise would have been charged on their weekly market.

The freedom of the villagers was repeatedly stressed, indicating how important the canons and Lord Walter expected it to be to the peasants they hoped to lure there. Lord Walter spelled out that no one of Hannape would be called to accompany him to a tournament, a battle, or other mounted excursion, except to defend Guise, an indication that in other circumstances peasants might be called on to join such an expedition. In addition, he noted, no one would lose their house in the village for a misdemeanor (*forisfacta*), and he himself would not impose any arbitrary *gîte* or demand to be housed. Mills and ovens would belong to the villagers. But these advantages had at least some limits, for Lord Walter said that he would exercise justice in the village, and he and Prémontré would jointly choose the mayor, who would swear allegiance to both of them every year.

The document, phrased as an agreement between Lord Walter and Prémontré,[12] does not say specifically that the peasants had negotiated for these freedoms. But in arranging for a new, free village, Walter and the canons must surely have known from the example of other new towns what peasants would want, what specific inducements might encourage them to come from all over the region to live at Hannape, as he stated should happen. He did note, however, that men of Guise itself could not move there, indicating that he did not want to lose any rents or dues he had previously been receiving while gaining new revenues from this new foundation. Whether the peasants directly made their preferences clear in this case, or whether Walter and the canons knew from examples seen elsewhere what peasants wanted, the result was the same: landlords wanted to gain highly valuable tenants, and they were willing to give away much in order to acquire their service. The powerful had clearly learned that inviting peasants with freedoms and low rents worked better to obtain their service than any attempt to compel them.

In both of the above cases, peasants were able to obtain considerable self-governance from the powerful, who granted them a charter spelling this out. Although scholars have tended to stress the decisions of landlords that led to such new towns, they should be seen as resulting at least in part from peasant

---

12. Lord Walter's family had a long history of generosity to Prémontré, as illustrated by documents in the canons' cartulary copied in proximity to this one.

collective action.[13] There were of course variations. As in the Hannape example, charters of franchise (or liberty) might be issued as an inducement to bring peasants to settle in a sparsely populated hamlet or in a brand-new village, laid out by a landlord who had more property than rent-paying tenants (the many places called Villeneuve in France today were mostly "new" in the twelfth century). Alternately, a commune could be established in an existing village, as a commune would be established in a city, by the inhabitants swearing to work together to govern themselves, and this commune would seek formal recognition and validation in a charter from a powerful lord, even the king.

Thus new towns (farming villages) and urban communes were in effect quite similar: both promised liberties to lower-status inhabitants who acted collectively. Recognizing new towns to promote settlement and land clearance was less potentially fraught for the powerful than recognizing urban communes, because the latter gave new independence to townspeople in an existing city, threatening the established order. This concern may be seen, for example, when the bishop of Auxerre persuaded King Louis VII to confirm in the 1170s that there should be no *communia* in his city, although the count had attempted to form one.[14] But new villages and communes both are indicative of the less powerful being able to negotiate successfully with the powerful. One of the most influential charters of liberty of the twelfth century was the so-called Customs of Lorris.[15]

The Customs of Lorris

The charters of franchise granted to new towns are evidence for the agency peasants were able to exercise and for its recognition by those who granted the charters. Yet scholars have tended to overlook the role of the peasants here. New towns have primarily been seen as markers of broad economic expansion, especially of the increase in commerce, rather than of peasant

---

13. A similar point is made by Reynolds, "Government and Community," pp. 100–105.

14. *Three Cartularies from Thirteenth-Century Auxerre*, ed. Constance Brittain Bouchard, Medieval Academy Books 113 (Toronto, 2012), pp. 64–65, no. 25. For the context of this attempted commune, see Yves Sassier, *Louis VII* (Paris, 1991), pp. 432–38.

15. Another influential charter was that originally granted to the farming village of Beaumont-en-Argonne, in Lorraine, in the 1180s by the archbishop of Reims. It was edited by H[enri] d'Arbois de Jubainville, "Loi de Beaumont (texte latin inédit)," *Bibliothèque de l'École des chartes* 12 (1851), 248–56. A colloquium was held in honor of its eight hundredth anniversary; *La charte de Beaumont*. Curiously, almost none of the papers from the colloquium refer to Beaumont, and the charter's particular provisions remain unstudied.

initiative.[16] It is indicative of how little attention has been given to peasant efforts at self-governance that the Customs of Lorris, the widely imitated list of the rights and responsibilities of the inhabitants of this "new town," have been rarely studied.[17] When scholars do mention them, the focus is typically on the roles of Kings Louis VI, Louis VII, and Philip II in authorizing them, in the context of the kings' drive to increase royal authority and revenues.[18]

The village of Lorris, located in the Gâtinais not far from Orléans, received a royal confirmation of its "customs" early in the twelfth century. The villagers were granted liberties and a great deal of control over their own economic activities, while most arbitrary dues and demands were eliminated. The Customs proved enormously popular and were adopted at scores of other villages across northern France during the following century.[19] The Customs were written in Latin, but the villagers clearly had someone, probably the local priest, who could translate for them. That the king himself would consider the inhabitants of a village competent to negotiate their dues and make a binding agreement of their responsibilities demonstrates the credit peasant agency was given.

The original grant of these Customs—the one given to the villagers by King Louis VI at the request of his friend Lord Blanchard of Lorris—was lost in a fire.[20] But these Customs were clearly significant, as indicated by the numerous occasions on which Louis made similar grants to other newly established villages. In the next generation, Louis VII, who had a palace by the village, confirmed the Customs of Lorris in 1155.[21] In 1187, after the fire that destroyed the charters of both Louis VI and Louis VII, Philip II

---

16. N. J. G. Pounds denies that peasants had any ability to negotiate or to resist burdensome dues; *An Economic History of Medieval Europe* (New York, 1974), pp. 164–74.

17. The only full-length scholarly work devoted to these Customs is well over a century old; Maurice Prou, *Les coutumes de Lorris et leur propagation aux XIIe et XIIIe siècles* (Paris, 1884). He treated the Customs as an indication of royal interest in improving agriculture and commerce and treats peasants as recipients of royal favor, not actors in their own right; ibid., pp. 17–20. Georges Duby never mentioned these Customs in his *Rural Economy and Country Life in the Medieval West*, trans. Cynthia Postan (Columbia, S.C., 1968). The Customs are also not mentioned by Werner Rösener, *Peasants in the Middle Ages*, trans. Alexander Stützer (Urbana, 1992).

18. For example, Jean Dunbabin, *France in the Making, 843–1180* (Oxford, 1991), pp. 273–75; and Elizabeth M. Hallam and Judith Everard, *Capetian France, 987–1328*, 2nd ed. (Harlow, Eng., 2001), pp. 182–83, 206–9.

19. Jean Richard, "Les courants de chartes de franchises dans la Bourgogne ducale (XIIe–XIVe siècles)," in *La charte de Beaumont*, pp. 107–8.

20. *Recueil des actes de Louis VI*, 3:356–57, no. 414. The editors here note this as a "lost charter."

21. Louis VII's confirmation is printed in *Recueil des chartes de l'abbaye de Saint-Benoît-sur-Loire*, ed. Maurice Prou and Alexandre Vidier (Paris, 1890), pp. 380–85, no. 168. The source for this edition is the later confirmation by Philip II.

confirmed the grant of Customs to the inhabitants of Lorris and granted these same Customs to a number of other villages.

Louis VII granted charters of franchise to many other villages in the years after his initial confirmation of 1155, explicitly saying that he was granting the Customs of Lorris.[22] Typical is a charter from 1163 in which Louis VII founded a new village, to be called Villeneuve-le-Roi (*Villa-franca-regia*), in northern Burgundy, and granted the village the Customs of Lorris, saying that he did so because he "wished there to be a great many inhabitants."[23] He recognized that the peasants saw attraction in regulations that gave them substantial freedoms.

The Customs of Lorris gave the inhabitants of the village an identity as a collective body, a body with rights and obligations that affected everyone, rather than having every family and every individual subject to different rents and customs. It was clearly anticipated that people would want to move to the village, because the Customs spelled out that anyone who moved to the parish and lived there for a year and a day, with no *clamor* raised against them, would become a full member of the community. If someone had been of servile status, this article appears to imply, he could shake free of that status by spending a year quietly at Lorris. Indeed, references to the Customs under both Louis VII and Philip II routinely referred to them as a charter of franchise or of liberty.[24]

The Customs also specified that anyone who sold his property at Lorris could move away without penalty, suggesting that there was no need to bind the inhabitants legally, because it was anticipated that they would want to stay, or that others would be eager to buy their property and move in. These inhabitants had clear expectations of what they would have to pay and what would be required of them. This certainty, the freedom from arbitrary demands, seems to have been even more important to the villagers than the actual amounts of rent.

And in fact the routine obligations specified in the royal charter for Lorris were quite minimal. The first item was the setting of rents: six pennies for a house in the parish and for an accompanying arpent of land.[25] Following

---

22. Prou, *Les coutumes de Lorris*, pp. 15–16, 18, 71–84. As an appendix, Prou lists all the villages that adopted the Customs of Lorris, whether by royal grant or grant by another lord. Louis VII had a palace at Lorris by 1152, though it is not known whether he constructed it or whether it was older; *Cartulaire général de l'Yonne*, 1:498, no. 343.

23. *Cartulaire général de l'Yonne*, 2:160, no. 145.

24. Prou, *Les coutumes de Lorris*, p. 67. The charter of Beaumont similarly said that someone who lived peacefully in the village for a year and a day would be free; "Loi de Beaumont," p. 253, no. 24.

25. Prou assumes this rent was paid to the king, but this is far from certain and is not specified in the charter; *Les coutumes de Lorris*, pp. 32–33. Rents were higher at Beaumont, twelve pennies a year, and were explicitly said to be paid to the archbishop; "Loi de Beaumont," p. 249, no. 1.

that, it was specified that none of the inhabitants would be expected to pay a *tonleium* or *consuetudo* from their crops or their animals or their vineyards, the terms used for dues that might be demanded fairly arbitrarily. Neither could any inhabitant be required to go on a military expedition taking him further than would allow him to go home at night.

Inhabitants would also not be charged tolls on specified roads leading out of Lorris. The assumption here is that those who lived in the parish would be taking their goods to market, and that their enterprise would generate enough revenue that a lord might well find tolls profitable. All of these specifications were intended to make the inhabitants' financial situation more predictable, so that the profits from their own efforts could not be siphoned off by the more powerful. Landlords often hoped to take advantage of the growing economy of the time by imposing tolls and tailles, but the spread of the Customs of Lorris makes clear that the peasants resisted, hoping to keep the fruits of the improved economy for themselves.

But the Customs also laid requirements on the inhabitants of Lorris. They agreed to pay for fifteen days' worth of food for the king and queen and also agreed that only the king's own wine would be sold with royal edict. Probably their biggest concession was that those with horses and wagons could be commandeered to assist in the king's grape harvest of his Orléans vineyards in the fall (that is, be subject to a corvée, *corvata*), and *villani* were expected to carry wood to be used by the royal cook. Although the inhabitants did not escape all financial or labor obligations, they were happy to settle on a manageable and predictable amount.

As well as economic provisions, the Customs had a number of articles concerning those who were charged with crimes. Fines were set, depending on the gravity of the offense. No one coming to the Lorris market was to be held captive or have his goods seized in the absence of a specific crime. The Customs clearly frowned on judicial duels, for fines were specified for those undertaking them, even if they settled their disagreements before the fight took place (though here the fine was less). No one was to be judged by any provost in the Gâtinais outside of Lorris, nor were any allowed to leave Lorris to seek justice in the royal domain.[26] But someone accused of a crime was permitted to offer a pledge (*plegium*) that he would be present on the day he was to be judged, essentially posting bail; someone offering such a pledge could not be held captive.

---

26. Curiously, Prou interprets the Customs as specifying that the inhabitants of Lorris would be judged solely by the royal provost; *Les coutumes de Lorris*, pp. 43–44.

Here it should be stressed that Lorris was a small community, and Blanchard of Lorris, at whose request the first royal charter for the community was granted, was not one of the great lords of the realm. And yet the villagers of Lorris were able to persuade three generations of kings to spell out their rights, especially their right to associate and create their own rules of local governance. The kings themselves granted away prerogatives, such as hearing cases or collecting tolls, in return for such concessions as receiving two weeks' worth of food a year or obtaining assistance in the grape harvest. That these different expectations could be spelled out like this is certainly a testimony to the peasants' ability to create a situation for themselves where arbitrary commands were replaced by knowable expectations. Blanchard of Lorris himself gained a village that prospered and that would, due to the Customs, be a magnet for other peasants hoping to move to a profitable location.

How did the inhabitants of Lorris achieve this? Payment was certainly involved, but if a group of peasants were cooperatively able to generate enough money to tempt a king, then they must be credited with initiative and forethought. The lords of the widespread villages where the Customs of Lorris were subsequently established must have seen the value of peasant tenants and wanted to attract them. An 1159 charter of Louis VII, in which he granted the Customs of Lorris to the village of Moulinet, specified that he did so in order to increase the local population, and similar sentiments are found in comparable royal grants to other villages during the next decade.[27]

The spread of the Customs of Lorris well beyond the Gâtinais over the course of the twelfth and early thirteenth centuries, and the frequency with which other great lords imitated the kings in making these grants,[28] demonstrates that peasant interest in determining their own communal identity and economic opportunities was not limited to one village. The Customs would of course be suitably modified in each location, changing, for example, the names of the roads out of the village where no toll was to be levied. But the rents and obligations specified in the Customs were remarkably stable. When two successive archbishops of Sens in the late twelfth century granted the Customs to the village of Villeneuve-l'Archevêque, for example, they specified again the six pennies in rent for a house and an arpent of land, as well as freedom from the taille and customary exactions. Any inflation in the preceding three generations had not altered the amount of rent the Customs of Lorris required. Although naturally there was no mention of feeding the

27. Prou, *Les coutumes de Lorris*, p. 16.
28. For examples, see Prou, *Les coutumes de Lorris*, pp. 88–99.

king and queen for two weeks, the archbishops did specify that private duels were not allowed and that the inhabitants would not be expected to go on military expeditions taking them more than a day's distance from home.[29]

Although study of this spread of the Customs well beyond Lorris has chiefly focused on the kings and great lords who granted the Customs, it should be stressed that these kings and lords were not just granting some generic charter in return for a payment. They were granting what was explicitly termed a charter of liberty. The local villagers must have found this valuable, or the Customs would not have been adopted in so many places, including in Champagne, where the counts were rivals to the French kings.[30] Scores of both new towns and longer-established villages spread all across Burgundy adopted these or similar customs during the twelfth and early thirteenth centuries.[31]

If the peasants of the various French villages that adopted the Customs of Lorris and other charters of liberty were, as is always assumed, paying for their charters, then they must have believed that this particular set of liberties was worth the price. The very spread of the Customs across northern France is a marker of peasant initiative. Villagers heard of the Customs, recognized their value, and did what was necessary to obtain a grant of these Customs for themselves.

The Commune at Vézelay

Both the Customs of Lorris and other communal movements indicate the eagerness of peasants and burghers of small towns to practice self-determination. They did not always adopt the Lorris customs, but they sought to create their own form of self-governance to resist what they considered subjection. Here the long quarrels between the abbots of Vézelay and the counts of Nevers are a revelatory example, for the quarrels were carried out using the inhabitants of the village and those who farmed the surrounding countryside as weapons against the other side.

The village of Vézelay stretches down the hill from the monastery, which is dedicated to Mary Magdalene. The house had roots in the ninth century

---

29. *Cartulaire général de l'Yonne*, 2:239–42, no. 225. A different new town that the archbishop founded around the same time, however, was expected to pay two solidi, which would be twenty-four pennies, for each house and arpent of land. The rest of the obligations followed the model closely. *Cartulaire général de l'Yonne*, 2:272–74, no. 254.

30. Prou, *Les coutumes de Lorris*, pp. 100–105.

31. Richard, "Les courants de chartes de franchises dans la Bourgogne," pp. 107–17.

and is now known primarily for its stunning Romanesque architecture.[32] Vézelay was more than a farming village, as it also served the pilgrims who visited the abbey, but the sources indicate that when the villagers banded together to oppose the powerful, they always included agricultural workers in their group. These villagers and peasants most commonly were on the side of the count in his quarrels with the abbot, but it is striking that both abbot and count claimed that only they could offer these men and women true liberty. An offer of *libertas* was the best inducement either side had.

The fraught relationship between the abbots of Vézelay and the men of the village and the surrounding countryside provides some of the best documented instances of peasant collective action. It is thus worth discussing in detail—especially as its implications for peasant action have previously been little noted.[33] The tensions between abbot and local populace stretched across the whole twelfth century, beginning in 1106, when Abbot Artald was murdered by the local inhabitants.[34] The motivation for this murder is now unclear, but it colored the abbey's relations with the local populace for the rest of the century. The men (*homines*) of Vézelay, as they are referred to in the sources, included both *burgenses*, those who lived within the walls of the little village or burg, on the hillside below the monastery, and the *rustici* of the surrounding countryside. The first call for a commune, which involved not just the villagers but the rural inhabitants of the region, took place in 1137. In 1152 these men of Vézelay declared a commune for the second time, in opposition to the abbot, with the support of the count of Nevers. These quarrels drew in many major political and religious figures, including the pope.

The first well-documented phase of the opposition by the *homines* of Vézelay against the abbot began in the 1130s, at a time when the present Romanesque church was being completed and the number of pilgrims rapidly rising. The abbot then was apparently treating all the people of the region in what they considered an arbitrary and greedy manner. They decided they would tolerate this no longer. Peasant concerns were at the forefront, for much of the quarrel was over crops and herds of animals. The details of this quarrel are known through an extensive agreement, overseen by some of

---

32. For its art and architecture, see, most recently, Conrad Rudolph, "Macro/Microcosm at Vézelay: The Narthex Portal and Non-elite Participation in Elite Spirituality," *Speculum* 96 (2021), 601–61.

33. The classic study of the extended quarrels is by Rosalind Kent Berlow, "Spiritual Immunity at Vézelay (Ninth to Twelfth Centuries)," *Catholic Historical Review* 62 (1976), 573–88. Interestingly, it remains essentially the only study.

34. *Monumenta Vizeliacensia: Textes relatifs à l'histoire de l'abbaye de Vézelay*, ed. R. B. C. Huygens, Corpus Christianorum continuatio mediaevalis 42 (Turnhout, 1976), p. 302, no. 19.

the major ecclesiastical leaders of the region, which settled the quarrel (at least temporarily) in 1137. The agreement spelled out the assertions made by both sides, the initial compromise that soon led to reopened quarrels, the complaints against the abbot, and the actions of the men that the abbot found so objectionable.[35]

According to the text of the agreement, in 1137 the bishop of Auxerre and the abbots of three Cistercian houses, along with the prior of Clairvaux, the abbot of Corbigny, and Count William II of Nevers, met to regulate the differences between Abbot Alberic and the men of Vézelay. These arbiters were, interestingly, all outsiders, though people whose centers of authority were located not very away. Vézelay was not a Cistercian house, being more closely aligned with Cluny, and it was in the diocese of Autun, not of Auxerre, though close to the diocesan border. Corbigny was an old Benedictine house in the diocese of Autun, most closely associated with Flavigny. The count of Nevers was also count of Auxerre and of Tonnerre, and although Vézelay was located very near where those counties' borders met, it was actually considered to be in the county of Avallon, which in the twelfth century was directly controlled by the duke of Burgundy.

The abbot initially claimed that he had not been receiving his rightful tithe of sheep, lambs, calves, pigs, wheat, and wine, the so-called "firstfruits." The men of Vézelay retorted that he had been taking a quarter of all of these rather than the appropriate one-tenth. Similarly, the abbot said that the peasants had been giving him inferior wine in place of the high-quality wine they owed him, and providing short measure in addition, and that they had been delaying delivery well past Saint Martin's day (November 11), when they were supposed to provide it. In response the peasants asserted that the abbot had been demanding money payments from them in lieu of wine and had been establishing the value of the barrels he was owed at far above market value. The abbot also said that every man who had any meadows within the *potestas* of Vézelay owed him one sheaf of hay for his horses, even if the peasants themselves had not yet cut the hay for their own use, and even if the abbot was not actually resident. The peasants replied that they owed such sheaves only when the abbot was at Vézelay. In addition, the men of Vézelay complained that the abbot fined them whenever one of their daughters married, restricted their traditional fishing rights, kept an inordinate amount of

---

35. *Cartulaire général de l'Yonne*, 1:313–23, no. 186. *The Vézelay Chronicle*, trans. John Scott and John O. Ward (Binghamton, N.Y., 1992), pp. 319–27.

grain when they ground flour at his mill, and sent his dean out to pick their grapes before harvest.[36]

These details not only indicate the variety of economic activities in which Burgundian peasants engaged in the first half of the twelfth century and the extensive mix of dues that they might owe, but they also reveal peasants and villagers who felt they were not being treated fairly. The abbot, they argued, was demanding far more than he was entitled to; they even brought out an agreement signed by Abbot Raynald a generation earlier to support their case, an agreement that Abbot Alberic dismissed out of hand. These peasants, along with the townspeople of the village of Vézelay, stood up not only to the abbot, their secular as well as spiritual lord, but also to the whole assemblage of powerful men brought in to settle the quarrel. They made their case for how unfair was their treatment, and the arbiters who heard their complaints took them seriously.

Now there were also details in the quarrel that show that some of the issues specifically involved the townspeople of Vézelay. For example, the abbot claimed that the townspeople had to allow those who came to the abbey at Easter and at the feast of Mary Magdalene to stay in their houses for free, whereas the townspeople insisted that they could rent out accommodations to pilgrims and merchant travelers for money, being required to put up only the count of Nevers with his retinue for free, and that only once every four years. Similarly, the abbot complained about the behavior of the money changers who would have catered to the abbey's visitors. The abbot also made a rather unspecific complaint about certain property attached to the *mensa* of both abbot and monks, called *corvate* and specified as held by both townspeople and *rustici*, for which apparently the required dues were not being paid.[37] The point here is that peasants and the *burgenses* of this village (even today, when it has outgrown its medieval walls, Vézelay has fewer than five hundred permanent residents) found common cause with each other.[38] Their complaints about the abbot were mingled together in the record of the agreement, even aside from the *corvate* that both held from the monks, indicating their solidarity with each other and also the lack of any distinction the arbiters found between peasants and small townsmen.

---

36. *Cartulaire général de l'Yonne*, 1:315–16, no. 186. *The Vézelay Chronicle*, pp. 320–21.

37. *Cartulaire général de l'Yonne*, 1:315–16, no. 186. *The Vézelay Chronicle*, pp. 320–21. It is possible that the *corvate* were arbitrary labor dues for which a monetary payment had earlier been substituted.

38. Some estimate Vézelay's twelfth-century population as twenty times its current size; for example, Rudolph, "Macro/Microcosm at Vézelay," p. 603. But this number would have to include all the *rustici* of the surrounding countryside, not only the villagers, to be plausible.

The arbiters settled these quarrels through compromise as was normal with twelfth-century dispute settlements,[39] offering each side something, trying to find a solution that would satisfy both the abbot and the thoroughly dissatisfied men from in and around Vézelay. The abbot was to receive no more than a tenth of the firstfruits as his tithe, and agreed that while he could put up visitors to the abbey in town at Easter and at the Feast of the Magdalene, he could do so only at his expense and could not impose on the same people every year. The inhabitants for their part agreed that the wine dues were to be paid on time and with good quality wine, or with the monetary equivalent of the value of fine wine; the abbot could take his sheaves of hay for his horses even if he were not resident; the *corvate* were to be returned to the abbot and monks; and the money changers were to use the weights and measures of Colonge. The men of Vézelay gained several important concessions in addition to having the abbot accept no more than a tithe of firstfruits and give up demands for free hospitality: young women were allowed to marry without payment of a fine; the burghers and peasants could fish, although they were to offer any salmon to the abbot; the amount of flour retained as the price of milling was to revert to the old standard; and no one was to surreptitiously pick someone else's grapes.[40]

This initial agreement was a good compromise, or at least the abbot so considered it. But it was not enough for the peasants and townspeople of Vézelay. According to the abbot, instead of settling down peacefully now that agreement had been reached, they determined that they could wrest even more concessions from him once the arbiters had left. Thus the townspeople (*burgenses*) and the peasants (*rustici*) swore an alliance (*confederatio*) with each other—which the abbot declared was actually a conspiracy (*conspiratio*).[41] Although the record does not use the term *communia*, the alliance they formed seems to have been something quite similar to the communes being established elsewhere in northern France, but with their own particular set of concerns. They wanted self-governance and they wanted to reduce some of the abbot's arbitrary demands, and swearing to act together seemed the best way to accomplish their goal. Initially they denied doing so, according to the abbot, but soon they started airing their grievances.

Several of their specific grievances at this point may appear as objections to the obligations laid on serfs. Indeed, some of the demands made by the

39. Constance Brittain Bouchard, *"Every Valley Shall Be Exalted": The Discourse of Opposites in Twelfth-Century Thought* (Ithaca, N.Y., 2003), pp. 94–112.

40. *Cartulaire général de l'Yonne*, 1:316–17, no. 186. *The Vézelay Chronicle*, pp. 321–22.

41. *Cartulaire général de l'Yonne*, 1:318, no. 186. *The Vézelay Chronicle*, pp. 322–23.

abbot seem to match what have been considered the classic markers of serf-dom. The burghers and peasants had already objected to fines being levied for their daughters' marriages, which might appear to be the same as *for-mariage*, even though in this case there is no indication that this fine was collected specifically when the young women married men from outside Véz-elay. The burghers and peasants now complained that when someone died, the abbot seized the person's house and goods unless the deceased's children were already living there. Although this seizure, which the abbot defended as the norm for both lay and ecclesiastical lords, was not called *mainmorte*, it certainly was the kind of demand given that name in the thirteenth century.

In addition, the men of Vézelay objected that the annual taille that they paid at the end of the year was both arbitrary and excessive. It would be much better, they argued, if four representatives could be elected from among the burghers and peasants, who would decide on an appropriate amount for the taille and consider each person's ability to pay. They had thought this pro-posal through enough to suggest that the four representatives would serve no more than one year in this role. The abbot, not surprisingly, would have none of it.[42]

It is striking that in spite of what might now appear as clear markers of servitude, the word *servus* never appeared. It had been gone for about a generation in Burgundian documents, as discussed in chapter 1, and it did not reappear here. The abbot never attempted to argue that those of servile status could not get out of these obligations. Instead, he relied on what had been done at Vézelay in the past and what other lords routinely expected in rents and revenue. He also treated the men of the region as worthy of receiv-ing a legal response: he did not and could not simply declare that they were his subjects and must do whatever he ordained.

In addition, complaints against the abbot that clearly had nothing to do with serfdom were mingled by the new *confederatio* together with those that might be so considered. The burghers objected that rents on abbey-owned houses in town had been going up, and when the money changers among them set up their benches in the street outside their houses, the abbot levied a fine. His response was that everyone had been raising their prices and that, besides, the streets were his, and anyone setting up in them should expect to pay. Both burghers and peasants complained that the abbot kept them from making donations of their land to a leper house, to which his reply was that he needed to preserve church property, suggesting that he considered their land not really theirs but the abbey's.

---

42. *Cartulaire général de l'Yonne*, 1:318–19, no. 186. *The Vézelay Chronicle*, pp. 323–24.

They complained that the abbot required a stiff payment before anyone could be buried, which the abbot categorically denied, as to admit it would have been admitting to simony, although he did suggest that some sort of small offering would not be amiss in the circumstances. They complained that he had been raising the rents, paid in wine, on their vineyards, and that he had set his own men to patrol them in an apparently menacing way, to which he replied that the amount he levied on each unit of land had remained the same, it only had appeared to increase because more land had been planted in vines, and that the guards were of long-standing tradition. Finally, they complained that the abbot was now charging rent on the old common pasture lands, to which he responded that if they could *prove* the pasture lands had once been free he would remit the rent, and also complained that he had set guards in the common woodlands, to which he responded that the peasants had been devastating the woods by overuse.[43]

Here the *rustici* and *burgenses* took the opportunity to try to improve their situation through a series of claims and complaints, complaints that earned them a response from the powerful. Once again the same set of arbiters assembled and sought to reach a compromise on all the issues, this time joined by a dozen castellans and a viscount, asked by the arbiters to come witness and give their assent to the final agreement.[44] The most important issue, at least from the abbot's point of view, was the *conspiratio* as he called it. Seven men, named in the attesting document, were elected from the peasants and townspeople to swear that they had not and would not establish any such "confederation, trust, or sworn pact" against the abbot and church.

Now in fact they had just done so, as everyone recognized, but the key point that allowed for compromise was the specification that the forbidden alliance not be established against the abbot and the church, *contra ecclesiam et abbatem*. That the group who had sworn together in confederation elected the seven and agreed that these would speak for all is indeed, and surely would have been recognized as such at the time, evidence that they were continuing to work through their sworn commune. As long as it was not a conspiracy specifically against *him*, the abbot let it pass, but collective action had clearly been established as a potent weapon for townspeople and peasants to use against what they saw as abuse.

The arbiters disposed of the new set of complaints and claims fairly briskly. Kin could inherit a house, they said, not merely the deceased's children already living there, as long as the deceased was a free person (*liber*) and the heir

---

43. *Cartulaire général de l'Yonne*, 1:318–20, no. 186. *The Vézelay Chronicle*, pp. 323–24.
44. *Cartulaire général de l'Yonne*, 1:320–23, no. 186. *The Vézelay Chronicle*, pp. 324–27.

intended to live in the house and received it from the abbot's hand—which doubtless meant agreeing to the rent owed. It is interesting to note that free townspeople, not only serfs, had apparently been obligated to pay *mainmorte*, even though it was not called *mainmorte*, and the mention in the document of free status was not accompanied by any mention of servile status.

The men of Vézelay gained the nod from the arbiters who declared that they could indeed give their property to the leper house, although the leper house was not supposed to sell it. Similarly, the abbot agreed that burials would not require a payment. A compromise was reached on the vineyards: the abbot's rents were deemed appropriate, but the men of Vézelay, not the abbot, would choose who patrolled the vineyards. Common pasturage and woods usage were reestablished as the peasants had demanded. The taille, however, was left in place, because it was concluded that it had traditionally been the practice. The peasants and burghers had not obtained everything they wanted, but neither had Abbot Alberic.

So this quarrel of 1137 problematizes the distinction between serf and free—because neither the abbot nor the confederation of burghers and peasants seemed to find the distinction significant or even worth mentioning. It also indicates that even those who were obligated to pay what have been taken as the classic markers of serfdom could and did have their complaints heard, taken seriously, and adjudicated at least in part in their favor by some of the most powerful men of that corner of Burgundy.

Although the quarrel between Abbot Alberic and the men of Vézelay was settled (reasonably) amicably, they had not forgotten their commune, their *confederatio*, which was not formally ended in 1137. Although members of the commune swore that they had no conspiracy against the abbot, collective action continued to be their principal line of defense fifteen years later, in 1152, when once again they declared a commune (calling it a *communia* as well as a *confederatio* this time) during bitter conflicts with Abbot Ponce, Alberic's successor.

The quarrel is known primarily from a contemporary history of Vézelay, written by Hugh of Poitiers, an unabashedly partisan monk of the monastery. Count William III of Nevers, son of the count who had helped arbitrate the 1137 settlement, had had long-standing quarrels with the abbot of Vézelay, claiming that he was the *advocatus* of the monastery, which the abbot vehemently denied.[45] According to Hugh of Poitiers, the disagreement over the advocacy of the monastery burst into open hostility due to one

---

45. For monastic advocates, see C. West, "Monks, Aristocrats, and Justice: Twelfth-Century Monastic Advocacy in a European Perspective," *Speculum* 92 (2017), 372–404; and Constance Brittain Bouchard, *Sword, Miter, and Cloister: Nobility and the Church in Burgundy, 980–1198* (Ithaca, N.Y., 1987), pp. 125–30.

man, someone whose family was from outside the region (*advena genere*), someone ignoble in his personal habits (*moribus ignobilis*), though wealthy (*locupletis*) due to his ability in the skilled trades. For good measure, he added that this man was poorly endowed by nature.[46] This man, Hugh of St.-Père, in spite of the monastic chronicler's efforts to denigrate him, does seem to have lived in the region—St.-Père is located in the valley just below Vézelay—and gives every indication of being a free man. Skilled and well-to-do, he decided, according to Hugh of Poitiers, to incite the count to claim the right to exercise justice at the monastery in the hopes that this would revive the commune and that he would be at the head of it.

Although Hugh of Poitiers tried his best to blame Hugh of St.-Père for all the disastrous events that followed, the monks may themselves been at least as responsible, even in his telling. The earlier low level of tension boiled up, according to Hugh of Poitiers, after a companion of Hugh of St.-Père was found chopping wood in a grove belonging the abbey, and the monk who found him tried to seize his axe. The man pulled the monk off his horse, but he ended up blinded shortly afterwards by the abbey's *clientes*, when the monk complained that he had been humiliated. The chronicler said that the count of Nevers took these events as an excuse to announce that he and only he could render justice against the abbot, on behalf of the now-blinded man, who he claimed as his own dear son (*filiolus*).[47]

After pillaging some of the abbot's farms, the count accused the abbot of imposing "new and unjust" requirements on the men of Vézelay. As these men began saying they should address the abbot on equal terms (*equipollenter*), Hugh of St.-Père supposedly invited the count to come to Vézelay.[48] The chronicler Hugh of Poitiers detailed some abortive efforts at making peace in the midst of further upheavals, including a blockade of the village of Vézelay, appeals both to Rome and to the king, and a certain amount of looting, but in spite of the abbot's best efforts the groundwork was laid for Count William to try to use the local men of Vézelay and their desire for a commune as weapons in his conflict.

---

46. Hugh of Poitiers, "Chronique" 2.9, in *Monumenta Vizeliacensia*, pp. 424–25. *The Vézelay Chronicle*, pp. 167–68.

47. This mention of a "dear son" has generally been taken as an assertion that the blinded man was the count's serf, especially as the count added that he could name the man's mother; for example, *The Vézelay Chronicle*, p. 170, n. 3. But in fact the count seems only to have been saying (accurately or not) that he knew this man, felt he was the man's patron, and cared about how badly the monastery had treated him. Another possibility is that the blinded man was the count's illegitimate son, but this seems less likely.

48. Hugh of Poitiers, "Chronique" 2.9–11, in *Monumenta Vizeliacensia*, pp. 425–28. *The Vézelay Chronicle*, pp. 168–73.

This buildup to the count urging the creation of a commune shows very active peasants and villagers, not satisfied with their treatment at the abbot's hands and ready to fight back. The chronicler tried to lay the blame on the wicked (as he characterized him) Hugh of St.-Père, but his wickedness played only a small part in the events. The peasants and townspeople themselves thought the abbot unjust in his treatment of the (unnamed) man blinded by the abbey's men, and they were disinclined to accept new burdens and dues. They clearly remembered their previous effort at confederation, which had won them several important concessions. Hugh of Poitiers was disturbed that the men should want to address the abbot on equal terms, but certainly they had no intention of being treated as suppliant or subservient. Far from being passive, these were men whom the count believed worth courting for their support in his own fights with the abbot.

In 1152 Count William approached the men (*homines*) of Vézelay, claiming to be very concerned about them and their subjection to the abbot.[49] The count lamented that Abbot Ponce, some "foreigner" from the Auvergne as he called him,[50] was oppressing the men of Vézelay with extortionist dues, while preventing William from assuring their safety as their *advocatus*. These problems would be solved, the count continued, if the men withdrew their allegiance from the abbot, swore a *confederatio* among themselves, and pledged their loyalty to him instead. He even sought to inspire them to do so by recalling, with apparent approbation, the murder of Abbot Artald back in 1106. Hugh of Poitiers, the chronicler writing the account, assured his readers that all the count's concern for the people's welfare was feigned, describing false tears and pretended compassion, but it is striking how he framed the count's appeal.

He had the count lament that the men of Vézelay lacked the "freedom" (*libertas*) that should have been their birthright. Even though Count William was addressing what the chronicler called the more powerful (*potiori*) men of Vézelay, he was not merely addressing merchants and artisans, for he stressed that they ought to be able to use the farmsteads, fields, meadows, woods, orchards, and vineyards in the surrounding countryside in full liberty. Vézelay was a village, not a city, and, as at Lorris, its inhabitants and those who lived in the surrounding countryside were concerned as much with farming as with commerce. Hugh's account, while underscoring the lack of a clear

---

49. Hugh of Poitiers, "Chronique" 2.17, in *Monumenta Vizeliacensia*, pp. 433–34. *The Vézelay Chronicle*, pp. 181–82.

50. Abbot Ponce did indeed come from the Auvergne. He was the brother of Abbot Peter the Venerable of Cluny. Bouchard, *Sword, Miter, and Cloister*, pp. 411, 431.

dividing line between prosperous peasants and small-town burghers, also indicates that he recognized a peasant desire for freedom—and knew that it was a powerful enough force that it could become a tool in quarrels between great secular and ecclesiastical lords.

For those living in and around Vézelay had the power to choose, either to take the "liberty" the count was offering them, along with what looks to the modern eye a lot like a classic commune, or else to stay under the authority of the abbot. Hugh continued his account by having the abbot make an impassioned argument to the same *homines*, telling them that when subject to the church they were really free.[51] As discussed in chapter 3, there had long been a sense that service to a church was less onerous (or at least more spiritually rewarding) than service to a lay lord, and the abbot fully exploited that sentiment.

The count, according to the abbot, wished not to free but rather to subjugate the men of Vézelay, press them into servitude (*servitutis*), whereas true *libertas* was to be found only under the dominion of the church. This argument was successful, at least initially. Hugh recounted that the men of Vézelay professed themselves faithful (*fideles*) to the abbot, only urging him to make peace with the count. Here the abbot, like Count William, is portrayed as recognizing that the villagers and peasants of the region had the ability to choose, to swear loyalty to one lord or another, to decide to swear to a mutual *confederatio* or to remain under the dominion of the church. Both suggested that the other wished to subjugate the peasantry and offered themselves as the best alternative to servitude and as a guarantor of liberty. Neither attempted simply to force the peasants to obey. They had to be persuaded.

According to the chronicler Hugh, the abbot's persuasion should have prevailed. But the dispute did not end. Wicked men, he said, induced the youths of the region to reject the abbot's version of liberty and follow the count instead. Even in his telling, the count's version sounds more appealing. The young men—criminally inclined, Hugh added, in case his assessment of them was unclear—abjured their loyalty to the abbot and instead swore mutual support to each other in the form of a *confederatio*, just as the count had urged them to do. The count, delighted, accepted their loyalty, promising he would always help and protect them as they established what Hugh called their "execrable commune" (*execrata communia*). This commune was explicitly self-governing. It had its own leaders (*principes*) and judges (*iudices*),

---

51. Hugh of Poitiers, "Chronique" 2.18, in *Monumenta Vizeliacensia*, pp. 434–35. *The Vézelay Chronicle*, pp. 182–83.

selected by the count but from among those who had mutually sworn to set up the commune. These were dubbed "consuls," the old Latin term that was sometimes used at the time for counts or magistrates. The traitorous men of Vézelay had, Hugh said sarcastically, thrown off from their necks the "yoke of ecclesiastical liberty" (*iugum libertatis aecclesiae*).[52]

Hugh's account is one of evil, deceit, forswearing, and detestable acts carried out by ungoverned youths. But it is also an account of peasant self-determination. The abbot had little beyond moral suasion with which to force the peasants to continue in service to Vézelay. The basis for any moral authority may well have been limited—Hugh's own account, even aside from the harsh accusations he records that the count made, suggests the abbot may have treated his peasants and townspeople badly. Secular power for monasteries always rested with their advocates—and Vézelay had rejected Count William's claim that he was their *advocatus*. Any monastery whose advocate turned on it was in trouble indeed.

Here it is striking that the count could not force the men of Vézelay to obey him any more than could the abbot. He had to appeal to their "prudence and magnanimity" (*prudentia et magnanimitas*). In other words, he recognized that they had agency, the ability to decide whether or not to join with him. The ability of these men of Vézelay to take matters into their own hands continued. Although, according to Hugh, the younger, more troublesome ones formed a commune, the older and wiser ones were initially determined to find a way to preserve peace and not break with the abbot. They went to the cardinals.[53]

This has not been seen as a particularly startling turn of events, but it should be if one perceives peasants as having little power. They went to the highest ecclesiastical lords, two cardinal legates who themselves sought to reconcile the abbot and the count. The cardinals, according to the chronicle, had no objection to meeting these *homines* of Vézelay. They offered their assistance, promising to encourage Abbot Ponce to give up the "novel and tyrannical" *consuetudines* he had been demanding. In the monastic chronicler's own account, their complaints were enough to persuade the cardinals that the abbot was a tyrant.

The cardinals' attempts at peace-making faltered, however, when the men of Vézelay demanded that the abbot remit the unwanted dues first, and he

---

52. Hugh of Poitiers, "Chronique" 2.19, in *Monumenta Vizeliacensia*, p. 435. *The Vézelay Chronicle*, p. 184.

53. Hugh of Poitiers, "Chronique" 2.20–22, in *Monumenta Vizeliacensia*, pp. 435–37. *The Vézelay Chronicle*, pp. 184–88.

demanded in turn that they first give up their commune and their allegiance to the count. The count himself continued to insist that the advocacy of the abbey was his by right and that he would make no concessions until he had this confirmed, even when threatened with excommunication. The men of Vézelay, according to the chronicler Hugh, stayed with the count and his promises of protection. The cardinals were no more able to impose a settlement on the peasants and townspeople than the abbot had been—or for that matter the count.

Hugh of Poitiers, who wrote as an eyewitness to all these events, continued with a series of increasingly violent and unpleasant developments, as the townspeople of Vézelay, whom he called *oppidani* and *burgenses*, plundered the church and burned houses, leaving the monks terrified.[54] A sentence of anathema had little effect. The abbot fled to Cluny, where his brother, Peter the Venerable, was abbot. Bishops, the pope, and the monks of Cluny all became involved before an uneasy peace was finally established, and the men of Vézelay gave up their *confederatio*, while the count and the abbot settled their differences. The final outcome was an agreement between Count William and Abbot Ponce, but it should be stressed that both men had seen the peasants and townsmen as valuable allies, men whose support they needed. Both promised that the men would be better off with themselves as lord, a case the count appears to have made more convincingly with his support for a commune.

Although the men of Vézelay do not appear to have won any major concessions from the abbot in the final agreement of 1152, beyond what they had already won fifteen years earlier, it is clear that they were a force with which all elements had to reckon, even cardinals. As their episode of plundering demonstrated, they were a group with a mind of their own and the possibility of carrying out real damage. Long before the peasant revolts of the fourteenth century, twelfth-century peasants and villagers fought back against what they saw as unfair treatment. Twelfth-century knights are well known as violent actors; after all, they were trained in violence. But peasants could be violent too. And they became central at Vézelay to the quarrel between abbot and count.

Communes, Mayors, and Judicial Rights

Although judicial rights, the question of who should judge malefactors, was not at issue in the 1152 quarrel at Vézelay, it frequently arose during the

---

54. Hugh of Poitiers, "Chronique" 2.23–28, in *Monumenta Vizeliacensia*, pp. 437–57. *The Vézelay Chronicle*, pp. 188–97.

negotiations over communes. Two generations after this quarrel between the abbot, the local inhabitants, and the count of Nevers, the establishment of village self-governance was at the center of a series of negotiations between a different count and monastery. This case was much less fraught than that of Vézelay, at least as far as it is recorded in surviving records, but the maneuvering between powerful secular and ecclesiastical powers should not obscure the role of the peasantry in trying to take control of their own lives. This case involved Count Peter of Auxerre and Tonnerre.[55] In the attesting charter, Peter gave to the monastery of Montier-la-Celle and its dependent church, which was located in the village of Stes.-Vertus, the dues he had been collecting from the inhabitants of that village. His long charter spelled out exactly what he had been receiving and how expectations would change once the monks would receive it instead.[56]

Peter said that he had been receiving the *gîte* and "ancient customs" (*antiquas consuetudines*) from the villagers of Stes.-Vertus, which his men and the mayor of the village had collected together: every year around All Saints day, they received from each hearth (*foca*) two bushels of grain, plus two solidi for each draft animal, or two solidi for other animals, or twelve pennies if the householder worked his fields by hand without a draft animal. The mayor was not expected to pay, presumably because of his role in helping to collect the grain and coin. This uniform payment was not a rent but, as the document said, a *gîte*, a payment expected of everyone in the village in return for protection. All of this income, Peter specified, would now go to the monks. Although the amounts might seem small, both Peter and the monastery of Montier-la-Celle took them seriously: if anyone did not wish to pay, the document specified, his land would be seized.

Although the document started as a pious donation, it quickly became a description of judicial courts, because the count was keeping his judicial rights in the village, even if giving the monks the annual "customary"' payments. Specifically, he said that he would continue to judge cases of murder, kidnapping, and theft, even though he stated that he would be doing so as a concession from Montier-la-Celle. But he clearly did not want to become

---

55. Peter had married the granddaughter of Count William III of Nevers, the count who had quarreled with Vézelay in 1152, and had thus become count of Nevers himself, but by 1203, the time of the agreement discussed here, he had yielded Nevers to his son-in-law, retaining Auxerre and Tonnerre. The three counties of Nevers, Auxerre, and Tonnerre were inherited by a series of women from the late twelfth to the late thirteenth century; Constance B. Bouchard, "Three Counties, One Lineage, and Eight Heiresses: Nevers, Auxerre, and Tonnerre, Eleventh to Thirteenth Centuries," *Medieval Prosopography* 31 (2016), 25–48.

56. *Recueil de pièces pour faire suite au Cartulaire général de l'Yonne*, ed. Maximilien Quantin (Auxerre, 1873), pp. 9–10, no. 21.

involved in minor infractions within the village, which primarily involved animals straying. Various amounts in pennies were specified as the fines for cows, steers, horses, or sheep running loose in a field, or for someone taking such an animal and keeping it overnight, presumably trying to pass it off as his own. But these infractions were not to be judged by the count, even though he specified that he would continue to be entitled to half the fines. Rather, such cases were to be judged by four "wise men," elected by the whole community of the village. A representative of the count would sit in on the proceedings, but the four villagers would pass the judgment, and the count himself would play no role in bringing malefactors before this court; that role was left for the mayor.

Hence this document suggests an initiative by the villagers of Stes.-Vertus to take control of at least some aspects of their own lives. The village mayor (*prior ejusdem villæ*) appears to have been appointed by the monastery. Villagers would henceforth take charge of infractions involving farm animals themselves. The count may have wanted to avoid presiding over peasant squabbles, but he would not have handed what he considered minor issues over to the villagers had they not pushed for it themselves. In many ways this was a variation of the establishment of a commune; the attesting charter spoke of the *communitas* of the village rather than specifically of a *communia*, but the idea was certainly similar. Although the document is phrased as a gift to a monastery, it was also a recognition of a village's collective action.

In addition, the charter mentions that the peasants had bought their way out of what they had considered an onerous burden. Previously Count Peter and his men had been able to demand a meal whenever they stopped in Stes.-Vertus. But now this demand was replaced by an annual payment of ten pounds, paid collectively by the men of the village. The peasants, through their own initiative, had been able to make what was expected of them far less arbitrary, turning what would have been an occasional unexpected demand into a payment that could be anticipated and planned for. They did, however, continue paying rents, even if not to the count. Peter said that all rents, which he detailed as land tax, tithes, mill fees, oven fees, water, and *census*, would be collected by the mayor, further indicating that the latter acted as the monks' agent. This mix of dues, which must have varied substantially according to (for example) how often someone ground grain at the mill, was addressed in general terms, with no effort to spell out amounts. Peter repeated that he would not attempt to collect any of these rents except with the express permission of the monks of Montier-la-Celle.

This document is an excellent example of the sort of source in which peasant agency may be found. It does not present itself as a description of

peasant action, as indeed do almost no documents. Rather, it is a pious donation that could be read for descriptions of the sorts of dues villagers might
be expected to pay or for detail on the handling of infractions in a society
without a modern legal structure. Yet here one finds active peasants, working with a mayor who might not be one of them but who stood between
them and the more powerful, managing to turn a change in the entity to
which they would pay dues into an opportunity to create their own version
of a commune with rights over justice.

A final example of a village commune able to successfully negotiate with
the powerful involves the commune (*communia*) of Crépy, near Prémontré. In
1206 the mayor of Crépy himself issued a charter attesting to the end of his
commune's quarrel with the monastery. The villagers and the monastery had
both been using some nearby hills for pasturage and for gathering building
stones, but now the canons of Prémontré wanted to clear the land for crops.
Rather than accepting this, the mayor and commune raised a *querela*, which
they and the monastery submitted to two arbiters, a canon of the church
of St.-Jean of Laon and the parish priest of Crépy. The attesting document
makes clear that the commune functioned as an equal to the monastery, ready
to reach an agreement (a *compromissum* as the document put it) but also not
accepting anything that they found harmful.[57]

In this case, the canons of Prémontré agreed that if they cleared the hills
for agriculture, they would pay the commune an amount equal to one-half
of the dues that the commune normally levied on such fields. If they planted
a vineyard, they would similarly pay one-half of the wine tax (*vinagium*). In
addition, the agreement specified that the canons would be able to harvest
wood in their adjoining woodlot only once in six years and then would be
obliged to leave at least twenty trees standing.

Although framed as a compromise, this agreement appeared to benefit the
commune. The mayor and commune were able to limit woodcutting even in
a woodlot they specified as belonging to the canons, and although they only
anticipated receiving half the fees from newly cleared fields, this was on land
that had been previously been treated as belonging jointly to the monastery
and the commune. The attesting document is known now because it was copied into Prémontré's cartulary a generation or two later, but it is surely significant that the document was written in the voice of the mayor, who thus had
the final word on what the agreement entailed. This peasant village, devoted
to agriculture, was able to use its collective power as a commune to negotiate
successfully with a large and highly respected monastery.

---

57. Soissons, Bibliothèque municipale, MS 7, fols. 38v–39r.

Quarrels between Crépy and Prémontré were not, however, at an end. Six years later, in 1212, the new mayor of Crépy issued a charter of his own attesting to a quarrel settlement; here the *communia* was also called a "peace" (*pax*), indicating its formal standing.[58] The quarrel involved the land and house of one Renald, a citizen of Crépy who had taken the habit at Prémontré before his death. This was apparently not just any piece of property but the location of a winepress that the villagers used. After extended discussion between mayor and monastery, the commune agreed that the canons of Prémontré could keep the property and operate the winepress there, charging what the attesting document called the "customary" fee to those who used it. In return for being able to keep Renald's gift, the canons would pay a chicken and a bushel of oats a year, a token amount that seems designed to act as a reminder that they had the property with its winepress only on suffrage.

The mayor's charter made a further specification that nothing in this agreement would detract from the commune's right to exercise *justicia* over everyone in the village, including over the monastery's servants who operated the winepress, even though those servants would be exempt from other local taxes. Even more importantly, Prémontré had to agree that it would not in the future acquire any further property at Crépy, or, if it received a gift in alms of property there, it would sell it to a villager within a year and a day. The commune, represented by its mayor, was thus able to negotiate a settlement that preserved the village's autonomy: no one else would exercise justice there, and property at Crépy would not be given away by anyone who felt a religious impulse. The collective action of a commune could be powerful, allowing villagers to interact with important ecclesiastics essentially as equals. Far from being passive recipients of the decisions of lords and great churches, they could and did negotiate for what they themselves wanted.

Charters of franchise, new towns, communes, all of them are markers of the ability of twelfth- and thirteenth-century rural inhabitants to seek improvements in their lot. In most cases, new towns were granted rights and freedoms because the powerful who controlled the land saw economic benefit in doing so. But they knew that benefit was contingent on peasants actually coming and settling in the new town, and that the most attractive inducement to lure them was an offer of (relatively) low and predictable rents, coupled with a sizeable amount of liberty and self-governance.

In other cases, such as Vézelay, villagers and peasants fought determinedly for what they considered their rights. These people may have been more

---

58. Soissons, Bibliothèque municipale, MS 7, fol. 36v.

aggressive than most in their response to what they saw as oppression. But their determination to end what they believed to be harsh dues and arbitrary demands earned them enough respect that the count of Nevers thought it necessary to recruit them in fighting his own battles with the abbot, and they were able to reach compromises adjudicated by powerful secular and ecclesiastical lords, including two cardinals.

The peasant search for better conditions and more predictable obligations is reflected in charters of franchise, for example in the royally approved Customs of Lorris. The peasantry of the high Middle Ages did not simply accept their condition but were determined to improve it, and the spread of communes and new towns demonstrates that through collective action and readiness to be heard in the courts of the powerful, they were often successful.

CHAPTER 5

Peasant Agency

Peasant dues, obligations, and payments, such
as those discussed in the previous chapters, may appear to the modern eye
as simply demanded by the powerful from the weak. But the record of what
may look like the imposition of obligations was often the product of long
negotiation. High medieval peasants appear to have realized that they were
in a period of at least relative strength during such negotiations: they out-
numbered the lords considerably, and they were the only source of their
rents or, for that matter, food. Their numerical advantage and essential roles
gave them the opportunity for initiative and resistance.

If peasants were routinely defeated by the powerful in their efforts at self-
determination, one would expect that the charters would normally record
the failure of their efforts. But in fact the ecclesiastical cartularies in which
peasants are found most commonly record them *winning*, or at least coming
to a compromise agreement they were willing to accept. Of course they did
not always triumph in their quarrels with the powerful, but the fact that the
charters record them doing so more often than they record the opposite is a
clear indication of successful peasant agency.

Peasant Initiative

So far I have discussed peasant initiative in situations where they established a commune, or changed landlords in being given to a monastery along with their land, or made pious gifts of their own. But these transitional moments were not the only ones in which peasants acted to improve their situation. Even those who had long lived on and worked the land could and did renegotiate the terms of their tenure. A charter from Bèze from around the year 1100 describes the discussions that took place between the abbot and the villagers of Bourberain, located a few kilometers from the monastery. That this charter was preserved in the monastery's cartulary indicates that the monks considered it a validation of their own rights. And yet nothing in it suggests that the abbot was able to impose his will on the peasants.

There had been a fire in Bourberain, and the villagers had been staying at the abbey while preparing to rebuild. The village was on monastery land, so the peasants requested official permission to build from the abbot. His reply, as recorded in the charter, seems unyielding. "May you never have houses in our territory, such as you used to have, unless you pay customary servile dues, such as our men and others who live under our authority pay. If you do not wish to, you shall never again receive permission to build from me."[1] But the villagers were not discouraged. Indeed, from the harsh tone of the abbot's reply, it would seem that he was concerned that rebuilding could be seen as an opportunity to improve tenure obligations, suggesting that he feared this as a real possibility.

After discussion among themselves, the villagers announced that they would each pay twelve pennies a year and all the old customary dues, except that they would no longer be required to cart wine from Gevrey, would not pay any arbitrary *tallia*, and would not be required to pay any new dues. In addition, they agreed that if they received any injury from the monks or

---

1. *The Cartulary-Chronicle of St.-Pierre of Bèze*, ed. Constance Brittain Bouchard, Medieval Academy Books 116 (Toronto, 2019), pp. 260–61, no. 204. "Absit ut umquam deinceps in nostro fundo ita mansiones habeatis sicuti actenus habuistis nisi consuetudinaria servitia reddederitis, sicut nostri et alii qui in nostra potestate consistunt. Si autem nolueritis, construendi ulterius licentiam a me non consequemini."

their men, they would take their case first to the abbot and only seek justice elsewhere if they could not receive it from the monastery officials.

The abbot signed the agreement—as did the villagers of Bourberain (or at least made their marks). Without defying the abbot they had negotiated a better arrangement for themselves: no more unexpected exactions, which they considered well worth twelve pennies a year, and no more onerous carting of wine from the far side of Dijon. It is also significant that the abbot seemed genuinely worried that they might sue him in someone else's court without first giving him a chance to respond to their complaints, indicating that even peasants bound to pay what he called servile dues had a right to legal recourse.[2]

The settlement of another case from Bèze from the same time indicates that the abbot had good reason to worry about peasants and their demands.[3] One Girald of Lux, a village just a few kilometers from the monastery, was said to be damaging property belonging to the monks and of seizing the tithes that should have gone to the monastery's church at Lux. This *villicus*, according to documents in the house's cartulary, objected to the *servitio* he owed the monks. He had been excommunicated for seizing the tithes, without result.

But in the end Girald's aggressive behavior paid off. He and the abbot reached a settlement, but the advantage was all on his side. The abbot determined exactly what land Girald held—he had apparently been claiming more than he really had—and agreed to cut in half the required rent in grain to which Girald had objected. Girald in turn agreed to stop stealing the tithes and was freed from anathema. The abbot said that he acted out of "mercy" and a desire to bring about "peace," and that this way Girald would remain "faithful" to the monastery. He added that this decrease in rent would not continue past Girald's own lifetime, but it was clear that he had given in to Girald's most important demands. Girald ended up free from excommunication, with his holdings confirmed to him, and his rents cut in half. If anyone in this case was imposing his will on the other, it was the tenant, not the landlord.

It is in the context of Girald's defiance of the abbot that one must read another document from Bèze from almost exactly the same time.[4] Here the abbot specified that one Deodatus of Neuvelle and his wife owed an annual head tax to the monastery, "just as do other *servi* and *ancille* of Saint Peter, four pennies for the men and two for the women." At first glance this

---

2. Jean Richard treats this agreement as a predecessor to later charters of franchise; "Les courants de chartes de franchises dans la Bourgogne ducale (XIIe–XIVe siècles)," in *La charte de Beaumont et les franchises municipales entre Loire et Rhin* (Nancy, 1988), p. 107.

3. *The Cartulary-Chronicle of Bèze*, pp. 282–83, no. 234.

4. *The Cartulary-Chronicle of Bèze*, pp. 299–300, no. 248.

seems nothing more than a simple description of the head tax the monks demanded. But one must ask, if this was the accepted norm, why was it found necessary to spell it out in a charter aimed at a specific couple, much less say that the couple had agreed that none of their sons, daughters, or descendants would deny this? The conclusion seems inescapable that they *had* attempted to deny it. Although in this case the serfs had been unable to get out of a due that they clearly found objectionable, in slightly different circumstances they might have been able to do so. This threat of peasant defiance was quite real and provided the motivation for the document's almost desperate closing insistence, "this written account will be taken as a testimony of truth forever."

These examples from Bèze all concern peasants negotiating with a monastery. But one should not assume that only monks, and not secular lords, were willing to deal with peasants. For even powerful laymen found themselves compelled to settle with peasants who argued for better conditions. For example, Count Gui of Nevers, Auxerre, and Tonnerre reached an agreement in 1174 with his tenants of Tonnerre, an agreement that hints at long negotiation between him and his tenants.[5] Tonnerre had been the seat of a county since at least the tenth century, and it was home to the old Benedictine monastery of St.-Michel, so it would have to be considered more than a farming village in the twelfth century. Yet it was not a city either, being instead a small town, larger than a village but substantially smaller than the cities of its region, like Troyes or Auxerre.[6] (Even now Tonnerre has fewer than five thousand inhabitants.) The whole agreement between count and residents of Tonnerre turned on grain, vegetables, and wine, indicating that the *homines* with whom Count Gui dealt were involved in agriculture. As was the case with the *homines* of Vézelay discussed in the previous chapter, the inhabitants of the small town and the peasants of the surrounding countryside made common cause.

Gui drew up the charter spelling out the agreement he had reached with the men of Tonnerre, starting with his promise no longer to demand the taille, an arbitrary payment, or other (undetailed) customary dues. The taille had doubtless been considered very onerous by the inhabitants of Tonnerre, which was why they were willing to make concessions to free themselves from it. They agreed that instead they would each year pay the count

---

5. *Cartulaire général de l'Yonne*, ed. Maximilien Quantin, 2 vols. (Auxerre, 1854–60), 2:259–61, no. 242.

6. For these small towns of Champagne/Burgundy, see Theodore Evergates, *Feudal Society in the Bailliage of Troyes under the Counts of Champagne, 1152–1284* (Baltimore, 1975), pp. 30–32.

one-tenth of their grain harvest, one-tenth of their vegetables, and one-tenth of their wine. The count noted that they had sworn (*jurabunt*) not to lie about the amount of their grain harvest or other agricultural products in calculating his tenth.

Here we see peasants being given credibility—their word would be accepted, essentially because the count had no alternative, although he did threaten them with fines if they were caught lying. The agreement, which the peasants appear to have negotiated entirely on their own, also specified annual rents: five solidi for a household, five solidi for someone from outside Tonnerre living there although not owning any house or land, and twenty-five for a Jewish household. The count retained rights of justice, and he specified that if he went on a military expedition, householders would either have to accompany him in person or send a representative, but beyond that the villagers of Tonnerre were essentially left to their own devices. The importance of this agreement is evidenced by the count swearing "by my hand" to observe it and make sure all his heirs did likewise, and by the notable number of high-ranking witnesses: as well as the count's wife, the countess, these included three bishops (Langres, Auxerre, and Nevers) and a dozen of the most powerful castellans of the region. The *homines* of Tonnerre were able to be taken seriously, have arbitrary demands replaced by set amounts they were willing to pay, and have their agreement with the count confirmed by the most important secular and ecclesiastical figures of their corner of Burgundy.

Peasants were especially likely to try to exercise usage rights, with or without a lord's permission, as attested by the number of documents in which they negotiated their way to a better position. Usage rights gave them access to resources of land other than what they rented or owned. When the monks of the Benedictine house of St.-Pierre of Chalon granted the Cistercians of La Ferté some wooded land along the Grosne River, the abbot of St.-Pierre specified that the *rustici* of the region would still be able to take their animals through those woods, to and from the river.[7] Although this specification was made rather laconically, in one sentence of the attesting charter, the monks of both houses must have realized the difficulties that would arise if these peasants were suddenly forbidden access to the river for their animals. These usage rights were important enough for the abbot of St.-Pierre to include them in his charter and for the scribes at La Ferté to include them when copying the charter into their pancarte.

---

7. *Recueil des pancartes de l'abbaye de La Ferté-sur-Grosne, 1113–1178*, ed. Georges Duby (Paris, 1953), p. 101, no. 100.

In another case from the early thirteenth century involving Pontigny, it took the bishop of Troyes to persuade the men (*homines*) of Villemaur to give up the usage rights, the *usuarium*, that they had been exercising in the Othe forest, contrary to the demands of the monks of Pontigny.[8] Although the men of Villemaur were ruled against, it is striking that the bishop did not merely rule that they were in the wrong. His attesting document said that they themselves had agreed to yield, that they had given up (*quitaverunt*) their claims and foresworn them (*abjurasse*). The document that the monks had copied into their cartulary to preserve the memory of their successful case suggests that the men had made their own decision to give up rights they had presumably been exercising for some time.

They might have been pressured into agreeing, but from the document's wording, doing so was at their own volition. They had long used Pontigny's woods for their own purposes, and their agreement to stop doing so was necessary, even if given grudgingly. Both the bishop and the monks recognized that it would have been impossible to force the peasants into stopping unless they themselves conceded. A ruling against them would not have been sufficient without that agreement.

Peasant Resistance

The same determination and collective action that allowed peasants to negotiate better terms for themselves allowed them to fight back against what they considered imposition and injustice. It is possible for scholars to read documents where peasants objected to their treatment by their lords in two ways: either as an indication of how badly peasants were treated, or as an indication that in spite of lords' best efforts at oppression, peasants were entirely capable of resistance. I would argue for the latter. This resistance was not always a last-ditch effort to put off the inevitable; it was sometimes successful.

Some documents record rather laconically the result of what must have been long and complicated negotiations between a lord or church and peasants who felt aggrieved. A case from the middle of the twelfth century at the Cistercian monastery of La Ferté suggests the ability of peasants to argue for what they perceived as rightfully theirs. The appearance of their claims to property in the documents, even in cases where they ultimately lost, indicates their doubtless well-founded belief that they might well win.

---

8. *Le premier cartulaire de l'abbaye cistercienne de Pontigny (XIIe–XIIIe siècles)*, ed. Martine Garrigues (Paris, 1981), p. 113, no. 38.

In this case, a man named Vitalis claimed as his a house that had once belonged to his late father-in-law, Robert Berengar.[9] While he was at it, he also claimed some property that his uncle had given the monks in alms, some additional land that he had held from Notre Dame of Beaumont, and two furrows (*seilluns*) of additional land, identified by the person who held the adjoining mansus. The quarrel was resolved when Vitalis, along with his wife Bonafilia (daughter of Robert Berengar), announced that he was giving up all his quarrels with the monks. Although the attesting charter does not give a reason for his decision to yield his claims, it is perhaps significant that immediately following this quarrel settlement in La Ferté's attesting pancarte, the scribe copied a threat of excommunication from the bishop of Chalon. The bishop said that anyone, "noble or ignoble, literate or illiterate, greater or lesser," who tried to seize any of the property spelled out in that pancarte would be excommunicated until he made satisfaction. Although most of La Ferté's twelfth-century pancartes included both threats and confirmations from the bishop of Chalon, this is the only example where such "ignoble" claimants were explicitly mentioned, suggesting that the threat was aimed directly at Vitalis. Both the bishop and the monks feared that lower-status, illiterate people might "violate" the gifts that had been made to La Ferté, as Vitalis had done.

But Vitalis did not give up easily. He appeared again in the monks' next pancarte, again claiming the late Robert Berengar's house as his.[10] In addition, he claimed between two and four furrows of land and additional pieces of property in each of four different villages, as well as a cartload of hay that was owed by someone else. This time, when he gave up his claims, the monks made him a countergift: a cow and a tunic. As a symbol of his agreement to the end of the quarrel, Vitalis brought a load of nuts on his donkey to the monastery. The attesting document was confirmed by Vitalis's wife Bonafilia, and, in the same way that a knight might refer to family members, he noted that the couple did not have any children who could have confirmed, presumably because they were too young.

The extent of Vitalis's claims and the tenacity with which he pushed them might cause some to suspect that he actually was a knight rather than a peasant. But nothing other than the sheer audacity with which he pursued what he wanted suggests other than peasant status. Clearly the bishop of Chalon, in his threats of excommunication, anticipated such claims from "ignoble, lesser" people. Vitalis wanted a house and he wanted strips of agricultural

---

9. *Recueil des pancartes de La Ferté*, pp. 88–89, no. 81.
10. *Recueil des pancartes de La Ferté*, pp. 93–94, no. 88.

land, not the sort of things over which a high-status person would imperil his soul. The income he tried to divert from the monks to himself was a cartload of hay. He symbolized his formal yielding of his claims by bringing a donkey-load of nuts. The monks satisfied him with a cow and a simple item of clothing. A further telling detail is that Durannus Beslers, identified as a *conversus* (lay brother) of La Ferté, played an important part in the *negotio* that led to the final settlement. *Conversi* were usually of peasant stock—he was most likely a friend or relative of Vitalis. Given all these markers of Vitalis as a peasant, the only reason to argue that he was not would be the assumption that peasants were never in a position to raise such claims. Here the bishop of Chalon would have disagreed.

A similar case of peasants resisting pressure is found in a 1220 document in the cartulary of the Cistercian house of Pontigny. It records an agreement between the monks and two women, mother and daughter, of the village of nearby St.-Gervais. They had been living in two houses, described as located next to the village well, houses that the cellarer of the monastery decided actually belonged to Pontigny, not to them. According to the document, with the intervention of the representative of the dean of the cathedral and of "other good men," the cellarer agreed to rent the two houses to the women for their lifetimes, for twenty solidi a year. They in turn agreed to pay twenty solidi immediately for needed repairs and confirmed that the houses would revert to the monks on their deaths.[11]

The distinct impression one has is that the monks had originally wanted to evict two peasant women who had been living in the houses rent-free (and who the monks thought had let them run down) but were persuaded to let them stay if they started paying rent. The dean's representative would not have been called in if the women had gone quietly, which they clearly had not. Instead, the document's brief summary of the agreement indicates that they had fought stubbornly, persuasively, and successfully to stay in what they considered their homes.

Such stubborn resistance appears frequently in the records. An example from the "Book of Serfs" of Marmoutier shows how much the line between free and serf could be negotiated by a determined peasant.[12] A charter from 1097 related that a shepherd, Otbert, had burned down one of the monks' granges a generation or so earlier. He did not have the wherewithal then to

<hr />

11. *Le premier cartulaire de Pontigny*, pp. 325–26, no. 314.

12. *Le livre des serfs de Marmoutier*, ed. André Salmon (Tours, 1864), pp. 101–2, 117–18, nos. 108, 127. See also Dominique Barthélemy, *The Serf, the Knight, and the Historian*, trans. Graham Robert Edwards (Ithaca, N.Y., 2009), pp. 58–61; and Paul Fouracre, "Marmoutier and Its Serfs in the Eleventh Century," *Transactions of the Royal Historical Society* 15 (2005), 37–38.

pay compensation, so instead, according to the 1097 charter, he voluntarily became a serf of the monastery, his own service becoming a form of payment. He agreed that he, his wife Plectrudis, and their children would all be serfs.

Now this story is complicated by the existence of an earlier charter, dating from the time that he became a serf (probably in the 1060s), that says nothing about arson or granges. It is indeed unclear how the memory of servitude as punishment became attached to Otbert, given that the charter issued at the time he became a serf has a different version of the process. It says rather that Otbert's first wife had been a serf (*ancilla*) of Marmoutier when he married her, even though Plectrudis, his second wife, was a free woman. This earlier charter says that the monastery insisted in a legal setting (*placitum*) that Otbert's servile status, acquired by his first marriage, was still in effect, and that Plectrudis agreed to accept servile status as well, putting four pennies on her head, rather than leave her husband. It is significant that the monks recognized that a free woman had a choice; the charter indicates that becoming a serf was her decision, not something that accrued to her automatically by a marriage to someone whose own servile status was at least open to doubt. But the story did not end there.

According again to the 1097 charter, Plectrudis later claimed that their son Vitalis had been born while she and Otbert were both still free and was therefore free himself. Her claim was ultimately unsuccessful because she backed down rather than proving it, as she initially announced herself ready to do, through the ordeal of hot iron. But it is important to note that someone who was both a serf and female had access to this form of legal proof, had she decided to go through with it.[13] In spite of his mother's understandable hesitation to undergo the ordeal, young Vitalis himself refused to recognize the monks' *dominium* over him. According to the charter recording the prolonged series of events, after a long time he finally "repented" and recognized himself as Marmoutier's serf, putting four pennies on his head. Even then he was not fully reconciled to his servile status and denied it again, only agreeing finally to recognize that he was indeed a serf, again by putting four pennies on his head, when he was old enough to have a son of his own.

---

13. For the frequency with which the ordeal was threatened but not undertaken, see Stephen D. White, "Proposing the Ordeal and Avoiding It: Strategy and Power in Western French Litigation, 1050–1110," in *Cultures of Power: Lordship, Status, and Process in Twelfth-Century Europe*, ed. Thomas N. Bisson (Philadelphia, 1995), pp. 89–123. He describes a similar case from Le Mans from around the same time, when a *famulus* offered to prove his point through the ordeal but backed out; ibid., pp. 89–90.

It is indeed possible that the quarrel may have continued into the next generation, at a time when many serfs were seeking to make themselves free, but we will never know, because the document recording Vitalis's second recognition of his servile status is the final entry in Marmoutier's "Book of Serfs." The case of Otbert's status, his wife's, his son's, and his grandson's, a disagreement that stretched out for some thirty years, indicates that serfs were fully capable of disputing their status and indeed had recourse to legal procedures in their effort to assert their freedom. Much as the monks of Marmoutier, and surely other lords, would have liked serfdom to be an inalterable state, the serfs themselves believed they had a legal right to dispute that status and acted on their belief. We have only the records of cases where the monks of Marmoutier were successful in establishing that someone was their serf, but it is possible that decades-long disputes like the case of Otbert, Plectrudis, and Vitalis may sometimes have ended with serfs keeping the freedom for which they long fought.

Peasants in Court

In the above case, Otbert and his family resisted at a low level for years, never letting a setback deter them permanently. But what happened when the more powerful turned violently on peasants? For there was surely plenty of that. One of peasants' best resources in such situations was to turn to other powerful lords, ideally in a legal setting. Here it is important not to let one's entirely appropriate sympathy for peasant grievances make one conclude that they were nothing more than helpless victims. And yet that has been the default position for scholars. In a classic study of peasant complaints before the court of the twelfth-century count-kings of Catalonia, the peasants are described as speaking with "tormented voices."[14]

But these cases cannot simply be read as the final cries of the powerless being crushed. To begin, they were able to bring their complaints about their castellan lords to the highest court of the land, that of the count-kings. Thus, as the study indicates, the Catalan peasants gained the attention of the one person who could counter those attacking them or imposing new dues on them. Scribes at court wrote out in great detail the names of the peasant claimants and the specifics of their accusations, down to the value of a stolen pig. The claimants emphasized the horrors to which they had been subjected, using their very weakness as a tool to gain the court's attention.

---

14. Thomas N. Bisson, *Tormented Voices: Power, Crisis, and Humanity in Rural Catalonia, 1140–1200* (Cambridge, Mass., 1998).

The count-kings were as interested in suppressing the upstart castellans as were the peasants themselves. Although the records do not indicate the final judgment of these cases, it is unlikely that any such records would have been preserved of cases that the court dismissed. The peasants were never assured of victory, and they were doubtless concerned about retaliation, but their "tormented voices" were very effective.[15]

This ability of peasants to gain a sympathetic response from a more powerful lord when abused by a lesser one is also found in the Burgundy-Champagne region. A case with striking similarities to the tormented voices of Catalonia arose at the monastery of Montier-en-Der in the late eleventh century.[16] The monks had property at the village of Ecot, located over fifty kilometers from their house, which they had granted *in beneficium* to a knight named Bencelin. This property included authority over the villagers there, which it seems Bencelin abused. A charter of Der's abbot recorded that the men (*homines*) of the village arrived at the monastery, asking to be taken under the abbot's direct dominion, complaining that Bencelin had tortured them so much that they had little faith that anyone would ever recover. Their voices were certainly tormented!

The men of Ecot also said they had managed to scrape together "from their poverty" (*paupertaticula*) twenty solidi, which they gave to the abbot. Moved by this desperate (and perhaps exaggerated) tale of woe, as well as by the money, the abbot agreed that henceforth the villagers would be subject only to the monastery, and that their village would not be granted *in beneficium* to Bencelin or to any other knight. Here we know that the peasants' own initiative and heartrending pleas were effective in freeing them from an abusive lord. Like the claimants in Catalonia, they were able to play off one powerful figure against another.

Similarly, a generation or so later, another charter from Montier-en-Der indicates that the men (*homines*) of Guindrecourt were able to get the abbot on their side in complaining about the local castellan. Calling themselves the men of Saint Peter (Der's patron saint), they persuaded the abbot that the castellan had used his position as monastic advocate to "extort" dues from them. They were convincing enough that the castellan, on his deathbed, was said to implore the abbot tearfully for a chance to make amends, in all humility. The charter spelled out what dues an advocate *was* allowed to collect:

---

15. See also M. W. McHaffie, "Law and Violence in Eleventh-Century France," *Past and Present* 238 (2018), 10–26. He suggests more broadly that many of the complaints about extreme violence found in medieval sources were part of an effort to ensure a court's proper attention.

16. *The Cartulary of Montier-en-Der, 666–1129*, ed. Constance Brittain Bouchard, Medieval Academy Books 108 (Toronto, 2004), pp. 232–33, no. 104.

six days of labor every spring in March, and a meal once a year if he came through Guindrecourt. Even this reduction in what he had been demanding was not enough for the peasants; they paid the dying castellan sixty solidi to "redeem" them from owing these obligations to him or his successors at all.[17] Here the men of Guindrecourt used both their connection to the abbot, for whom the castellan was acting as lay advocate, and his own fears while dying to negotiate a freedom from what they had considered serious impositions.

As this case indicates, the relationship between a group of peasants and someone who was supposed to be in charge over them was always potentially fraught, whether the man in charge was monastic advocate or castellan's provost. The peasants often faced their most serious abuses not from great lords but from lower-level administrators who took advantage of their position. In another example from Montier-en-Der from the early eleventh century, a document says that the Viscount Dudo had inflicted unspecified damages (*tortitudines*) on the monastery's men (*homines*) at Vouciennes.[18] Vouciennes was some fifty kilometers from the monastery, so the monks would have had to give oversight of their men there to someone more local. Although the document does not specify how the monks had learned about the viscount's wrongdoing, it must have been from their own men, those suffering from it, as was the case with the men of Ecot. According to the document, the viscount expressed suitable remorse, and in return the monks gave him advocacy over their men and property at Vouciennes. Specifically he was given certain judicial rights in the area.

At first glance this might seem like rewarding bad behavior. If those of Vouciennes had hoped to remove the viscount from any authority over them one can assume that this was not the outcome they had wished, but the monks may have felt they had few options. The men who had complained to the abbot did, however, get certain concessions: they were declared to be free, with no "servitude" owed to the viscount, even if they were subject to his justice. As monastic advocate, he was supposed to protect and defend the monks' men, the abbot specified. This example then shows both the difficulties peasants might have dealing with a local strongman and their ability to lessen these difficulties, at least potentially, by appeal to a higher authority.

And sometimes the higher authority was not even the peasants' ultimate landlord but rather the diocesan bishop, to whom both peasants and their landlord might turn for help. In an example from the Auxerrois at the beginning of the twelfth century, a group of villagers (*homines* and *habitatores*),

---

17. *The Cartulary of Montier-en-Der*, pp. 294–96, no. 150.
18. *The Cartulary of Montier-en-Der*, pp. 136–38, no. 43.

tenants of a monastery, joined with the monks in complaining to the bishop
of Auxerre about a local lord. Here, by joining forces, monks and peasants
were more effective than either group would have been alone. According to
their complaint, Lord Itier of Toucy had been both committing crimes and
extorting unjust dues from the villagers, abuses that to them had little distinction. Their hope that the bishop, the chief moral authority in the region,
would side with them was well placed, for the bishop ordered the lord to stop
demanding the taille, to end what was characterized as kidnapping, arson,
and thefts, to cease requiring that the villagers provide him with wooden
chests and stools, to stop demanding to be put up in houses belonging to
the monastery, and to give up his insistence that villagers be judged in his
own court.[19] Having three powerful authorities over them, the bishop, the
monks, and Lord Itier, was an advantage for the villagers, because they could
maneuver to pit one against the other. A monastery did not want a local castellan making demands on its peasants, and the bishop was the person best
positioned to make such abuses stop.

In another example where peasants were able to use one lord against
another, in the middle of the eleventh century the men of several villages of
the Jura (county of Burgundy) managed to free themselves from what the
attesting document called "unjust" obligations.[20] In this case the villagers,
here called simply *homines*, were considered to be the men of the monastery
of Romainmôtier, but they were also said to be subject to the *bannum* of
Lord Amalric of Joux, located much closer to them than was the monastery. The castle of Joux (both then and now) commands the narrow gorge
that is one of the few ready routes through the Jura mountains, connecting
with the route over the Great Saint Bernard pass, one of the most important
connections between medieval France and Italy. To maintain the gorge as a
usable route, fairly constant maintenance was required, and Lord Amalric
said that he and his three predecessors had all required the men of the neighboring villages to "dig out and restore" it whenever it needed excavating and
rebuilding.

This kind of road work was doubtless the most onerous obligation that
Amalric put on the men, but it was not the only one. In addition, they were
expected to help track down brigands (*latrones*) and help construct new roads
into the adjacent forest. If they did not do so, they were required to make
amends to the lord of Joux. Even though Romainmôtier considered these

---

19. *Cartulaire général de l'Yonne*, 1:221, no. 117.
20. *Le cartulaire de Romainmôtier (XIIe siècle)*, ed. Alexandre Pahud, Cahiers lausannois d'histoire
médiévale 21 (Lausanne, 1998), pp. 134–37, no. 35.

villagers the monastery's men, since they lived in the region of Joux they fell under the *bannum* of the region's lord, which was why he and his predecessors had been demanding and receiving the unpaid labor that he now renounced under the title of "unjust customs."

The settlement was reached in the court of the archbishop of Besançon, acting in accord with the count of Burgundy, clearly a highly powerful pair of individuals. Before them, Lord Amalric detailed and repudiated the work he had required the villagers to perform. Strikingly, the document did not say that the monastery of Romainmôtier itself had appealed to the archbishop. Indeed, the monks' prior (the house was a Cluniac priory) was absent from the proceedings; the villages were situated a sizeable distance from the monastery, which is located over the modern border from France into Switzerland. Rather, the document, even though it was copied into the monks' twelfth-century cartulary, suggests that it was the villagers themselves who had argued that they were being treated unjustly.

Most likely they had made their case to the count, for the count paid Lord Amalric five pounds in recognition of his renunciation of his demands on the villagers. The prior of one of Romainmôtier's dependent houses also gave him five pounds. One can see why this prior and the archbishop, as churchmen, would see a lessening of secular demands on a monastery's men as appropriate, but it is harder to see why the count would have played such a central role unless he himself had been approached by the peasants involved.

This suggestion is given further likelihood by the detail that the count guaranteed to Lord Amalric that he would "receive justice" if the men of the villages in question attacked the men of Joux. Amalric himself was a dependent of the count, so the peasants had found exactly the right person to help them against him. Because they were supposed to be the men of Romainmôtier, they could be sure of the archbishop being at least potentially interested. By complaining to their banal lord's lord, they were able to persuade Amalric to give up demands that had apparently been made for several generations and that must have been quite valuable. Behind the text of an agreement in which Amalric detailed banal rights he was now renouncing, one can glimpse the initiative of peasants who could use one lord against another.

Although the prior of Romainmôtier was not directly involved in this settlement, he did become involved two or three decades later, when Lord Amalric attempted once again to force the nearby peasants to work rebuilding his road through the gorge. This time the prior objected to this unjust claim (*calumnia*), ordering Amalric to cease and showing him the earlier charter attesting to his agreement. Undeterred, Amalric insisted he would never back down unless the prior would prove him wrong in a duel. Such an undertaking would have been highly irregular, and the duel never took place—Amalric's friends talked him out of it, after extensive discussion. Instead, the prior gave Amalric forty solidi (that is, two pounds), and he declared himself satisfied.[21] (His acceptance of this relatively small monetary settlement suggests he realized he was in the wrong demanding the prior submit to a duel.) The attesting charter is quite short in this case, so it is harder to see to what extent the peasants themselves may have rallied support from the powerful. But there can be no doubt that both the prior of Romainmôtier and the count of Burgundy, who witnessed the agreement, had intervened to protect the peasants. Their motivation might have been concern for their own position of authority or even animus against Lord Amalric, rather than disinterested concern for peasant welfare, but from the point of view of men no longer being forced to provide unpaid road work, the result was the same.

Drawing the peasants' lord into a quarrel could make him advocate for them in court. For example, in 1202 the *homines* of the village of Fouchères, near Sens, became involved in a dispute with the monks of St.-Jean of Sens.[22] They had extended their fields into the neighboring territory (*territorium*) of Villebras, where it appears that some of the land was cultivated on behalf of the monastery. The monks felt aggrieved by this incursion and raised a complaint. The peasants' lord, Milo of Pougy, came to their assistance. He negotiated with the monks to allow the men currently cultivating fields at Villebras to continue to do so, although no additional people would be allowed without the abbot's explicit permission. In return, he said, his men would go to St.-Jean to settle their quarrels and have the abbot supervise the sale of their produce. In addition, the peasants would pay a rent of two solidi and an obol for each arpent of land they cultivated there, every year on the feast of Saint Remigius. The monks' representative would also be the first at harvest time, counting out the sheaves (*gerbas*) that would go to the monastery before the peasants could collect their own grain. The abbot did, however, promise safe passage of the peasants' harvest back from the fields.

Milo of Pougy not only negotiated the settlement of the *controversia* but drew up the attesting document, sealed it himself, and had his wife Isabelle formally agree. A quick reading of his charter might suggest that he and the monks decided between them what the local peasants were allowed to do. But to do so would overlook several key details, including that all the

21. *Le cartulaire de Romainmôtier*, pp. 137–38, no. 36.

22. *Recueil de pièces pour faire suite au Cartulaire général de l'Yonne*, ed. Maximilien Quantin (Auxerre, 1873), pp. 6–7, no. 15.

indications are that the men of Fouchères had started expanding their fields and raising grain on land not theirs due to their own initiative, and that, after what the charter suggests was a fairly long time, their lord was able to negotiate their right to continue to do so, paying only a fairly minimal rent. Milo himself wanted to present himself as a good lord to his peasants, and he does not appear to have gained anything from the settlement, other than carrying out what he himself most likely and the peasants doubtless considered his responsibility, protecting and supporting them.

As this case shows, sometimes peasants took the initiative, proceeding as they wished, and defending themselves later. The modern phrase comes to mind: It is easier to seek forgiveness than permission. In another example from the early thirteenth century, the villagers of Sacy, near Auxerre, decided to cut down a woods and plant crops. The monks of the Cistercian house of Reigny were distraught when they discovered this, because they had been enjoying woods usage, gathering firewood, cutting timber for building, pasturing their herds, and doubtless collecting nuts, honey, berries, and the like.[23] Although the woods was not the monks', they had been granted usage rights there by the lord whose land it was. The abbot immediately attempted to take the villagers to court, arguing that he acted out of authority delegated to him by apostolic authority, already an indication of how seriously a monastery had to take peasants.[24]

But the peasants did not easily accept that they were at fault. When the quarrel was finally ended by compromise in 1220, a compromise reached before Bishop Henry of Auxerre, the bishop said that the settlement had required a great deal of both time and money. The peasants agreed to pay compensation, but they could keep the land they had cleared, and the monks allowed them to clear some additional land belonging to the monastery, on the condition that the monks could pasture their animals there (presumably after harvest). Although the bishop's charter spoke of a compromise, the villagers of Sacy had indubitably prevailed. They had in essence compelled the monks to sell them some cropland, both the land they had cleared for planting and some additional land, after having stubbornly resisted making any sort of payment to the monastery. From the monks' point of view, continuing to fight the peasants was more effort than it was worth.

Sometimes peasants were able to fight back unaided against what they considered unjust impositions, reaching a resolution without even having to

---

23. A twelfth-century grant of woods usage in this region to the monks of Reigny specifically mentioned the house pasturing their flocks there; *Cartulaire général de l'Yonne*, 2:61–62, no. 57.

24. *Recueil de pièces pour faire suite au Cartulaire général de l'Yonne*, p. 106, no. 240.

wait for a sympathetic court. An example is provided by a charter from Bèze, where around 1145 the lord of Tilchâtel claimed a *homo* dependent on the monastery, whom the charter called "a man of Saint Peter." The man, named Aldric, put up his own defense. The lord of Tilchâtel, located less than ten kilometers from the monastery, argued that after Aldric's brother died, Aldric had taken up the brother's money and property, including a mansus subject to the lord. Aldric argued on the contrary that he had never lived there nor taken his brother's money. His stubbornness ultimately prevailed. The case was settled through mediation, after Aldric gave the lord four pounds and ten solidi. The lord's wife was sought out separately; she agreed to the "peace" that had been established between her husband and Aldric.[25]

The case is now known because the settlement was written up in a document copied into Bèze's cartulary, but it is noteworthy that the monks were not the principal actors in keeping Aldric and his service for themselves. The document said this agreement was reached with the mediation of wise men, but it is striking that there was no judicial ruling. Rather, Aldric himself, to whom the document attributes the settlement, took matters into his own hands, finding a compromise that would leave both the monks and the lord of Tilchâtel satisfied, and himself the man of Saint Peter, a status he clearly preferred to being a castellan's man.

Aldric's initiative was far from unusual. In an earlier case where peasants took matters into their own hands, three serfs of the Touraine claimed in the second half of the eleventh century that they ought to have a share in their grandparents' inheritance of land, houses, and vineyards, held from Marmoutier. The monks refused, even though their grandparents had been serfs of Marmoutier, because they, due to their mother's marriage to a serf of the count of Anjou, were considered Angevin serfs.[26] The case stretched out over some years, as the brothers Hilduin, Gui, and Herbert initially brought a formal case against the abbot of Marmoutier for what they felt was their rightful property, and then, when he rejected their case, threatened the monks with violence (*violentia*), to be administered by Fulk, count of Anjou.

First, however, they had to persuade Fulk to interfere on their behalf. He held a court with his faithful men and ruled that Hilduin, Gui, and Herbert were *his* serfs, thus not entitled to hold property that would have marked

---

25. *The Cartulary-Chronicle of Bèze*, pp. 376–77, no. 327.

26. *Le livre des serfs*, pp. 108–10, no. 116. See also Fouracre, "Marmoutier and Its Serfs," pp. 39–41. Fouracre discusses the tense relations between the count and the monastery at the time, which this case surely complicated.

them as serfs of Marmoutier. The three told Fulk brusquely that if he would not seek justice on their behalf they would do so themselves. The count did eventually request the abbot to give his serfs a share of the inheritance but was rebuffed. Not dissuaded, the three brothers went back to the monastery, where a new abbot had been elected. According to the account in Marmoutier's cartulary, they tried a series of complaints and claims without success, until finally the abbot, to restore peace (*pax*), gave them fifteen pounds of silver and accepted them into the monastery's spiritual "benefits and society." The three brothers agreed not to bring any more claims, in a formal process before many witnesses in the monks' chapter house. Count Fulk himself attended and promised that he would expel them from his lands and castellanies if they tried to reopen the quarrel.

Here the three serfs making their claim acted at their own initiative, eventually with partial success, even though they never did obtain any of their grandparents' property. The account of the quarrel in the cartulary gives the family the dignity of a history, with individuals named. The fifteen pounds of silver and the spiritual benefits of being associated with Marmoutier were significant prizes. In the meantime, the process had indicated that serfs had inheritance rights—the brothers' cousins inherited without any problem— and that they and their claims had enough validity to gain them formal hearings in both the monks' and the count's courts and even the count's reluctant assistance. They sought what they considered rightfully theirs, and even though they did not reach their ultimate objective, everyone around them, both secular and lay, had to take them seriously.

Peasants could and did go to court to defend themselves against others of their own status as well as against the powerful. A striking example from Bèze in the first decades of the twelfth century indicates that being a dependent of a sympathetic lord could be a true advantage in these cases as well. One Peter of Pouilly was a dependent of the monastery, as indicated by the fact that when he decided to marry, the woman was formally donated to the monks to serve them as Peter did, as *Sancti Petri femina*, even though the donation charter specified that she would remain free (*libera*). When Peter's brother Aldo demanded a share of the market stall Peter controlled, insisting that it had been their father's and he was entitled to a share, Peter insisted instead that his father had given him the entire market stall at the time of his marriage. The case was settled by the abbot of Bèze, before his monks. Peter brought with him as witnesses both his mother and two officers of the monastery. Although Abbot Girard surely tried to rule fairly, it is not surprising that he decided in favor of Peter, a man of Saint Peter. Aldo not only lost and had to provide oath-helpers, he had to pay his brother thirty pounds in damages.[27] In this case having a lord whom Peter of Pouilly served meant that he had access to a definitive and positive ruling, which he might not have had if merely working for himself. Men in positions like this were able to turn the disadvantages of a lack of independence to their advantage at least some of the time.

Peasants' Failed Cases

Above I have given a series of examples where the peasants prevailed. They cannot have always done so, but the point is that they should be seen as people with the desire and capability to fight back against oppression using more than passive resistance. Even records of failed cases that peasants brought to court indicate their ability to press for what they considered rightfully theirs. When the powerful who managed to defeat peasants in such a case recorded their triumph in a charter, they clearly wanted a permanent record. This was especially true if they had the charter copied into a cartulary. For powerful lords or churchmen, prevailing in court was not a preordained outcome. They needed a record because they recognized that, without it, the peasants might well press their case again.

A complicated case of this sort arose in the middle of the twelfth century at the village of Bligny, near Autun.[28] Two members of the cathedral chapter of Autun had received a regular income from the village, administered by the village mayor, a man named Walter, and by Gui, the dean of nearby Vic. Mayor Walter presents an example of the great variety of sorts of people who might now be referred to as peasants. He clearly was more than a simple *rusticus*. He had most likely been appointed mayor by the cathedral canons as their agent. But his interest and sympathies clearly lay with the villagers, not with the canons.

The attesting charter records that, at least according to the canons, they had agreed with Mayor Walter that he would collect sixty solidi in rent from the village for them, of which he could keep five. He argued that even if he could not collect the full sixty, he was still entitled to his five. The canons disagreed, specifying that if overall rents declined, so should his share, and that all he was entitled to was one penny out of every solidus collected (there were twelve pennies in a solidus). So far this might appear like an agent for the more powerful just looking out for himself, but there are also clear signs that he was much closer to the villagers than to the churchmen of Autun.

---

27. *The Cartulary-Chronicle of Bèze*, pp. 368–69, nos. 319–20.

28. *Cartulaire de l'église d'Autun*, ed. A[natole] de Charmasse (Paris, 1865), pp. 98–99, no. 2.13.

The diminishing rents from the village seem suspicious at a time of rapid economic growth, especially as the charter mentions people from outside moving to Bligny and not being subject to the canons, suggesting population growth. Even more notably, Walter flatly denied that the villagers of Bligny owed any wine to the canons, even though the latter insisted that this had been legally established and that he was supposed to collect it. He, backed up by the dean of Vic, gave every sign of seeking to reduce the dues of the villagers.

The case quickly became extremely messy. According to the canons' indignant account, Walter said he could settle the question without any representatives sent by the canons, because he himself was acting with their authority. He further said that newcomers to Bligny would be heard in his court, not the canons', and also denied that the latter had any right to pasturage or hay in Bligny. The dean of Vic additionally complicated the case by asserting that he alone could decide which of the fields at Bligny could be cultivated for the canons' own food; the canons said that the dean's father, who had presumably preceded him in office, had asserted the same thing but had peacefully yielded his claim. Walter, the charter added, had not been paying any rent for his house, even though he was supposed to pay two pennies a year. A day for a hearing before the entire cathedral chapter was finally set, with the intention of settling the case. But the charter closed with the rather self-satisfied statement that the witnesses were all there, the canons were ready to present their evidence, but the mayor and dean did not appear.

By not appearing they lost their case, but the point should not merely be that they lost. They had asserted rights it seems fairly clear they did not have, and their assertions had to be taken seriously. They had been invited to prove their contentions before the canons for whom they theoretically worked. The charter, drawn up by the triumphant canons, implies that Walter and Gui had very weak claims from the beginning, but clearly these could not be summarily dismissed. Lower-status people like these could still expect to be heard if they raised plausible objections to what was expected of them. There is no sign that Walter and Gui were punished for attempting to claim more for themselves than the canons believed they were owed, even though they skipped the formal hearing on their case rather than try to support claims they would have known were unsupportable. They ultimately had to accept their obligations, however grudgingly, but the point should be that they felt it worth a try to assert what they wanted. They certainly had the ability to attempt it.

For it was not always easy to prevail against determined peasants in court, as is demonstrated by a case between the religious house of Dilo, near Sens, and the local peasantry.[29] In the 1180s the canons of Dilo protested that the peasants of nearby Vaudeurs were using a road that ran along a valley next to their grange, and that this was harmful to them and their enterprise. The archbishop and the abbot of St.-Remi of Reims were called in to settle the quarrel and ruled in favor of Dilo. That the case reached the level of the archbishop's court indicates that it was impossible simply to dismiss the claims of determined peasants without strong support from the most important ecclesiastical figure of the region.

And even that was not enough, for the men of Vaudeurs continued using the road, to the distress of the canons of Dilo, presumably because it was the most direct and easiest route for them. For close to twenty years they continued to "molest" the canons' grange, as the attesting charter put it. The archbishop's *officialis* threatened the men with excommunication, but even this sanction had no immediate effect. Finally the peasants came to the archbishop's court, asking to be freed from excommunication and offering to settle with the canons of Dilo, but this was not surrender. They mounted their own complaint, saying that they had always used this road, and insisted that the case be judged by four "wise men," to whom all sides gave the authority to make a decision, including the now-retired abbot of St.-Remi who had ruled against the peasants in the first place. The judges ruled in favor of the peasants but concluded that they should pay four pounds a year in amends for the damage to the canons' grange. This settlement lasted for only a few months, however, for the peasants decided that they did not want to pay the four pounds and promised the canons that they would find other roads to use if they did not have to pay.

But even now the dispute was not settled. Fifteen men from the village of Vaudeurs, including the mayor, swore to the canons that they would not use the disputed road again, but it quickly became clear that there was no other road that would take them where they needed to go without crossing at least some of Dilo's land. Rather than going back to the archbishop's court, or the judgment of the four "wise men," the peasants negotiated their own settlement with the canons, still accepting that they would not use the main, disputed road but finding a compromise on the other available routes. All parties agreed that if the men and their animals damaged Dilo's land or crops while using the side roads they should pay amends.

The amounts were specified depending on the damage, from eighteen pennies up to a few solidi, certainly less than the four pounds a year the villagers had found too burdensome. The inhabitants of Vaudeurs were not

---

29. *Recueil de pièces pour faire suite au Cartulaire général de l'Yonne*, pp. 16–17, no. 24.

able to continue to use the road through the valley that they clearly preferred, as evidence their resistance to finding other routes even when excommunicated. But this loss was not a humiliation. Eventually they were able
themselves to negotiate a mutually acceptable agreement with the canons of
Dilo, allowing them to travel and move both produce and their herds, paying
only if some specific (and presumably avoidable) damage ensued.

Here one could say that the peasants had ultimately lost, because they
never did gain clear access to the road they preferred, but the real point is that
even a case recorded in a church's cartulary as a win over its tenants, those
tenants had negotiated their way to a better situation. Not even the most
powerful churchmen of the diocese of Sens were able simply to impose their
will. It was impossible even for the powerful to ignore peasants or to force
them into subjugation.

A case from Clairvaux where the peasants lost nonetheless demonstrates
their ability to advocate for themselves, even before the most important lords
of the region. The men (*homines*) of Longchamp had been insisting that they
had usage rights at Perrecin, which would have included such activities as
pasturing and wood gathering. The monks of Clairvaux, however, did not
recognize any such rights. This conflict (*querela*) was brought in 1150 before
Henry, count of Bar-sur-Aube and future count of Champagne.[30] Henry
ruled summarily against the men who had been, according to the monks,
encroaching on their land. He ordered that the men of Longchamp never
raise the issue again and indeed that their heirs were not to do so either.[31]

This might appear merely as an example of the powerful (here the monastery of Clairvaux) forcing local peasants to give up something to which
they had thought they were entitled. But it is important that the monks
could not simply forbid the peasants their *usuarium*—rights to pasture and
gather wood. They had to bring in Henry, the most important secular lord
of the region, to get a definitive ruling, and Henry's decision was witnessed
by other regional lords, including the count of Reynel. Far from having no
recourse but to yield, the men of Longchamp were persistent enough to
require a ruling by the greatest secular power the monks could muster before
their ultimate loss.[32] The ability to be heard in the count's court shows that

---

30. For Henry, see Theodore Evergates, *Henry the Liberal: Count of Champagne, 1127–1181*
(Philadelphia, 2016).

31. *Recueil des chartes de l'abbaye de Clairvaux*, ed. Jean Waquet et al. (Troyes, 1950–82), pp. 46–47,
no. 20.

32. Usage rights at Perrecin must have been highly desirable. Some twenty years later the bishop
of Langres announced that two brothers, whose status is not given but who were presumably also

these men could not be simply overruled or disregarded. In other circumstances, they might have won, and the monks knew it.

In yet another case where peasant claims were adjudicated up to the highest regional authorities, the monks of Pontigny complained in 1200 that the *homines* living in certain villages along the Serein River, on the far bank from the monastery, had been improperly crossing the river and taking timber and other forest products from the monks' woods. The case was adjudicated by the bishop of Paris and by the royal constable, after the monks had the countess of Vermandois bring their complaint forward.[33] This was a major court case; the countess produced seven witnesses and the monks five more. In addition, the monks produced an earlier charter of Count William of Nevers attesting that no one from those villages had any usage rights in those woods. The peasants produced no witnesses; perhaps they were not expected to do so, in a case that seemed predetermined to go against them. Yet an assertion of a monopoly in the woods, as the monks put forward here, was not enough by itself if the local peasantry found violating that monopoly advantageous to themselves. Even though the peasants in this case were ruled against, their position was strong enough that it took a number of highly placed secular and ecclesiastical leaders to make them concede. One may perhaps doubt how effectively the ruling could be enforced.

An early thirteenth-century case settled before the king similarly indicates that peasants did not necessarily lose just because they were the weaker party; rather, they were able to have their complaints heard in court, even the highest court in the kingdom.[34] The quarrel had arisen between the cathedral chapter of Auxerre and their men (*homines*) at Merry and Eglény, two nearby villages, and involved the chapter's imposition of an arbitrary taille (*tallia*), as opposed to normal rents and customary dues. The villagers agreed in the settlement before the king that they would pay the taille, but only under certain circumstances. The chapter had, it seems, been imposing it whenever they needed a little extra money, and the villagers had strenuously objected.

They were willing to pay the taille, the villagers said, if the chapter hosted the king himself or the pope, or if it was needed for defense of the realm. This, they said, was long practice. But where they objected was the chapter trying to raise money if they decided to purchase something for their own use. According to the agreement overseen by the king, if the chapter wished

---

peasants, gave up long-standing and highly disputed claims to *usuagium* in the woods there; *Recueil des chartes de Clairvaux*, p. 156, no. 146.

 33. *Recueil de pièces pour faire suite au Cartulaire général de l'Yonne*, p. 3, no. 6.

 34. *Recueil de pièces pour faire suite au Cartulaire général de l'Yonne*, pp. 45–46, no. 101.

to buy something with a price below one hundred pounds, they would not impose a taille to help pay for it. Only if they planned to buy something more expensive would they be able to do so, and in this case the dean would appoint four cathedral canons to investigate the price, try to negotiate it down, and swear that they would use money raised through the taille solely for this particular purchase. The villagers thus would still be subject to some arbitrary levies, but the chapter would have to go to extraordinary lengths to prove that such levies were justified.

The cathedral chapter had gone to Paris to have the king formally rule for them, but it is crucial to note that this royal ruling, presumably confirming an agreement that the principals had worked out themselves, was not a clear win for the canons. Their ability to raise money from their tenants in these villages was limited in this agreement. That they accepted these limits, and treated the decision as a win worth having the king confirm, indicates that they realized they could not simply force their will on their tenants. Without the agreement over how and when they could levy the taille, they might have been unable to force their *homines* to pay it at all. It is also worth noting that some of the peasants appear to have actually gone to Paris, because King Philip said that the agreement had been reached before him, and his chamberlain recorded their words. When a powerful and wealthy cathedral chapter needed the king to confirm that they could still levy the taille, and when the peasants paying the taille could stand before the king and gain limitations on their required payments, one must recognize the reality of peasant agency.

Peasants as Legitimate Witnesses

The ability of peasants to be heard in court is indicative of those courts' willingness to take their testimony as credible and serious. In resolving disputes even among the powerful, the word of peasants could be decisive. During the 1140s Lord Gaucher of Salins attempted to claim a *femina* named Pontia as in servitude to him. His claim is known because she was, as it turned out, actually the *femina* of the Cluniac house of Romainmôtier, and the monks recorded the end of the quarrel in two separate charters in their cartulary.[35] But Lord Gaucher was forced to give up what the charters called an unjust claim not merely due to ecclesiastical pressure. Pontia herself, identified by the names of her parents as well as her husband, played a central role in disputing these claims, as did her husband and her natal family.

---

35. *Le cartulaire de Romainmôtier*, pp. 173, 176–77, nos. 64, 66.

Lord Gaucher is recorded as having recognized that she was a dependent of Romainmôtier, not his, because of the testimony (*testimonio*) of her blood relatives (*consanguinei*). Pontia's husband Lambert seems to have organized the oaths of her brothers or cousins, who were individually named. Even though these relatives can barely have escaped from servitude themselves—Pontia was referred to at one point as a handmaiden (*ancilla*) of St.-Pierre of Romainmôtier—their testimony was crucial in resolving the quarrel. Their oaths were delivered before the count of Burgundy and several of the other most powerful lords of the Jura. Pontia and her family were able to avoid becoming subject to one of the most important men of the region not only because their (preferred) lord was a highly respected monastery, but because they themselves were able to swear and have their testimony accepted.

Peasants were especially valuable as witnesses when landlords needed to determine where borders between property lay. They not only knew, but they could swear to it in court. Those who lived on the land and worked the fields had to have a detailed knowledge of where one person's land stopped and another's started. Both lay nobles and church leaders respected peasant knowledge of such matters. Indeed, because peasants were by far the most numerous part of the rural population, the powerful had little choice but to respect their memories and perceptions when there were no written records on which to rely.

In one significant case, the monks of the Cistercian house La Ferté tried to determine the exact borders of their lands a generation after their monastery was founded.[36] The monks called on the duke of Burgundy and the count of Chalon, successors to the counts who had established the monastery in the first place, to define their borders again. The duke and count called on their provosts, and the provosts in turn asked for help from all the male inhabitants of the closest villages (*homines vicinarum villarum*). Only with their testimony and memory of how the borders had originally been laid out were the monks able to designate exactly what was and was not their land—in this case clearly needing the insights peasants could provide. Not only was peasant testimony allowed in court, here it was sought. The powerful may have looked down on the poor and less powerful, as has indeed always been the case, but they needed the peasants, sometimes for their testimony as well as their labor.

For the modern reader, one of the most striking aspects of the charters that record instances of peasant agency is how normal the scribes found it. No

---

36. *Recueil des pancartes de La Ferté*, pp. 90–91, no. 82.

one expressed surprise or shock that peasants should move from one village to another, clear new crop land with or without permission, choose their own marriage partner, try to negotiate their way out of serfdom or out of arbitrary dues, and insist that their grievances be heard. The peasants seemed accomplished at maneuvering between different powerful people, able to use one against another.

Indeed, when confronting a hierarchy schooled in the Christian tradition, their very political and economic weakness could become a tool. When the Catalan peasants complained to the count-king about their castellan lords, speaking with "tormented voices," they were assured of a hearing. They were not assured of success, but those in power would at least feel compelled to hear them. Peasants could take their grievances to a court, whether the local bishop's, a count or duke's, even sometimes the king's. In court peasants might give testimony on their own behalf, even offer to prove a point through the ordeal. Their testimony was indeed sought out as highly valued when great landowners were disputing where borders might lie, because their knowledge of the land was respected.

Of course peasants did not always win their cases. But then neither did the powerful. Even when they lost, the charters that recorded the outcome made sure to insist that the case should not arise again, often accompanied by curses—because everyone knew that the peasants were always capable of new claims and assertions. These claims were most successful when, as became increasingly common, they pitted the powerful against each other or worked together collectively. Whether stubbornly and quietly resisting or noisily arguing in court, peasants had to be respected and taken seriously. And much of the time the powerful showed that respect by letting them alone to pursue their own activities.

Conclusion

The preceding chapters have included a great many examples of peasants negotiating for better conditions, demanding what they believed to be theirs, and maneuvering between the demands of different lords. The evidence is necessarily uneven, since few peasants of the high Middle Ages appear in the surviving sources. But both the number and the variety of examples I have been able to assemble across just one region of France make clear that peasants then exercised self-determination and actively resisted oppressive treatment.

In spite of a great deal of excellent scholarship over the last hundred years on the rural economy and society, medieval peasants still often appear to inhabit an unchanging world in many a popular work or textbook: living in a hut in a village clustered around a castle (or at least a large manor house), forced to show obedience to their lord at all times and compelled to pay him a heavy rent in labor and produce. The male serfs are seen heading out to the manor's field with their oxen every morning, the women sewing or dairying or performing other feminine chores for the manor. This is the world of the fictionalized peasant Bodo that Eileen Power created a century ago, in turn based heavily on Charlemagne's "Capitulare de villis."

But high medieval peasants were not ninth-century peasants any more than they were the rebels against servitude of the fourteenth century. There were far more villages than castles in late twelfth-century France, many of them self-governing "new towns" where the lord was distant if there was a lord at all. Peasant rents could be negotiated in the high Middle Ages, at least at significant transition points, and those plowing with oxen were not termed serfs. In long-established villages as well as the newly created ones, the records show peasants who were neither passive nor helpless.

The peasants discussed in the preceding chapters were unusual *because* they appeared in the documents; they did *not* appear in the documents because they were unusual. That is, if not typical in having their deeds recorded on parchment, there is nothing inherently distinctive about these peasants. They sought to better themselves, they felt aggrieved when they were treated unfairly by the more powerful, and they tried to find ways to improve their situation. When these acts were recorded, they were treated as entirely normal. The spottiness of peasants' appearance in the documents may well owe more to the scribes who did—or did not—find these peasants' actions worth recording than it does to what the peasants were actually doing. Further study of records from other regions should similarly reveal a great many examples of peasant initiative and independent action.

Spotty or not, the documents portray people who were essential to the functioning of the society and economy of high medieval France—and, crucially, were understood by elites to be essential. Aristocrats might look down on them, even mock them for their poverty and lack of sophistication, but they could never ignore the peasantry. These men and women were neither expendable nor interchangeable. When they appear in the records, it is almost always as individuals, with names, with family connections, and with personal histories. That many monasteries routinely found it necessary to record in writing their agreements with their peasant tenants—and that Marmoutier created a whole cartulary specifically to record their interactions with their serfs—underscores these people's importance.

The peasantry was far from uniform: some were farmers and others artisans, some bound by legal servitude and others completely free, some destitute yet others wealthy enough to have serfs of their own. They were capable of improving their status as they saw it, making themselves serfs of a church in some eleventh-century cases, or buying their liberty if servile. A few might rise to become provost for a monastery or mayor of a village, even though most could never aspire to a position of authority. Even within the same village, different individuals or different family members would be expected to owe different amounts of rents and dues. One cannot take the requirements spelled out for one individual or family or for one village and assume they were normative.

In spite of this diversity, medieval peasants recognized that collective action would often be necessary in opposing the powerful. They were entirely capable of organizing themselves, whether in creating a commune, adopting the Customs of Lorris, raising money to buy their way out of onerous dues, building a village church, or complaining to a court that they were being downtrodden. Especially at turning points, such as a fire or a transfer of lordship from a layman to a church, peasants could renegotiate their obligations. Here, as in many other instances in which they worked to better their position, they found ways to bargain with the more powerful, whether by stubborn resistance, buying their way out of arbitrary requirements, or playing one lord off against another. They found many more options to affect their situation than the foot-dragging, false compliance, or pilfering available to modern subjected peoples. As the chronicler of Vézelay put it in horrified tones, they intended to negotiate with the powerful as equals.

Peasants themselves may not have been powerful, but they were certainly not powerless. They may have sometimes been treated harshly, but the records describing abuses such as the seizure of peasant property or the infliction of physical violence called these shocking and unheard-of (*inaudita*) acts of cruelty, carried out by godless men who had violated the social order and deserved severe punishment. Such depredations were neither common nor broadly accepted in high medieval France. It would be a mistake to take peasant complaints of gross mistreatment in the records as routine, as such complaints were designed to elicit sympathy and concern. They are indicative of peasant strategies to maneuver their lords into seeing the peasants' enemies as also theirs. Their daily life was extremely difficult, but it was not hopeless.

Even without support from among the local elite, peasants could and did bring their grievances to the attention of high office holders and regional courts. No one seemed to find it odd for peasants to bring their cases to court, and it was assumed that they could swear oaths either for themselves or as witnesses, or even volunteer to undertake trial by ordeal. Although they were never assured of victory, there were plenty of examples in which they triumphed. Their very weakness inspired powerful aristocrats and church leaders, who liked to present themselves as defenders of the poor and the weak, to take up their case.

French peasants of the high Middle Ages are found in the records choosing their own spouses, inheriting from family members, and opening up new lands to agriculture, and the scribes who wrote charters attesting to important transactions took it for granted that these were normal activities. Peasants appear in the sources as (at least irregular) churchgoers, who considered close association with a monastery an advantage. They might even, as *conversi*, join the new monastic orders themselves, as the brothers who did all the heavy work, and a few actually became priests. Some peasants were also of course capable of mocking ecclesiastics or trying to steal the offering, but nothing in the records suggests any actions worse than those of the multitude of knights found in every monastic cartulary, trying to appropriate the monks' property or carry out harmful projects. The peasant version of religion was by necessity simpler than that of the better educated, but it was neither pagan nor, by medieval standards, superstitious.

It is well known that the high Middle Ages were a time of rapid economic growth, and the peasantry were the driving force behind it. Much has been made of technological improvements: better plows, windmills, drainage, and crop rotation. It is understood that urban growth was only possible when the rural population produced enough surplus food to feed the city dwellers. But surely the peasants themselves deserve credit for adopting new techniques, expanding the arable, and finding ways to produce enough to sell their surplus in town. Most appear to have had a landlord, but there were far too many of them in comparison with the elites for the landlords to have directed them all in finding new ways to grow more and better crops—especially as there are many examples of landlords finding out after the fact what their tenants had been doing. The scores of "new towns" scattered across northern France were sites where the peasants organized themselves, where a mayor or provost might answer to a distant landlord but all important decisions had to be made locally.

The documents sharply undercut the assumption of some historians that the expansion of the economy in the eleventh and twelfth centuries was accompanied by a new, harsher subjection of the peasantry. Rather, the records suggest that the peasants found this a time of new opportunity. If the high Middle Ages did see the emergence of more oppressive lordship, it also witnessed peasants, perhaps in reaction, working actively and often successfully to better their condition. The same peasant initiative recorded in documents attesting that a woman had formally agreed that she was subject to someone new, or that a couple had established that they were free and not serfs, or that a group of villagers had freed themselves from *mainmorte*, should be credited with the improved agricultural economy of their time. It was the labor of peasants, labor they themselves readily undertook as providing significant advantages for themselves, that made possible the flowering of the high Middle Ages.

Is the picture I have presented here too sunny? I do not believe so. Scholars from Georges Duby to Thomas Bisson have expressed entirely appropriate sympathy for those whose lives, by our standards and even by theirs, were often "nasty, brutish, and short" (to misappropriate Hobbes). But to treat medieval peasants only as victims does them a serious disservice. They opened up new agricultural lands and entered into complicated agreements on the dues this land would pay. They negotiated, they fought back. Sometimes they lost in spite of their best efforts. Sometimes they lost even before a contest began. But there was always the possibility of taking action, and we deny them their dignity if we do not take their efforts seriously.

Those who had easy access to the written word, not surprisingly, were those whose records remain. We know much more about the churchmen and powerful lords who had their actions preserved in writing than we do about the vast mass of the illiterate population. But these records also include lower-status people, often playing a significant role in the proceedings. Certainly not all peasants could exercise control over their own lives, but we should not conclude that none did. If one assumes that peasants were marginalized and silent, then the infrequency of their appearance in the records can be taken as proof of this. However, a close reading of the documents in which peasants do appear indicates that they may have been subject to harsh expectations and had a material existence no modern Westerner could tolerate, but they did not accept their position passively. They could and did exercise real agency: negotiating for better conditions, fighting back against whatever they considered overly burdensome, sometimes manipulating even the highest courts into seeing matters from their point of view. The powerful in the high Middle Ages fully recognized this agency. It is time for more of us who study medieval people to do the same.

BIBLIOGRAPHY

Manuscript Sources

Paris, BnF, MS nouv. acq. fr. 8664, documents from La Bussière.

Paris, BnF, MS nouv. acq. fr. 8677, 8680, eighteenth-century copies of documents from Maizières.

Soissons, Bibliothèque municipale, MS 7, thirteenth-century cartulary of Prémontré; available at https://bvmm.irht.cnrs.fr/mirador/index.php.

Vesoul, Archives départementales de la Haute Saône, H 409, documents from Theuley.

Printed Primary Sources

Adalbero of Laon. *Poème au roi Robert*. Ed. Claude Carozzi. Paris, 1979.

Aliscans. Ed. Erich Wienbeck, Wilhelm Hartnacke, and Paul Rasch. Halle, 1903.

Andreas Capellanus. *On Love*. Ed. P. G. Walsh. London, 1982.

Baudri of Dol. "Vita B. Roberti de Arbrissello." PL 162:1043–58.

"Capitulare de villis." MGH Capit. 1 (1883; rpt. 1984), pp. 82–91.

Cartulaire de l'église d'Autun. Ed. A[natole] de Charmasse. Paris, 1865.

Le cartulaire de Marcigny-sur-Loire (1045–1144): Essai de reconstitution d'un manuscrit disparu. Ed. Jean Richard. Dijon, 1957.

Le cartulaire de Romainmôtier (XIIe siècle). Ed. Alexandre Pahud. Cahiers lausannois d'histoire médiévale 21. Lausanne, 1998.

Cartulaire général de l'Yonne. Ed. Maximilien Quantin. 2 vols. Auxerre, 1854–60.

Cartulaires de l'abbaye de Molesme. Ed. Jacques Laurent. Vol. 2, *Texte*. Paris, 1911.

The Cartulary-Chronicle of St.-Pierre of Bèze. Ed. Constance Brittain Bouchard. Medieval Academy Books 116. Toronto, 2019.

The Cartulary of Flavigny, 717–1113. Ed. Constance Brittain Bouchard. Medieval Academy Books 99. Cambridge, Mass., 1991.

The Cartulary of Montier-en-Der, 666–1129. Ed. Constance Brittain Bouchard. Medieval Academy Books 108. Toronto, 2004.

The Cartulary of St.-Marcel-lès-Chalon, 779–1126. Ed. Constance Brittain Bouchard. Medieval Academy Books 102. Cambridge, Mass., 1998.

Chartes de l'abbaye de Saint-Étienne de Dijon de 1155 à 1200. Ed. Georges Valat. Paris, 1907.

Chartes et documents concernant l'abbaye de Cîteaux. Ed. J. Marilier. Rome, 1961.

Cistercian Lay Brothers: Twelfth-Century Usages with Related Texts. Ed. Chrysogonus Waddell. Cîteaux: Commentarii Cistercienses, Studia et Documenta 10. Brecht, Belgium, 2000.

Galbert of Bruges. *Histoire du meurtre de Charles le Bon, comte de Flandre*. Ed. Henri Pirenne. Paris, 1891.

Les gestes des évêques d'Auxerre. Ed. Guy Lobrichon et al. 3 vols. Paris, 2002–9.

Guibert of Nogent. *Autobiographie*. Ed. Edmond-René Labande. Les Classiques de l'histoire de France au moyen âge 34. Paris, 1981.

Lebeuf, Abbé. *Mémoires concernant l'histoire civile et ecclésiastique d'Auxerre et de son ancien diocese*. New ed. by A[mbrose] Challe and M[aximilien] Quantin. Vol. 4, *Recueil de monuments, chartes, titres et autres pièces inédites*. Auxerre, 1855.

Liber miraculorum Sancte Fidis. Ed. Auguste Bouillet. Paris, 1897.

Le livre des serfs de Marmoutier. Ed. André Salmon. Tours, 1864.

"Loi de Beaumont (texte latin inédit)." Ed. H[enri] d'Arbois de Jubainville. *Bibliothèque de l'École des chartes* 12 (1851), 248–56.

Monumenta Vizeliacensia: Textes relatifs à l'histoire de l'abbaye de Vézelay. Ed. R. B. C. Huygens. Corpus Christianorum continuatio mediaevalis 42. Turnhout, 1976.

Le premier cartulaire de l'abbaye cistercienne de Pontigny (XIIe–XIIIe siècles). Ed. Martine Garrigues. Paris, 1981.

Raoul Glaber. *Opera*. Ed. John France et al. Oxford, 1989.

Recueil de pièces pour faire suite au Cartulaire général de l'Yonne. Ed. Maximilien Quantin. Auxerre, 1873.

Recueil des actes de Louis VI, roi de France (1108–1137). Ed. Jean Dufour. 3 vols. Paris, 1992–93.

Recueil des chartes de l'abbaye de Clairvaux. Ed. Jean Waquet et al. Troyes, 1950–82.

Recueil des chartes de l'abbaye de Saint-Benoît-sur-Loire. Ed. Maurice Prou and Alexandre Vidier. Paris, 1890.

Recueil des pancartes de l'abbaye de La Ferté-sur-Grosne, 1113–1178. Ed. Georges Duby. Paris, 1953.

Robert of St.-Marien. *Chronicon*. MGH SS 26:226–87.

Suger. *Vie de Louis VI le Gros*. Ed. Henry Waquet. Paris, 1964.

Three Cartularies from Thirteenth-Century Auxerre. Ed. Constance Brittain Bouchard. Medieval Academy Books 113. Toronto, 2012.

Twelfth-Century Statutes from the Cistercian General Chapter. Ed. Chrysogonus Waddell. Citeaux: Commentarii Cistercienses, Studia et Documenta 12. Brecht, Belgium, 2002.

Walter, Johannes von, ed. *Die ersten Wanderprediger Frankreichs*. 2 vols. Leipzig, 1903–6.

Secondary Sources

I do not include here a few tangential works cited only once or modern translations of medieval sources. If I cite several articles from a volume of collected articles, I here include only the volume itself, leaving the individual articles to the footnotes.

Arnold, Ellen F. *Negotiating the Landscape: Environment and Monastic Identity in the Medieval Ardennes*. Philadelphia, 2013.

Arnold, John H. *Belief and Unbelief in Medieval Europe*. London, 2005.

Arnoux, Mathieu. *Le temps des laboureurs: Travail, ordre social et croissance en Europe (XIe–XIVe siècle)*. Paris, 2012.

Baldwin, John. *The Government of Philip Augustus: Foundations of French Royal Power in the Middle Ages*. Berkeley, 1986.

Barthélemy, Dominique. *The Serf, the Knight, and the Historian*. Trans. Graham Robert Edwards. Ithaca, N.Y., 2009.

Barton, Richard E. *Lordship in the County of Maine, c. 890–1160*. Woodbridge, Suff., 2004.

Bennett, Judith M. *History Matters: Patriarchy and the Challenge of Feminism*. Philadelphia, 2006.

——. *A Medieval Life: Cecelia Penifader and the World of English Peasants before the Plague*. 2nd ed. Philadelphia, 2021.

Berkhofer, Robert F., III. "Marriage, Lordship and the 'Greater Unfree' in Twelfth-Century France." *Past and Present* 173 (2001), 3–27.

Berlow, Rosalind Kent. "Spiritual Immunity at Vézelay (Ninth to Twelfth Centuries)." *Catholic Historical Review* 62 (1976), 573–88.

Bisson, Thomas N. *The Crisis of the Twelfth Century: Power, Lordship, and the Origins of European Government*. Princeton, 2009.

——. *Tormented Voices: Power, Crisis, and Humanity in Rural Catalonia, 1140–1200*. Cambridge, Mass., 1998.

Bloch, Marc. *Les caractères originaux de l'histoire rurale française*. New ed. Paris, 1999; rpt. 2006.

——. *Feudal Society*. Trans. L. A. Manyon. Chicago, 1961.

——. *Slavery and Serfdom in the Middle Ages*. Trans. William R. Beer. Berkeley, 1975.

Bonnassie, Pierre. *From Slavery to Feudalism in South-Western Europe*. Trans. Jean Birrell. Cambridge, 1991.

Bouchard, Constance Brittain. *"Every Valley Shall Be Exalted": The Discourse of Opposites in Twelfth-Century Thought*. Ithaca, N.Y., 2003.

——. *Holy Entrepreneurs: Cistercians, Knights, and Economic Exchange in Twelfth-Century Burgundy*. Ithaca, N.Y., 1991.

——. "Medieval French Peasants: The New Frontier?" *Haskins Society Journal* 30 (2018), 213–30.

——. "Peasants and Polyptyques in the Ninth Century: The Peasant Hermod." *Medieval People* 36 (2022), 1–22.

——. "Restructuring Sanctity and Refiguring Saints in Early Medieval Gaul." In *Studies on Medieval Empathies*, edited by Karl F. Morrison and Rudolph M. Bell, pp. 91–114. Turnhout, 2013.

——. *Rewriting Saints and Ancestors: Memory and Forgetting in France, 500–1200*. Philadelphia, 2015.

——. *Spirituality and Administration: The Role of the Bishop in Twelfth-Century Auxerre*. Speculum Anniversary Monographs 5. Cambridge, Mass., 1979.

——. *"Strong of Body, Brave and Noble": Chivalry and Society in Medieval France*. Ithaca, N.Y., 1998.

——. *Sword, Miter, and Cloister: Nobility and the Church in Burgundy, 980–1198*. Ithaca, N.Y., 1987.

——. "Three Counties, One Lineage, and Eight Heiresses: Nevers, Auxerre, and Tonnerre, Eleventh to Thirteenth Centuries." *Medieval Prosopography* 31 (2016), 25–48.

Bowman, Jeffrey A. *Shifting Landmarks: Property, Proof, and Dispute in Catalonia around the Year 1000*. Ithaca, N.Y., 2004.

Brunel, Ghislain, and Serge Brunet, eds. *Les luttes anti-seigneuriales: Dans l'Europe médiévale et moderne*. Toulouse, 2009.

Burnouf, Joëlle, et al. *Manuel d'archéologie médiévale et moderne*. 2nd ed. Paris, 2020.

Burton, Janet, and Julie Kerr. *The Cistercians in the Middle Ages*. Woodbridge, Suff., 2011.

Campbell, Bruce M. S. *English Seigniorial Agriculture, 1250–1450*. Cambridge, 2000.

Carrier, Nicolas. *La vie montagnarde en Faucigny à la fin du moyen-âge: Économie et société, fin XIIIe – début XVIe siècle*. Paris, 2001.

La charte de Beaumont et les franchises municipales entre Loire et Rhin. Nancy, 1988.

Cooper, Lisa H. "Agronomy and Affect in Duke Humphrey's *On Husbondrie*." *Speculum* 95 (2020), 36–88.

Davis, Adam J. *The Medieval Economy of Salvation: Charity, Commerce, and the Rise of the Hospital*. Ithaca, N.Y., 2019.

Deanesly, Margaret. *A History of the Medieval Church, 590–1500*. 1925; rpt. London, 1989.

Donkin, R. A. *The Cistercians: Studies in the Geography of Medieval England and Wales*. Toronto, 1978.

Dubois, Jacques. "L'institution des convers au XIIe siècle: Forme de vie monastique propre aux laïcs." In *I laici nella "Societas christiana" dei secoli XI et XII*, Miscellanea del Centro di studi medioevali 5, 183–216. Rome, 1968.

Duby, Georges. *The Age of the Cathedrals: Art and Society 980–1420*. Trans. Eleanor Levieux and Barbara Thompson. Chicago, 1981.

——. *Love and Marriage in the Middle Ages*. Trans. Jane Dunnett. Chicago, 1994.

——. *Rural Economy and Country Life in the Medieval West*. Trans. Cynthia Postan. Columbia, S.C., 1968.

——. *La société aux XIe et XIIe siècles dans la région mâconnaise*. 2nd ed. Paris, 1971.

——. *The Three Orders: Feudal Society Imagined*. Trans. Arthur Goldhammer. Chicago, 1980.

Dunbabin, Jean. *France in the Making, 843–1180*. Oxford, 1991.

Epstein, Steven A. *An Economic and Social History of Later Medieval Europe, 1000–1500*. Cambridge, 2009.

Epuresco-Pascovici, Ionut. *Human Agency in Medieval Society, 1100–1450*. Woodbridge, Suff., 2021.

Evergates, Theodore. *Feudal Society in the Bailliage of Troyes under the Counts of Champagne, 1152–1284*. Baltimore, 1975.

——. *Henry the Liberal: Count of Champagne, 1127–1181*. Philadelphia, 2016.

Farmer, Sharon. *Communities of Saint Martin: Legend and Ritual in Medieval Tours*. Ithaca, N.Y., 1991.

——. *Surviving Poverty in Medieval Paris: Gender, Ideology, and the Daily Lives of the Poor*. Ithaca, N.Y., 2002.

Firnhaber-Baker, Justine. "The Social Constituency of the Jacquerie Revolt of 1358." *Speculum* 95 (2020), 689–715.

Fleming, Robin. *Britain after Rome: The Fall and Rise, 400 to 1070*. London, 2010.

——. *The Material Fall of Roman Britain, 300–525 CE*. Philadelphia, 2021.

Fossier, Robert. "Rural Economy and Country Life." In *The New Cambridge Medieval History*, vol. 3, edited by Timothy Reuter, pp. 27–63. Cambridge, 1999.

——. "The Rural Economy and Demographic Growth." In *The New Cambridge Medieval History*, vol. 4, pt. 1, edited by David Luscombe and Jonathan Riley-Smith, pp. 11–46. Cambridge, 2004.

Fouracre, Paul. "Marmoutier and Its Serfs in the Eleventh Century." *Transactions of the Royal Historical Society* 15 (2005), 29–49.

France, James. *Separate but Equal: Cistercian Lay Brothers, 1120–1350.* Collegeville, Minn., 2012.

Freed, John B. *Noble Bondsmen: Ministerial Marriages in the Archdiocese of Salzburg, 1100–1343.* Ithaca, N.Y., 1995.

Freedman, Paul. *Images of the Medieval Peasant.* Stanford, 1999.

——. *The Origins of Peasant Servitude in Medieval Catalonia.* Cambridge, 1991.

——. "Peasants, the Seigneurial Regime, and Serfdom in the Eleventh to Thirteenth Centuries." In *European Transformations: The Long Twelfth Century,* edited by Thomas F. X. Noble and John Van Engen, pp. 259–78. Notre Dame, Ind., 2012.

Freedman, Paul, and Monique Bourin, eds. *Forms of Servitude in Northern and Central Europe: Decline, Resistance, and Expansion.* Turnhout, 2005.

French, Katherine L. *The Good Women of the Parish: Gender and Religion after the Black Death.* Philadelphia, 2008.

Geary, Patrick J. *Furta Sacra: Thefts of Relics in the Central Middle Ages.* 2nd ed. Princeton, 1990.

Genicot, Léopold. *Rural Communities in the Medieval West.* Baltimore, 1990.

Guyotjeannin, Olivier, Laurent Morelle, and Michel Parisse, eds. *Les cartulaires.* Mémoires et documents de l'École des chartes 39. Paris, 1993.

Hallam, Elizabeth M., and Judith Everard. *Capetian France, 987–1328.* 2nd ed. Harlow, Eng., 2001.

Hamilton, Bernard. "Religion and the Laity." In *The New Cambridge Medieval History,* vol. 4, pt. 1, edited by David Luscombe and Jonathan Riley-Smith, pp. 499–533. Cambridge, 2004.

Hanawalt, Barbara A. *The Ties that Bound: Peasant Families in Medieval England.* Oxford, 1986.

Head, Thomas. *Hagiography and the Cult of Saints: The Diocese of Orléans, 800–1200.* Cambridge, 1990.

Head, Thomas, and Richard Landes, eds. *The Peace of God: Social Violence and Religious Response in France around the Year 1000.* Ithaca, N.Y., 1992.

Higounet, Charles. *Défrichements et villeneuves du bassin parisien (XIe–XIVe siècles).* Paris, 1990.

Hilton, Rodney. *Bond Men Made Free: Medieval Peasant Movements and the English Rising of 1381.* New York, 1973.

Hoffmann, Richard C. *An Environmental History of Medieval Europe.* Cambridge, 2014.

Hyams, Paul R. *Kings, Lords, and Peasants in Medieval England: The Common Law of Villeinage in the Twelfth and Thirteenth Centuries.* Oxford, 1980.

Jordan, William Chester. *From Servitude to Freedom: Manumission in the Senonais in the Thirteenth Century.* Philadelphia, 1986.

Kaeuper, Richard W. *Medieval Chivalry.* Cambridge, 2016.

Keene, Derek. "Towns and the Growth of Trade." In *The New Cambridge Medieval History,* vol. 4, pt. 1, edited by David Luscombe and Jonathan Riley-Smith, pp. 47–85. Cambridge, 2004.

Klapisch-Zuber, Christiane, ed. *Silences of the Middle Ages.* A History of Women. Cambridge, Mass., 1992.

Kreiner, Jamie. *Legions of Pigs in the Early Medieval West.* New Haven, Conn., 2020.

Lambert, Malcolm. *Medieval Heresy: Popular Movements from the Gregorian Reform to the Reformation.* 3rd ed. Oxford, 2002.

Langdon, John. *Horses, Oxen and Technological Innovation: The Use of Draught Animals in English Farming, 1066–1500.* Cambridge, 1986.

Lauwers, Michel. "Le 'travail' sans la domination?" In *Penser la paysannerie médiévale, un défi impossible?*, edited by Alain Dierkens, Nicolas Schroeder, and Alexis Wilkin Paris, 2017. Kindle edition.

Lifshitz, Felice. "Beyond Positivism and Genre: 'Hagiographical' Texts as Historical Narrative." *Viator* 25 (1994), 95–113.

Little, Lester K. *Religious Poverty and the Profit Economy in Medieval Europe.* Ithaca, N.Y., 1978.

Loveluck, Chrisopher. *Northwest Europe in the Early Middle Ages, c. AD 600–1150: A Comparative Archaeology.* Cambridge, 2013.

Lynch, Joseph H. *The Medieval Church: A Brief History.* New York, 1992.

McCormick, Michael. "New Light on the 'Dark Ages': How the Slave Trade Fueled the Carolingian Economy." *Past and Present* 177 (2002), 17–54.

McHaffie, M. W. "Law and Violence in Eleventh-Century France." *Past and Present* 238 (2018), 3–41.

Mollat, Michel. *The Poor in the Middle Ages.* Trans. Arthur Goldhammer. New Haven, Conn., 1986.

Moore, R. I. *The First European Revolution, c. 970–1215.* Oxford, 2000.

Newman, Martha G. *The Boundaries of Charity: Cistercian Culture and Ecclesiastical Reform, 1098–1180.* Stanford, 1996.

Nicholas, David M. *The Growth of the Medieval City: From Late Antiquity to the Early Fourteenth Century.* Harlow, Eng., 1997.

Panfili, Didier. "Les convers cisterciens: Frères ou serfs? Du discours à la pratique sociale (vers 1130–vers 1230)." In *Labeur, production et économie monastique dans l'Occident médiéval de la Règle de Saint Benoît aux Cisterciens,* edited by Michel Lauwers, pp. 403–56. Turnhout, 2021.

Poly, Jean-Pierre, and Eric Bournazel. *The Feudal Transformation, 900–1200.* Trans. Caroline Higgitt. New York, 1991.

Postan, M. M. *Essays on Medieval Agriculture and General Problems of the Medieval Economy.* Cambridge, 1973.

Pounds, N. J. G. *An Economic History of Medieval Europe.* New York, 1974.

Power, Eileen. *Medieval People.* London, 1924.

Prou, Maurice. *Les coutumes de Lorris et leur propagation aux XIIe et XIIIe siècles.* Paris, 1884.

Raftis, J. A. *Peasant Economic Development within the English Manorial System.* Montreal, 1996.

Rennie, Kriston R. *Freedom and Protection: Monastic Exemption in France, c. 590–1100.* Manchester, Eng., 2018.

Reynolds, Susan. *Fiefs and Vassals: The Medieval Evidence Reinterpreted.* Oxford, 1994.

——. "Government and Community." In *The New Cambridge Medieval History,* vol. 4, pt. 1, edited by David Luscombe and Jonathan Riley-Smith, pp. 86–112. Cambridge, 2004.

Rider, Jeff. *God's Scribe: The Historiographical Art of Galbert of Bruges.* Washington, D.C., 2001.

Rider, Jeff, and Alan V. Murray, eds. *Galbert of Bruges and the Historiography of Medieval Flanders.* Washington, D.C., 2009.

Rio, Alice. *Slavery after Rome, 500–1100.* Oxford, 2017.

Rösener, Werner. *Peasants in the Middle Ages.* Trans. Alexander Stützer. Urbana, 1992.

Rubenstein, Jay. *Guibert of Nogent: Portrait of a Medieval Mind.* New York, 2002.

Rubin, Miri, ed. *Medieval Christianity in Practice.* Princeton, 2009.

Rudolph, Conrad. "Macro/Microcosm at Vézelay: The Narthex Portal and Non-elite Participation in Elite Spirituality." *Speculum* 96 (2021), 601–61.

Sassier, Yves. *Louis VII.* Paris, 1991.

Schofield, Phillipp R. *Peasants and Historians: Debating the Medieval English Peasantry.* Manchester, Eng., 2016.

Scott, James C. *Weapons of the Weak: Everyday Forms of Peasant Resistance.* New Haven, Conn., 1985.

Seale, Yvonne, and Heather Wacha. "The Cartulary of Prémontré: People, Places, and Networks from Medieval to Digital." *Medieval People* 36 (2022), 353–71.

Searle, Eleanor. "Seigneurial Control of Women's Marriage: The Antecedents and Function of Merchet in England." *Past and Present* 82 (1979), 3–43.

Southern, R. W. *The Making of the Middle Ages.* New Haven, Conn., 1953.

Sutherland, Samuel S. "The Study of Slavery in the Early and Central Middle Ages: Old Problems and New Approaches." *History Compass* 18, no. 10 (2020), https://doi.org/10.1111/hic3.12633.

Tellenbach, Gerd. *The Church in Western Europe from the Tenth to the Early Twelfth Century.* Trans. Timothy Reuter. Cambridge, 1993.

Tucker, Joanna. *Reading and Shaping Medieval Cartularies: Multi-Scribe Manuscripts and Their Patterns of Growth.* Woodbridge, Suff., 2020.

Van Houts, Elisabeth. *Married Life in the Middle Ages, 900–1300.* Oxford, 2019.

Verhulst, Adriaan. "Quelques remarques à propos des corvées de colons à l'époque du Bas-Empire et du Haut Moyen Age." In *D'une déposition à un couronnement, 476–800: Rupture ou continuité dans la naissance de l'Occident medieval,* edited by Institut des Hautes études de Belgique, pp. 89–95. Brussels, 1975.

Vinogradoff, P. *The Growth of the Manor.* London, 1905.

Weber, Eugen. *Peasants into Frenchmen: The Modernization of Rural France, 1870–1914.* Stanford, 1976.

West, C. "Monks, Aristocrats, and Justice: Twelfth-Century Monastic Advocacy in a European Perspective." *Speculum* 92 (2017), 372–404.

West, Charles. *Reframing the Feudal Revolution: Political and Social Transformation between Marne and Moselle, c. 800–c. 1100.* Cambridge, 2013.

White, Stephen D. *Custom, Kinship, and Gifts to Saints: The "Laudatio parentum" in Western France, 1050–1150.* Chapel Hill, N.C., 1988.

——. "Proposing the Ordeal and Avoiding It: Strategy and Power in Western French Litigation, 1050–1110." In *Cultures of Power: Lordship, Status, and Process in Twelfth-Century Europe,* edited by Thomas N. Bisson, pp. 89–123. Philadelphia, 1995.

Wickham, Chris. *Land and Power: Studies in Italian and European Social History, 400–1200.* London, 1994.

Wolf, Eric R. *Peasants.* Englewood Cliffs, N.J., 1966.

Wright, Sharon Hubbs. "Medieval European Peasant Women: A Fragmented Historiography." *History Compass* 18, no. 6 (2020), https://doi.org/10.1111/hic3.12615.

INDEX

www.ingramcontent.com/pod-product-compliance
Lightning Source LLC
Chambersburg PA
CBHW020048230825

31529CB00035B/1703